Mad Cow Was Over the Moon

The Fourth Year in Rural Galicia

Liza Grantham

BY THE SAME AUTHOR

***Mad Cow in Galicia* memoir series:**

Mad Cows and Englishmen: at large in Galicia
How Now, Mad Cow? The Second Year in Rural Galicia
'Til Mad Cow Comes Home: The Third Year in Rural
Galicia

The complete Shakespeare plays in everyday verse:

A Play by Any Other Name… Omnibus Edition

But ask the animals, and they will teach you,
or the birds in the sky, and they will tell you…

Job 12:7

CONTENTS

Thanks are due, as always, to the Varela family for their friendship and generosity; without them and their *rubia galega* cows there would be no story to tell.

Chapter 1

A Stitch in Time

It's April, but the dusting of frost on the lawn is more typical of an English winter than a Galician spring. A cuckoo calls its vernal ostinato from the nearby oakwood, and blackbirds peck purposefully in the hardened soil. The air, though crisp, is filled with the sound of birdsong and a dove flutters out of the fig tree, up into the forget-me-not sky. A chill wind stirs the broom and ripples the blossom on the apple trees, yet the chestnut, with its majestic strength remains still.

I shiver, pushing my hands deeper into my pockets, as I gaze out across the valley where the distant mountains are crowned with pine. There was a time when Paradise had seemed as distant as those mountains, but Fate had led us, trusting, hoping, believing, to Galicia, our home.

It was three years since my husband, Gary, and I had abandoned the sun, sea and sands of Gran Canaria for the verdant landscape of Galicia in northern Spain. Spending a long weekend in the region one summer had left us spellbound, and less than a year later we had returned to buy the house of José Val. Our dream home was a nineteenth century stone farmhouse in a tiny hamlet tucked away in a valley. We were surrounded by nothing but fields and forests as far as the eye could see.

Cutián was a typical Galician *aldea*; sparsely populated, with less than a dozen houses along a country lane. Apart from ourselves, the only permanent residents were Maruja, Javier and their son, José Manuel, at the farmhouse, and Carmen, the elderly widow whose garden bordered ours. Másimo, Solina and Begoña stayed in the village at weekends, and Alfonso the taxi driver came over every other evening to tend to his rabbits, chickens, bees and veg. There was also an Englishman, Paul, who came for only a few weeks a year, to spend time with nature and soak up the sun.

For five weeks that first summer, we'd scrubbed and painted, repaired floorboards, clad ceilings and cobbled together a motley assortment of furniture. In December we'd moved in, along with our eight-week-old German shepherd puppy, Anxo, and our two-year-old, cup-of-tea-coloured moggy, Scholes. We'd hired local tradesmen to build a new roof, replace the dangerous electrics, and plumb in hot running water. We'd cleared bracken and bramble, dug out a vegetable plot, added fencing and installed a cockerel and hens.

As we headed into the second year, we were ready to embark on the journey to self-sufficiency. Gary had dug, composted and weeded tirelessly throughout the winter and put in all manner of seeds and plants in the spring. As gardeners we were green, but the metaphor stopped at our fingers; by the end of the summer, few of our vegetables had thrived. Unlike the vegetable harvest, our egg supply had been abundant, and I was keen to progress to raising animals for meat. We didn't have enough space for sheep or pigs or cows, so I was limited to breeding smaller livestock. We invested in a pair of rabbits and introduced a brooder to our existing flock of laying hens. As we neared the end of our second year, our female rabbit, Doe, had presented us with what would be the first of many litters of babies and Mrs Brown, our broody hen, had hatched our very first batch of chicks.

The following April, undeterred by our previous disappointments, we were eager to travel further along the road to self-sufficiency. Armed with greater experience, we began our third year confident of success. Alas, Mother Nature takes a dim view of complacency, and nothing could have prepared us for the misfortune and heartache that lay ahead. Whilst our veg thrived, our livestock suffered. We lost chicks to a weasel, a turkey to infection and rabbits to poisoning. If that wasn't bad enough, there was far, far worse to come. During the autumn, our beloved Anxo had taken poorly. His illness was brief but fatal; no words could ever describe the pain I felt when he crossed over the Rainbow Bridge. Without a canine companion I sank into despondency, but my spirits were lifted when we brought Lenda, a German shepherd puppy, into our home. Towards the end of winter, we added a further four-legged member to the family; much to our surprise, we were adopted by Másimo's ginger kitten who we called Fred. Over the last four months Fred had wormed his way into our affections. Másimo hadn't batted an eyelid when I'd asked if we could keep him and have him neutered. Scholes had accepted him like a long lost brother, and the house of José Val was now his home.

With such a disastrous year behind us, I hardly dared imagine what the next twelve months would bring. Nevertheless, despite the cruel blows that Fate had rained on us, there was much to be thankful for. I was regaining my positive outlook and hoped that better times lay ahead. For the first time, the pantry and freezers were packed to the gunwales with the fruits of our harvest, and out in the garden we had a litter of rabbits and a trio of chicks.

Although I still grieved for Anxo, I was learning to look to the future. I took comfort in Lenda's companionship and was frequently moved to laughter by the antics of Scholes and Fred. We had a good relationship with our *galego* neighbours, and I'd forged a bond with Maruja, who had become a true friend. We'd made the acquaintance of some great English ex-pats and, after an initial period of semi-isolation, we were beginning to enjoy a social life again.

With my optimism returning, I was ready to embrace the next chapter in our erratic and extraordinary life. What better time to start than on the anniversary of our signing for the house? With no regular income, a lavish celebration was out of the question, so we'd settled on an evening in the garden, chatting over our beers and soaking up the late April sun. As it had turned out, the evening, for me at least, had brought with it an excitement of epic proportions. Keen to begin our revels, I'd opted to take Lenda for a shorter walk, abandoning our usual route in favour of a quick trek up through the woods. The outcome had been nothing if not astounding; out in the *campo*, with twilight approaching, Lenda and I had come face to face with a boar.

I stubbed out my cigarette and lifted the kettle from the cooker. The heavy thud of footsteps signalled that Gary was coming down the stairs. I shivered as I poured water onto the teabag. My teeth chattered and I cursed inwardly; perhaps I should have lit the range after all. I heard the stairs door creak open and, seconds later, Gary came into the kitchen. Lenda rushed to greet him, wagging her tail.

'Morning,' I murmured, as I passed him his cuppa.

'Morning,' he yawned. 'What's the matter? Your hands are shaking, is it nerves?'

I looked at him, puzzled. 'Nerves? I don't know what you mean.'

'I thought you might be worried about going over the fields. You know, after what happened last night.'

'Last night? Ah, the *jabalí*. Don't be daft, I'm not nervous. I've not long been out to do the rabbits and chickens. There's frost all over the garden. I'm shivering 'cos I'm bloody cold.'

'Frost, eh? Who'd have thought it? Yet the sun's shining and the sky's a brilliant shade of blue.'

'It's Galicia. You should know by now – the weather defies all reason. Listen, it's time I walked Lenda. It won't stay cold for much longer. It's going to be a lovely warm day.'

'Are you taking a stick?'

'A stick? Why?'

'If there's a *jabalí* lurking about out there you'd be better to take precautions. If I were you I'd…'

I gave a derisive sneer. 'Hark at you. There've always been *jabalí* "out there" and it's taken me three years to see one. The chances are, it'll be another three before I see one again. Anyway, boars are nocturnal – they'll all be snoring their heads off by now.'

Gary looked at me despairingly. 'You don't see the danger, that's your trouble. I read about them in *El Progreso* – they've been known to kill.'

'Rubbish. They've been known to *injure*. Hunters get gored now and then, it's hardly the same. I'm sure last night was a one-off – maybe a mother out foraging while her young were asleep. I'll be as safe as houses – we'll be back on our usual route today.' I grabbed my fleece from the coat rack. 'Right, if I'm not back in two hours send a search party. And ring *El Progreso*. "Killed by a

Boar" would make a brilliant headline. They'd have their doom-and-gloom fix for the day.'

I opened the back door, and Lenda bounded out and disappeared around the corner of the barn.

'Don't forget the stick!' called Gary. 'Take mine – it's by the bench!'

Ignoring him, I closed the door behind me and inhaled deeply. It was a sure sign that it was Saturday morning; the floral bouquet of Solina's laundry was drifting over on the wind. I listened for the familiar sound of shouting and laughter but heard only birdsong and the distant thrum of a chainsaw; silence prevailed at number fifteen. It was a safe bet that Másimo was already busying himself in one of the *fincas*. I felt a tremor of excitement; if I passed him on my way to the *campo* I'd be able to tell him about the *jabalí*. Along the track, I caught up with Lenda, who was snuffling for pee-mails left by the dogs from the farm. As I neared the stream, I heard a familiar whistling coming from over the crumbling stone wall. Sure enough, there was Másimo in his shirt sleeves, digging fervently with a mattock in the frozen soil.

'*Hola*, Masi,' I called. '*Buenos días*.'

'*Buenos días*, Elisa,' he beamed. 'I'm getting rid of the weeds.'

I smiled to myself. Trust Masi. His efforts were completely pointless. Next weekend the whole village would be sowing and planting in earnest, and José Manuel would drive over in the tractor and plough the entire area ready for the beans. Másimo was a typical rural *galego*; he simply loved to be down in the *finca*, whistling and perspiring as he hoed between the kale. I trod gingerly over the steppingstones and made my way over to the makeshift pallet gate. As Lenda shot off up into the eucalyptus wood, I made my announcement with pride.

'Masi, I've seen a *jabalí*!'

Masi stopped hoeing, put one hand on his hip and looked at me squarely. 'Today?'

'No, yesterday, in the evening when I was taking Lenda for a walk.'

'Was it dark?'

'No. It was still daylight. The sun was low in the sky, but it hadn't set.'

Masi chuckled and shook his head. 'It couldn't have been a *jabalí*, Elisa. They only come out at night.'

'But I saw it. It had tusks.'

'They were probably antlers, Elisa. It must have been a deer.'

I was about to protest but thought better of it. Masi would talk for hours if he was given an opening, so I nodded in agreement and set off after Lenda, through the eucalyptus woods and up into Javier's five fields.

When I called Gary in at breaktime, he was frowning. It didn't bode well. Nine times out of ten, a frown meant a problem. Nine times out of ten, a problem meant a spend.

I plonked his coffee down in front of him. 'Go on then, what's wrong?'

'It's Sophie.'

I breathed a sigh of relief. I was fond of Sophie, but she wasn't *our* cat, she was Másimo's. Whatever fate had befallen her, it wasn't going to cost us a cent.

'What's happened?'

'I think she's in pain. She was writhing about on the floor in the barn, and Fred was standing over her, mewing. It looked for all the world as if he was worried about her. He's not left her side all morning. I think he's scared.'

I reached for my tobacco. 'Poor Sophie. I've been dreading this happening. Dear, oh dear.'

'What do you mean? It's not something serious, is it? Is it contagious? What about Scholes and Fred?'

I stifled a giggle and looked at Gary, forcing myself to keep a straight face. 'Oh, it's serious, alright. But you needn't worry. I'm sure Scholes and Fred will be safe.'

I began to roll a cigarette and watched as his brow furrowed.

'I don't understand.'

'Sophie's in oestrus.'

He looked blank.

'She's in season, Gary. She's ready to mate.'

'She can't be. She's the same age as Fred. They must only be six months old at the most.'

I thought back to when Sophie and Fred were kittens. They were no more than eight weeks old when they'd arrived at number fifteen. That was back in September and it was now April. I counted on my fingers and was taken by surprise. 'Crikey, Gary, they must be nine months old!'

It was then that the realisation hit me. If Sophie was sexually mature, then Fred would be too. The time had flown by and we still hadn't got round to having him neutered. If we acted quickly, we might yet save Sophie from becoming a mum. I'd been too hasty in thinking her predicament wouldn't affect us. Gary's frown really *had* been a portent; this was going to cost us money after all. I took a deep breath and looked at him.

'We'll have to get Fred done.'

'I know. We agreed on that weeks ago, and Masi's already told you it's no problem. We'll book him in for June.'

I sighed. 'June's no good, Gary – he'll be nearly a year old by then. He needs doing *now*, for Sophie's sake. If we can get him in at the vet's for Monday, we might still be in with a chance.'

'It's out of the question, Liza. It won't be happening this month, *or* next month. It'd take us well over budget. It'll *have* to wait until June.'

I lit my cigarette and inhaled deeply. When the animals were going to cost money it only ever ended in a row. I had to persist; I wanted to do right by Sophie. Apart from that, I could see no reason why Fred couldn't be neutered now.

'I don't see why. If I keep the shopping list frugal we should have enough left in the kitty.'

He grinned annoyingly. 'The kitty. Very good.'

I glared at him. '*Gary*. I'm being serious. '

His smile faded and he looked stern. 'Listen. The MOT's due in May. The basic charge isn't much, but if they find a problem…'

'Wait a minute. What do you mean, *May*? You told me the van had been MOT'd two months before you bought it. That was back in January. It won't need doing 'til November this year.'

'Sorry, but you're wrong. A van's different to a car. It has to be MOT'd every six months.'

'You're joking!'

'I'm not. I thought I'd told you…'

'I can assure you, you didn't. That's all we need. First the screeching brakes, now this bombshell. I'm beginning to rue the day you ever bought the bloody van.'

'Even if we *could* afford it, it wouldn't make any difference.'

'Of course it would. It'd stop Sophie being mated. Fred's hardly going to be jumping all over her when he's just come out of surgery. He'll be laid up on the sofa, licking his wounds.'

'And what about Posster?'

'Posster? I don't see what Posster's got to…' my voice faltered as the relevance dawned on me. 'Shit,

Gary! I hadn't thought about Posster – you're absolutely right!'

In my haste to eliminate the most obvious threat to Sophie, I'd completely forgotten that Fred wasn't the only tomcat in Cutián. Posster, a stray who looked uncannily like Scholes, had appeared in the village two years ago. We'd named him and fed him, but he and Scholes had become arch-rivals; all hell broke loose whenever the twain should meet. Eventually Posster had installed himself at the top of the village. Alfonso had a couple of cats to keep the mice down. They were both females and Posster had claimed them for his wives. Now a seasoned Romeo, it was only a matter of time before Posster got wind of Sophie's 'condition'. It was a foregone conclusion we wouldn't be able to save her from motherhood after all.

After lunch I took the rubbish up to the village wheelie bin. I was hoping Maruja would be on the doorstep when I passed the farmhouse; undeterred by Masi's reaction, I couldn't wait to tell her about the boar. Luna and Pastor, the retired cow dogs, were asleep on the doorstep but there was no sign of Maruja. The sound of the telly blaring out from the kitchen said she was working indoors. On the way back, I struck lucky; as I neared the corner she was coming out of the back door. Flea-pelt the housedog-cum-guineapig was flapping and yelping around her heels.

'*Buenos días*, Maruja,' I called.

'*Buenos días*, Elisa. Isn't it cold?'

'It's bitter,' I nodded. 'This morning there was frost on the lawn.'

'It's always the same in April. It can change so quickly. Yesterday it was warm until dusk.'

'Yes, it was like summer. We sat out in the garden. I've been dying to see you. While I was out with Lenda, I saw a boar.'

'A *jabalí*? Where?'

'In the field past the *río* and up through the oak woods.'

'Our *campo*? The one that slopes upwards just past the stream?'

'That's the one. I didn't realise it was yours though. I thought...' I was about to say that I'd seen Tonito herding his cows there on several occasions but thought better of it. Tonito, his cows and his underweight German shepherd, Pastora, had recently left the *aldea*. He wasn't quite the full ticket and I didn't want to cause him any strife.

'You didn't know it was ours because we don't take the cows there very often. It's not so far from the mountains – are you sure it wasn't a wolf?'

'I'm positive. I was as close to it as I am to that telegraph pole.'

Maruja peered towards the telegraph pole on the corner. Her brow furrowed. 'It *could* have been a boar, I suppose.'

At that moment, Javier emerged from the kitchen.

'Elisa thinks she saw a *jabalí*,' Maruja told him.

He peered at me. 'In the *campo*?'

'Yes,' I nodded. Like Maruja, Javier didn't look convinced. 'Lenda chased it into the forest, then seconds later it chased Lenda back into the field.'

'Are you sure it wasn't a dog?'

'Not unless you get dogs with tusks on.' I regretted it before the words had even left my mouth. Rural Galicians' humour differs greatly to that of the English; my neighbours had no grasp of irony and, sure enough, Maruja took me at my word.

'There aren't any dogs with tusks on Elisa. If it had tusks it was a *jabalí.*'

When Javier nodded his agreement I smiled gratefully, pleased that they'd finally accepted my tale. He looked at me and reeled off something in rapid-fire *galego*. I gaped at him blankly; I'd long since given up asking him to slow down.

'That was too fast for Elisa,' frowned Maruja. 'Tell her again, but slowly, so she'll understand.'

Javier chuckled and rattled it off just as quickly as before. I looked from one to the other.

'Javier said,' began Maruja, helpfully, 'you'll need to be careful. They've been known to kill people. The females are dangerous when they've got young.'

When we settled down with our beers that evening I told Gary about the neighbours distrusting my story, and how they'd eventually given me the benefit of the doubt.

'There you go,' he said smugly. 'You were lucky. I told you they could kill.'

I shrugged dismissively. 'Javier exaggerates – like you. Anyway, talking of killing, it's about time you made a start on the rabbits. Three tomorrow, three on Monday and three on Tuesday. The time's gone by so quickly – they're nearly four months old.'

'Never. It doesn't seem five minutes since I did the last lot. Have we eaten them all?'

'We have. There were the stews, the barbecues… oh, and the curry. I thought I might use a couple in the week. I fancy trying something different – I don't suppose you've got any ideas?'

'Didn't Nina give you a recipe when we saw her at the ex-pats' get-together? Something from Indonesia? That's one you still haven't done.'

'Crikey, Gary, you're right. I'd forgotten all about it. She didn't give it to me though, she was going to send it in an email. I'll go into Monterroso with you tomorrow.

You can drop me at the office and I'll use Maribel's computer. I bet she'll let me print it out as well.'

Living out in the middle of nowhere meant that, technologically speaking, we were cut off from civilisation. There was no mobile signal in the *aldea* so, twice a day, Gary would walk up to the church at the top of the village to check for messages and missed calls. The chances were that an internet signal would have been likewise unattainable, but on our limited budget such luxuries were out of the question and we hadn't bothered to find out. When we'd bought the house, Maribel, our estate agent had told us we could use the computer in her office. I didn't like to take advantage and only went in to check my emails once in a blue moon.

'Why don't you use the one in Antas?'

I looked at him like he was bonkers. 'You what?'

'You must remember? There's a bar near the Casa de Cultura that's got a computer with internet. It's like the ones in the *salon recreativo* in Las Palmas – you just put your money in the slot.'

'You've never mentioned it. How long has it been there? Honestly, Gary, this is the first I've heard.'

'Really? I could've sworn I told you months ago. I noticed it one market day in Antas. The main street was busy so I drove round the back roads instead.'

'I wish I'd known sooner. Now I do, the world's my lobster. I tell you, Gary – it'll change my life.'

On Monday morning Gary dropped me off at Cafe-Bar Olga before continuing into Monterroso to do the weekly shop. When I walked into the bar, I scanned the seating area but saw no sign of a computer. There was a lose-a-small-fortune fruit machine in the corner and a cigarette machine by the door. Gary would be at least an hour in

Monterroso; I crossed my fingers and hoped he hadn't got it wrong.

'*Buenos días*,' smiled a woman with a mop and bucket, appearing from a door marked *Aseos*. 'It's cold this morning, isn't it? What would you like?'

The mention of 'cold' struck a chord and I shivered instinctively. A steaming hot chocolate seemed like a good idea.

'*Chocolate, por favor*,' I answered. 'Is there a computer in here?'

The woman nodded and pointed to a doorway to the side of the bar. 'It's through there.'

I made my way through to a dimly lit games room. There was a coin-in-the-slot table-football game in the centre and more fruit machines to one side. Tucked away in the darkest corner was a tiny, high-backed computer desk. The monitor and keyboard occupied most of the tabletop, along with a used cup and saucer and a scrunched up serviette. To my surprise and delight there was a scattering of cigarette butts on the floor. I squeezed myself into the cramped space and was pleased to find that the seat was deceptively comfy. I was even more pleased to see that a euro would buy me an hour.

By the time Gary returned I was sitting outside smoking a third cigarette and reading through the jottings I'd made in my notebook.

'Any luck?' he asked me.

'Yes,' I beamed. 'It's been a great success. The No Smoking law doesn't apply in the games room; the woman who brought my hot chocolate didn't bat an eyelid when she saw me lighting a fag.'

'I meant the recipe.'

'Ah, yes. I've got that *and* I've had *loads* of messages. Most of them were from October, to wish me a happy birthday. Do you realise, it's the first time I've used the internet in almost seven months?'

'Crikey. It just goes to show you can live without all this new-fangled technology. There's something to be said for living in the past.'

'They haven't got a printer,' I continued, 'but I had plenty of time, so I've jotted the recipe in my book. If you kill the last three rabbits tomorrow, I'll do us *conejo indonesio* for lunch.'

'Sounds great. I've got some news as well.'

'Go on.'

'I've had a message off Rose. She's got some gardening jobs for me. They'll take three days, maybe longer. She's asked if I can start the first week in May.'

'That's fantastic. Does this mean we can have Fred neutered before June after all?'

'I don't see why not. Rose wants to pay me on a daily basis, so she doesn't get into a mess.'

I chuckled. Dear old Rose. Hanging on to her readies just wasn't her forte. Zany and impulsive, she lurched from one disaster to another. She was also generous and quick-witted, and we loved her to bits.

'I'll need to find a decent vet then,' I said. 'Now the Monterroso surgery's closed, we'll need to go further afield. I'll ring round some of the ex-pats, someone's bound to be in the know.'

'If you wait until the first of May, you can ask at the get-together. I can start at Rose's on the second, one day won't be such a big deal.'

'That's a brilliant idea. You never cease to amaze me. Every once in a while you show these rare glimmers of genius...'

'You want to be careful – I could always change my mind.'

I went out to the barn just after daybreak on Wednesday morning. The smell of garlic and chilli that oozed from my pores and clung to my clothes was testament to how successful my tamarind rabbit had been. It also served to remind me that there were only two rabbits to clean out and feed this morning and, until Doe's forthcoming litter began to venture from the nest, I could enjoy the reduction in workload for the next four weeks. Heartened by the thought, I hummed cheerfully as I scooped feed into a bucket. Moments later, I was hauled from my reverie by an almighty yowl. I glanced round to see Sophie wearing the look of an angry tiger, as a smug-looking Posster dashed out through the door. All hopes of protecting Sophie had just become futile; she'd be having her first litter of kittens in June.

Tamarind Rabbit (Indonesian-style)

Fry finely chopped onions,
Some garlic pulp too;
Add red chilli peppers
(Or powder will do).

Now stir in brown sugar,
And tamarind paste,
Soy sauce, and some lime zest,
And season to taste.

Deep-fry rabbit portions
(In batches, of course),
Then toss them 'til coated
In tamarind sauce.

Serve up with fresh salad
And plenty of rice.
(Or if you feel reckless,
French fries would be nice!)

Chapter 2

Good Vibrations

On Saturday morning I was pulling on my wellies when I heard the thrum of a tractor. It was barely daylight outside so I knew for certain it couldn't be José Manuel. Up at the farmhouse he and Javier would only just be stirring. Maruja would be down in the kitchen making breakfast; *sopa de leche* for herself and Javier, and cereals for José Manuel. Alfonso only came to the village in the evenings, and Carmen would still be tucked up in bed. That left only Másimo; why was he chugging about in a tractor at the crack of dawn? Determined to find out, I gave a final tug to my stubborn left wellie and grabbed my fleece from the hook. Instructing Lenda to stay in the kitchen, I was about to open the back door when I heard a resounding thud. It seemed to be coming from the other side of the passage wall, in the two storey annexe which had once been part of the house. I stood stock still and listened. I could still hear the chugging of the tractor, but nothing more. I was beginning to think that I'd imagined it when the sound came again. This time it was louder, and I was certain I'd felt the floor beneath me vibrate. Could it be an earthquake? I'd read about tremors in *El* doom-and-gloom *Progreso*; they weren't uncommon in the north-western corner of Spain. Rural Galician houses weren't built with underground foundations, and if the house came down we'd be buried beneath hundreds of tonnes of stone. We'd be crushed in an instant like the slugs that squidged underfoot in the dewfall. Worse still, we might even be buried alive. We'd be safer outside; I *had* to wake Gary. I opened the stairs door and the thud came again. This time there was no mistaking the vibration as the floor pulsed beneath me. There was no need to call Gary, within seconds he appeared at the top of the stairs.

'Liza! What the fuck are you *doing*? Sometimes you're so selfish! You *knew* I was still asleep!'

'There's an earthquake!' I yelled. 'Get some clothes on! You'll need to be quick – shoo Scholes and Fred through the cat-hole! I'll get Lenda – we *have* to get out of the house!'

I called Lenda from the kitchen and ushered her out through the back door and up into the garden. Másimo's tractor was still chugging away round the corner. I was considering warning him but I didn't want to leave Lenda alone. After what seemed an eternity, Gary appeared at the gate.

'You were ages,' I frowned. 'Did you get the boys out?'

'Fred went, but Scholes was being awkward. I couldn't shift him. He's under the bed.'

'You're joking! I can't believe you'd just leave him! Stay here with Lenda – I'm going back in.'

As I began to push past him he started laughing.

'Liza, calm down. There won't be any more tremors. Come on, there's something I want you to see.'

Reluctantly I followed him out of the gate and down to the corner.

'Look,' grinned Gary, pointing.

Masi was making *very* slow progress with the tractor. Instead of steering it back through the gate he was bashing repeatedly into the wall of number fifteen. Suddenly the cause of our 'earthquake' became clear.

After lunch I took the rubbish up to the wheelie bin. Maruja was standing on the farmhouse doorstep, minus her chequered pinny, and wearing trousers tucked into her socks. Her change of apparel marked a very special occasion; the family were going to plant their spuds.

'*Hola*, Maruja,' I smiled. 'Are you off to plant your potatoes?'

'*Hola*, Elisa,' she chuckled. 'You knew because of my trousers. I'll never get used to wearing them. I'm glad it's just once a year.'

I was about to reply when a protracted, ear-splitting 'BEEEP!' filled the air. It was followed by a familiar rumbling as Javier's old tractor pulled up at the top of the lane. It occurred to me that Maruja might be able to shed some light on Masi's shenanigans earlier on.

'We saw Másimo in his tractor this morning,' I ventured. 'He seemed to be having some trouble.'

'Ah, yes,' she nodded. 'There was a problem with the steering wheel – it would only turn one way. José Manuel went down to fix it, but Javier's been grumbling. We're behind with the planting and that means his lunch will be late.'

As if to confirm her story the persistent beeping came again. Maruja waved her arm in acknowledgement.

'You'd better go,' I smiled. I knew from experience that Hell hath no fury like a hungry man.

On the first of May I was up bright and early. I couldn't wait for the ex-pats' get-together in Monterroso; Nina and Marcus would be going, and I was dying to tell them about my coney cordon bleu. It wasn't the only reason I was keen for our outing; I was hoping that someone would know of a good veterinary clinic. Finding a vet would take us a step closer to neutering Fred.

Since Fred had first curled up on the sofa in February, he'd changed beyond all recognition. Back then, he'd flinch if I so much as approached him but only two months later, he just couldn't have enough fuss. Inside the house, he had become my shadow and even in the garden he was never far from my side. When I sat on the sofa he'd jump into my lap, writhe in ecstasy and purr loudly. The bond was mutual and I loved him almost as much as I loved Lenda and Scholes.

'White rabbits!' I shouted, when I heard the stairs door open.

'Cheat,' yawned Gary, as he came into the kitchen. 'I hadn't even got through the door – I didn't stand a chance.'

'Tough,' I grinned, as I passed him his cuppa. 'Happy *Día del Trabajo*. When I was a kid we called it Maypole Day.'

'I remember. All the mums made maypoles and we took them to school.'

'Yes, and the nearest Monday was always a bank holiday. I never understood that, I prefer the way they do it in Spain.'

'How d'you mean?'

'Having the holiday on the actual date, no matter what day of the week it is.'

'Ah, I've got you. Yes, it makes more sense.' As he reached for his tobacco his brow began to furrow. 'Shit.'

'What's the matter?'

'It's bank holiday *today*.'

'And?' I knew what was coming. Driving through Monterroso in the holiday traffic was bound to bring on Gary's Irritable Driver Syndrome. I reached for my tobacco and waited with bated breath.

'Monterroso will be *heaving* with traffic. It'll be a bugger finding somewhere to park.'

'Here we go. That old chestnut. Next thing you'll be saying "Can't we leave it 'til next month?" I know what you're like.'

'Well now you come to mention it…'

'Don't you *dare*. I've arranged to meet Nina and Marcus. It's all organised – I sent her a message. And anyway, we *have* to find a vet for Fred.'

Despite the cold nights, the days were already feeling like summer and the May Day crowds were out in their droves. Gary, however, had no difficulty parking on the wasteland behind the Hotel Río Ulla. By the time we'd parked up and strode the short distance to the main street, he was in a surprisingly good mood. He waved cheerily to the throng of ex-pats who were mingling out on the terrace, before turning to me, smiling, 'I think a coffee first, don't you?'

Inside, the hotel was surprisingly quiet, and we made our way straight to the bar. We ordered two coffees and Gary made a beeline for the football paper. I watched idly as the coffee machine hissed and bubbled, while the waitress clattered about with the cups.

'Hello,' boomed a voice from behind us. It was Marcus, but there was no sign of Nina. I tried hard to disguise my disappointment. She must have decided to stay at home.

'Morning,' I smiled.

'Actually,' said Marcus solemnly. 'It is afternoon.' His face broke into a broad grin. He leaned over towards me and whispered conspiratorially. 'Gary and I will get the coffees. Nina is waiting outside for you. She has a surprise.'

Filled with curiosity, I made my way back through the bar. Out on the terrace, I couldn't see Nina to begin with; a crowd had gathered around her and it didn't take long to find out why.

As people began to drift back to their tables I headed over to Nina who was clinging for all she was worth to the end of a leash. At the other end was a boisterous black Labrador puppy; Marcus was right, it was indeed a surprise. The pup was bounding with energy, her tail wagging ten to the dozen as she leapt repeatedly at the onlookers' legs. There were shouts and shrieks, and it didn't take long for the stragglers to head back to their coffees. Eventually, only a couple of seasoned dog lovers lingered behind.

'Isn't she gorgeous?' laughed Angela, wiping drool from her hands with a tissue.

'You cannot have her,' chuckled her husband, Luc, in his heavy Belgian accent. 'We have enough dogs already. This one would make five.'

'Lulu's not going anywhere,' smiled Nina. 'She cost us nine hundred euros. Marcus says she's the love of his life.'

As I was making Lulu's acquaintance, Gary and Marcus came out with the coffees. I couldn't help but notice that Gary had stuffed the football paper under his arm. Nina tied Lulu's leash to the railings and sighed wearily. 'Lulu exhausts me. I have to sit down.'

Angela and I moved over to sit on the windowsill, where we lit cigarettes.

'However do you cope with four dogs?' I asked her, looking over at Lulu who was still leaping up and down. 'Do you walk them two at a time?'

'No chance,' she laughed. 'I walk off towards the woods at the end of our garden and shout, "Who's coming?" Most of the time they'll all decide to join me, but once in a while – usually when it's raining – Nacho and Benji will stay behind.'

'And sometimes they go without her,' chuckled Luc, who'd been listening from the table. 'We have given up trying to keep them in.'

'I'm not happy about it,' added Angela, 'but the garden's so massive – it'd cost us a fortune to fence it. I'm on tenterhooks 'til they all come home safely. Two years ago Nacho was gored by a boar.'

'Never!' I gasped. 'My God, how awful!'

Luc shook his head. 'She exaggerates. There was a cut on his side. The vet said it *might* have been made by a tusk.'

'I see,' I nodded. 'A boar chased Lenda only the other week. It was way too close for comfort. For a few seconds I thought it was coming for *me*.'

'Oh dear,' frowned Angela. 'You need to be careful. The females can be vicious when they've got babies. They've been known to kill.'

I glanced across at Gary, expecting to hear "I told you so". To my relief he was poring over the football results with Marcus. I wondered if Angela might know of a vet close to home.

'Do you know of a veterinary clinic locally?' I asked her.

'Yes,' she nodded. 'The closest one to here's in Taboada. I haven't been there but people say it's very good.'

'You don't happen to know the name of it, do you?'

'I don't. But Nina will know, she's been there with Lulu.'

'Brilliant,' I smiled. 'Thanks ever so much.' I stubbed out my cigarette and went over to the table.

'Your coffee will be cold,' laughed Marcus. 'Come on, sit down.'

'Angela was saying you use the vet in Taboada. Could you give me the name?'

'It's Vet Oporto,' said Marcus. 'I think Nina has the number in her phone.'

'I do,' nodded Nina. 'But hold on a second.' She rummaged about in her handbag and pulled out a card. 'Here,' she said. 'You can keep it. The vet's a young woman and she's lovely with dogs.'

'That's great,' I beamed. 'Oh, and thanks for the recipe you sent me. I made it with rabbit instead of chicken. It was truly divine.'

'I'll send you some more if you like the Indonesian flavours. Hey, that's an idea – why don't you come over on Sunday for a meal? If it's nice we'll sit out in the garden. Bring Lenda with you. It would be good for Lulu; we could eat while we watch the dogs play.'

On Wednesday morning I'd only just made my coffee when I heard Gary stirring in the bedroom above. There was a downside to his going over to work at Rose's; he had to set off early and I wouldn't have the first hour of the morning to myself. I consoled myself with the fact that it wouldn't take him *that* long to smoke a fag and drink a cuppa. It wouldn't be too much of a pain really: I filled a saucepan with water, the least I could do was boil him a couple of eggs.

'Morning,' he yawned as he lurched into the kitchen.

'Morning,' I smiled cheerily. 'I'm boiling you some eggs.'

'Eggs? I couldn't eat breakfast at this time of morning. Leave 'em in a bit longer – if you hard-boil them they'll do for my tea.'

It was all I could do not to hurl the wretched egg-cup at him. Instead I continued to smile. 'I wonder what Rose will give you at lunchtime. You can bet your bottom dollar it won't be the luxury fare you had at Verna's. I reckon you'll get bread and cheese.'

He grimaced. 'I hope not. I'll be there at least eight hours – I'll need proper grub. Anyway, she did say "I'll make lunch for you." It's bound to be something cooked.'

I frowned to myself. I couldn't help thinking that Gary was being optimistic. Rose *talked* a good cook, but I knew she went out most days for a *menú del día*. Still, if that was what she'd told him, who was I to argue? Better to be safe than sorry though; I'd make sure his tea was ready for when he came home.

After a second cuppa, Gary set off for Vilabeira. As soon as the car disappeared around the corner I went out to see to the rabbits and the hens. Over in Warren Place (the rather grandiose name we'd assigned to the rabbit pens) Bravo Buck was already thumping on the floor of his hutch.

'Wait a minute, Buck,' I called as I stepped into Doe's enclosure. 'Doe gets priority – she's eating for ten.'

I didn't know for certain, of course, but it seemed a reasonable assumption; in her previous four litters, Doe had given birth to nine babies each time. I opened the hutch and she bounded down the ramp, out into the crisp May morning. With only five days remaining until the arrival of the bunnies, she was looking decidedly huge.

Down in the chooks' run, the day had already started; inside the henhouse the hens were scuffling and squabbling, and Wayne, our tiny cockerel, was crowing for all he was worth. As I walked into the enclosure, Waynetta the contrary banty hen fluttered down from her favourite tree. I'd given up trying to put her away with the big hens; she was wayward and flighty, and a law unto herself. When I opened the door of the house, the rest of the wives flapped their way noisily over to the feeder, while Wayne sidled up to them, eager to mate. I ducked under the damson trees and opened the smaller house known as 'the maternity wing' and Mrs Brown and her chicks hopped out into their little run. At nine weeks old they were almost ready to be released into the grown-ups' enclosure. There were two nameless blond cockerels and Humbug, a brown stripy hen.

As I made my way back up the garden I spotted Fred by the herb bed sniffing at the sage.

'Morning, Fred,' I called.

Fred looked across at me, and I stooped instinctively, expecting him to trot over for a rub. He didn't. He turned his back to the herb bed, his tail raised rigid. His back-end trembled as he sprayed on the sage.

It was well after six when Gary arrived home from Rose's. I heard the van before I saw it; the infernal screeching of brakes proclaimed its headway through the village long before it pulled up by the barn. When Gary stepped out into the lane he looked bedraggled and exhausted. I was pleased I'd had the foresight to fill the fridge up earlier; I had a hunch that the first thing he'd be wanting was an ice-cold beer. As it happened, it wasn't.

'I'm starving,' he announced as he slammed the van door shut. 'I could eat the back out of a sofa. I've got loads to tell you, but first things first – what's for tea?'

'Don't you remember? You said you'd have the hardboiled eggs I did this morning. I've made you cheese butties as well.'

His face was a picture. 'You're joking, aren't you? I had cheese sandwiches for lunch.'

'I did warn you, but you wouldn't have it. I'm not cooking now, it's nearly time to walk Lenda. It's only one night – you'll have to make do.'

I could have feigned sympathy, but why should I? He wasn't the only one who'd been grafting; we'd opted for a back-to-basics lifestyle and that meant no washing machine. It hadn't been a bundle of laughs doing the winter duvet by hand.

There was a lot of huffing and chuffing as Gary heaved the heavy barn doors open. Back in the kitchen I rolled myself a ciggie while he was parking the van. I listened as the engine started and the van reverse-screeched into its parking space. A terrible thought occurred to me as the barn doors banged to. I'd expected Rose to renege on Gary's hot dinner, but what if she'd reneged on his wages too? Fred's operation was no longer about protecting Sophie, but it was no less urgent. If Fred had begun to spray in the garden it was only a matter of time before he was doing it indoors. I needn't have worried; when Gary came into the kitchen he pushed four blue notes into my hand.

'Eighty euros,' he mumbled. 'And believe me I've earnt it. I've told Rose I'll need the day off on Friday. Tomorrow you can ring the vets.'

I felt like hugging him, but one look at his sweat-drenched, mud-caked tee shirt caused me to think again. 'Brilliant,' I beamed. 'I'm ever so grateful. I'll take a rabbit out now to defrost for tomorrow, then you can tell me all about your day.'

As Gary dove into his feeble picnic I filled a big saucepan with water. I was about to drop the frozen rabbit into it when Gary shouted, 'Don't!'

I stared at him. 'Don't what?'

'You can't put frozen rabbit in water. You'll give me food poisoning if you defrost it like that.'

Hadn't I told him a thousand times to butt out when it came to culinary matters? I gripped the handles of the saucepan and inwardly seethed. I looked at him squarely.

'Utter rubbish. If the meat's in a sealed bag, and the water's changed regularly, it's perfectly safe. Anyway, I thought there was something you were dying to tell me. I've got half an hour before I take Lenda; come on, let's hear your news.'

Gary was a pushover when it came to basic psychology; my diversion tactic worked a treat.

'To cut a long story short, I think Rose has gone mad.'

'Pardon?'

He swallowed and wiped egg from his mouth with is hand. 'Mad. You know – nuts, potty, bonkers. I think she's lost the plot.'

'That's hardly news is it?' I chuckled. 'The reason we love her is 'cos she's such a crackpot. She's one of the funniest people I know.'

I watched in disgust as he picked a sliver of eggshell from his teeth and dropped it into the ashtray.

'This is different. She's been off on a madcap spending spree. She wants a forest, an orchard and a veg plot – and she wants them *now*.'

'So you've been digging?'

'Digging, barrowing, carrying breezeblocks – you name it. She's had all sorts of stuff delivered. She's got this hare-brained scheme to grow a food forest and make raised beds.'

'That doesn't sound loopy. She's got plenty of land to go at. I'd say it's a jolly good idea.'

'I'm not saying it isn't, but it's the urgency of it that's scary. She's been spending money hand over fist.'

That *was* a worry. I only hoped Gary would finish working before the coffers ran dry.

On Thursday morning I went up to the church before I walked Lenda. I was keen to book Fred in for Friday; the clinic would be closed all weekend. I punched in the number from Nina's card and it was the vet herself that answered. When I asked if I could bring in a cat the next day to be sterilised, I heard the shuffling of paper, then a long pause.

'Is it a female?' she asked me, eventually.

'No,' I replied. 'It's a boy.'

'Ah, good. In that case there's no problem – if you can get here by ten I can fit him in. No food after midnight, but he can have water all night. You'll be able to collect him at two.'

I thanked her and was about to ring off, when I realised there was something I'd forgotten. I could just imagine Gary's face if I hadn't enquired about the price.

'How much will it cost?' I asked hurriedly.

'It's eighty euros.'

I grinned like a nincompoop. Talk about serendipity; it was a weight off my mind.

When Gary arrived home that evening he looked hot and sweaty but cheerful, nonetheless.

'You look happy,' I smiled. 'Better day?'

'Much better, thanks. Did you manage to book Fred in at the vet's?'

'Yes, Ten o'clock. He's inside now and…'

'How much?'

'Eighty euros.'

'Fucking hell.'

I glared. 'I don't want him going out, so I've blocked the cat-hole. He's not to have…'

He held his hand up. 'Whoa! Hold on. Let me get showered and changed out of my work clothes and then you can tell me the rest.'

'Right-o. I'll put your dinner on. I've made rabbit tikka masala and Bombay spuds.'

He looked sheepish. 'I'll pass, if you don't mind. A sandwich will do me. Rose made a giant chicken tagine for lunch.'

I was about to protest but thought better of it; if he had it warmed up tomorrow it would save me a job.

That evening, poor Gary must have heard the vet's instructions at least a dozen times.

'Now you won't forget, will you?' I said, as we went up the stairs at bedtime. 'He mustn't leave the bedroom no matter how much he hollers. He categorically *mustn't* have access to food.'

Up in the bedroom I closed the door firmly, satisfied I'd left no stone unturned. Fred had fresh water and a clean litter tray and he'd sleep in his usual place on the bed. The cat carrier was already down in the passage, lined with a plush, fluffy towel. Scholes would be spending the night on the sofa in the living room, but it wouldn't be a hardship. He was driven by his belly and would be perfectly happy as long as he had access to food.

I turned out the light switch and shuffled under the duvet. Fred was already in dreamland, oblivious to the fate that lay ahead. I reached through the darkness and clicked the button on the alarm clock. There would be no danger of oversleeping; everything would go smoothly for Fred's big day.

That night I dreamed that everyone in the village was going out to plant potatoes. I set off up to the farmhouse, but Másimo's tractor was blocking the lane. As I stood behind it, water began to gush out in torrents from the exhaust pipe. I tried to move, but my feet felt like lumps of hardened clay. I was seized by panic and watched in horror as the water poured into my wellies and splashed out over the sides. I shouted for help, but the tractor began to reverse and gave out a spine-tingling, high-pitched beeping. As the tyres crept closer, I knew I was a goner and the beeping resounded like a death knell in my ears. I awoke with a jolt, but the beeping continued. For a split second I was certain I'd died. I came to my senses when Fred stretched and rolled over on the duvet above me. The terrifying noise was the alarm clock, and today was Operation Bye-Bye Balls. As I drew my legs up towards me I was aware of the strangest sensation. I wasn't wearing waterlogged wellies, yet my feet still felt cold and damp. I sat up sharply, and Fred toppled sideways from my hip bone. I reached down to the bottom of the bed and recoiled in horror. The duvet was drenched.

'Shit!' I cursed. For a moment I sat motionless in the darkness. What on earth was I going to do? I could hear Fred purring and felt his head buffeting my arm. 'Poor Freddie,' I murmured. 'It isn't your fault. You couldn't get out through the cat-hole when you needed a wee.'

At that moment Gary stirred and groaned. 'What time is it?'

'Half past six. There's been an accident. Fred's wet the bed.'

He groaned again. 'Very funny. Go back to sleep.'

'Gary, I'm being serious. You can lie in a pool of piss if you want to, but I'm getting up.'

Down in the kitchen my mind was working overtime. Somehow I'd have to strip the beds, launder the duvet, its cover and the mattress protector, and have them dried before bedtime tonight. On top of that, there was the small matter of sponging and drying a damp mattress. What should have been a day of celebration was going to be one heck of a long haul.

It was after eight o'clock when Gary finally surfaced. I was *not* in a good mood.

'About bloody time,' I huffed, plonking his mug down on the marble surface.

'It's eight o'clock,' he yawned. 'I'm early. Anyway, what's got into *you*?'

'I've been waiting to strip the bed. In case you'd forgotten, Fred peed in the night.'

'I hadn't forgotten. I didn't realise you were being serious. My side was dry.'

'Bully for you. Right, I'm going to fetch the bedding down and leave it in soak before I see to the chooks and the rabbits. After that, I'll be taking Lenda, so getting Fred into his basket and off to Taboada will be down to you.'

Two hours later the duvet, its cover, and the mattress protector were hanging on the clothesline dripping a syncopated lament onto the lawn. It was all I could do to curtail my tears from joining the ensemble; if the breeze didn't turn to gusts before lunchtime we were doomed. The veg plot was decked out absurdly in flaccid white regalia; a pair of wet sheets and matching pillowcases were draped over the wire fence. Whilst the bed linen fiasco was tantamount to a crisis, the mattress situation wasn't nearly so desperate. The duvet had borne the brunt of Fred's transgression, leaving the mattress, apart from a small damp patch, unscathed. I'd sponged it with soap suds before hoisting it from the bedstead, dragging it through to the living room and shoving it up through the open window, where it was now balanced precariously, overhanging the lane.

By lunchtime, the wind was blowing lustily from the north, sending puffs of gossamer cloud across an otherwise clear blue sky. The stuff on the line was billowing proudly, while the sheets flapped a greeting to the bean sticks that had appeared inside the fence.

'Very nice,' said Gary, as he mopped the last traces of curry from his plate with a slice of Bimbo.

I looked away in an effort to disguise my disapproval. It never failed to amaze me that he could defile my culinary wonders with such unwholesome junk.

'Right, I'm going to rig up the netting and poke the peas in. When I've finished it'll be time to fetch Fred. Are you sure you don't want to come?'

'I'm positive, thanks. Everything but the duvet should be dry by then. I'll haul the mattress in and start to make up the bed. It's blowing like billy-o at the moment, so if it keeps up all afternoon we'll be as right as ninepence by tonight.'

By teatime the bed had been restored to its former glory and Fred, as I'd predicted, lay on the sofa licking his wounds. The vet had prescribed a five day course of antibiotics and said that we didn't need to keep him indoors.

'Are you unblocking the cat-hole at bedtime?' asked Gary when we settled down with our beers that evening.

I shook my head. 'No. He can stay in for a couple of days so the wounds don't get dirty. I'll let him out on Monday if all goes well.'

'Don't you think you're being a bit overcautious? You already know he won't use the tray.'

'It's not a case of he *won't* use the tray, he didn't use it because we hadn't trained him. Poor Fred, it must have confused him – he's always been able to go out through the hole. I'm sure that what happened last night was a one-off. Anyway, he won't be sleeping in the bedroom tonight, I'll leave him in the living room with Scholes.'

'Right. And next you'll be telling me that Scholes will show him the ropes.'

'That's what I'm counting on. Don't underestimate him – he's a clever lad.'

In the wee small hours I was roused from my slumber by a curious scratching and scraping. I lifted my head from under the duvet and held my breath. It wouldn't be the first time I'd been woken by the scurrying of mice in the roof space, but as I listened more closely it was clear that the noise wasn't coming from above. If I wasn't mistaken something was scrabbling about in the living room. I shuddered, wondering if it might be a rat. I eased myself out of bed and crept softly over the floorboards.

Pushing down gently on the door handle, I took a deep breath and pulled it ajar. The streetlamp outside cast a milky light through the window, illuminating the cause of the disturbance. My fear was unfounded; a large, ginger 'rat' was using the tray.

Liza Grantham

When the Earth Moves

They say that the moment will come for each girl
When a man will appear who will capsize her world.
He'll quicken her pulse, leave her head in a whirl,
When the earth moves.

Her heart will pump faster and quicken its beat,
Her efforts to fight it will end in defeat.
She'll fall for his patter, be swept off her feet,
When the earth moves.

He'll strike in a way that she'd never expect,
He'll give her no warning or time to suspect,
He'll knock her for six with a lasting effect,
When the earth moves.

He might be as close as the man from next door,
Who hasn't made quite such an impact before;
The mem'ry will stay with that girl ever more,
When the earth moves.

Chapter 3

Sunday Guests

On Sunday morning I awoke to the sound of purring; since Fred had used the litter tray he'd been allowed in the bedroom again. After a quick trip to the bathroom I was ready for coffee and a cigarette, but I paused by the cat-hole when I reached the bottom of the stairs. It wasn't quite forty-eight hours since Fred's operation, but he'd been taking his antibiotics like the perfect patient and all that remained of his wounds were two tiny black scabs. Scholes had spent noticeably less time outdoors during Fred's brief confinement, proving beyond doubt that the pair had become great pals. On what promised to be a glorious day, it seemed only fair that they should make the most of the sunshine. I took a deep breath and unblocked their exit; it was time for my brave ginger Ninja to venture outside. Ten minutes later, I was out on the bench with my coffee. I couldn't help but marvel at how quickly spring was turning into summer; we hadn't had a frost for five days now and the sweet Williams in the rockery were already in bloom. Lenda lay at my feet, and her tail thumped when I leaned forward to stroke her. Now ten months old, she was no longer a puppy. I wondered what she'd make of the boisterous Lulu when we drove over to Nina's in the afternoon.

Unlike the previous weekend, this morning there was no hint of seismic activity. Amidst Solina's shouts and Begoña's laughter there was no mistaking Masi's cheerful whistling. There would be no threat from the ram-raider at number fifteen today.

I was lighting my second cigarette when I heard the stairs door open and Gary appeared on the step.

'Morning,' he yawned, shielding his eyes from the sunshine.

'Crikey,' I grinned. 'You're early. If you've come for the Monster Trucks display, too late – it's been and gone.'

'You what?'

'It doesn't matter, I was joking. Seriously, couldn't you sleep?'

'Not a hope. Fred was purring down my lughole. I noticed you've opened the cat-hole, but I don't think Fred's caught on. Anyway, shouldn't you be making my cuppa?'

'I still don't see why we have to take Lenda,' moaned Gary at breaktime. 'It's not as though we'll be out for hours.'

'Don't be so miserable. Nina specifically asked us to bring her. It's company for Lulu and it'll do Lenda good too.'

'It's alright for you – you're not the one driving. It's distracting having a dog leaping about in the back.'

'She won't "leap about" – you do talk nonsense. Anyway, we can't make the same mistake with Lenda as we made with Anxo. In case you hadn't realised, it's seven months since she was last in the van.'

When Anxo had taken poorly in September, no amount of coaxing would get him into the car. In the end we'd given up and arranged a home visit; it wasn't until his condition became really serious that we were able to hoist him in and drive him over to the vet's. We'd vowed to accustom Lenda to travelling right from the start, but somehow the months had flown by and she hadn't been out of the village since her inoculation. This afternoon's outing was a chance to start as we meant to go on.

By two o'clock, Gary was looking decidedly grouchy. It was way past his usual lunchtime and Nina had said she'd serve dinner at four. To make matters worse, the weather was scorching; he was desperate for some fodder and an ice-cold beer. At two thirty I popped Lenda out to the garden before nipping back inside to pack a bottle of wine and some cans of lager. I stood the bag out on the bench and told Gary I needed the bathroom. He was growing impatient and stood jingling his keys by the barn.

'I'll be two minutes,' I told him. 'You could get Lenda into the van while you're waiting, and that bag of booze can go in as well.'

Ten minutes later we pulled out of the *aldea*. I was on the back seat with Lenda, who was sprawled out with her head on my knee. As we joined the main road, the valley fell away to a patchwork of fields and woodlands. Sunlight filtered through the canopies of oak trees, casting a haphazard arrangement of stripes on the road. I sank back in my seat, enjoying the colours of the late spring landscape and the sensation of warmth on my arms. I was almost nodding off when I felt the van slowing. I opened my eyes as the jingling of cow bells and the screeching of brakes filled my ears. Lenda clambered into an upright position, turned around clumsily and began to scrape at the door.

'It's alright, Lenda,' I said. 'They're *vacas*. You know they won't hurt you – you've seen them before.'

Gary brought the van to a halt at the roadside. When he turned off the engine, Lenda relaxed. We waited as the convoy of cows plodded forwards. After what seemed an age they sauntered off at a fork up ahead. We set off once more, and Lenda remained calm until we came to Randulfe. The tight twists and turns sent the brakes into a full-blown recital; for Lenda the shrieking falsetto was too much to bear. She leapt at the back windscreen, clawing at the headrests. Her body trembled as she whined and panted. Poor Lenda; she was beside herself with fear.

'For fuck's sake!' growled Gary. 'Can't you control her? *Now* what's she doing? Make her lie down!'

'I'm *trying*,' I retorted. 'She can't help it, she's scared.'

'I *knew* this would happen! You wouldn't bloody listen! I told you it was a bad idea!'

'It's not her fault. She hates high-pitched noises. She was okay 'til she heard that bloody screech.'

'*What* screech? You're not still moaning about the brakes, I hope?'

'I'm not moaning. I'm stating a fact. The van's a wreck – I rue the sodding day you bought it. She'd have been fine if we'd still had the car.'

As the road straightened out, Lenda grew calmer. I coaxed her back onto my lap and ruffled her ears. The brakes were quiet for now, but the van was filled with a stony silence. I was tempted to suggest we abandon the visit; we'd only been on the road ten minutes and a whole hour's drive still lay ahead. I gazed out of the window and indulged myself in indignant contemplation. I watched the occasional car cruise past and tried to imagine the passengers inside. I pictured couples, relaxed and smiling, with classics playing on the radio, gasping with pleasure and surprise as they took in the view. We didn't fall into the bracket of chattery wives and jovial husbands; as happy travellers went Gary and I didn't quite fit the bill.

It seemed an eternity before we finally pulled up at San Pedro. I breathed a heartfelt sigh of relief as Gary eased the van up onto the village green. As we drew to a halt, Lenda hurled herself at the farside window, squashing my drum of tobacco inside my bag on the seat.

'Can't you bloody control her?' seethed Gary.

Resisting the urge to retaliate, I gritted my teeth and glared.

As he pulled on the handbrake, I pushed the door open. Lenda lurched round and lunged forwards across my lap. My efforts to restrain her were futile; still gripping the lead I left the car sideways and landed up on the grass. I was dusting myself down when Gary approached from the driver's side.

'Where did you put the bag with the drinks in?'

'On the bench. I told you before I went up to the bathroom. The last thing I said was, "you can load that bag."'

'I don't be*lieve* it. Nobody turns up for dinner without a bottle. They're going to think we're really mean.'

'They won't think anything of the sort. You'll only have one beer anyway because you're driving and with Lenda to see to, I'll probably do the same.' I took a deep breath and looked him in the eye. 'Look, it's not often we go out visiting – can't you just stop being grumpy and enjoy the afternoon?'

'Over here!' boomed a voice, just in time to save us from a domestic.

I glanced over gratefully, to where Marcus was waving wildly from the gate. Grabbing Lenda's lead I ignored Gary and set off across the green.

'Are you alright?' chuckled Marcus. 'You have an unusual way of getting out of a car.'

'I'm fine,' I nodded. 'It's an English thing, but we only do it on Sundays. It's a good job really, it doesn't half hurt my arse.'

In the meantime, Gary had strolled up behind me. He'd swapped his misery-guts face for an expression of warm affability; he looked like a kindly vicar dropping round for afternoon tea.

A door on the side of the house opened and Lulu charged out like a whirling dervish, barking loudly and wagging her tail.

'Hi,' called Nina, from the doorstep. 'What are you waiting for Marcus? Open the gate and let them in.'

Marcus hoisted open the giant pallet that served as a makeshift gate. From that moment onwards, all pleasantries were out of the question; Lenda and Lulu flew into a state of doggy delirium and it quickly became apparent that no human was safe.

'I think the garden,' boomed Marcus, authoritatively.

'Follow me,' smiled Nina, 'I'll show you the way.'

She led us towards a door that opened into a small courtyard, surrounded by high stone walls with peach-coloured roses clambering along the top and trailing haphazardly over the sides. The dogs hurtled through, almost upending a table laid out with plates, cutlery and glasses, and out through an archway on the opposite side.

'Come on,' said Nina. 'Let's go with them into the garden. We'll be able to keep an eye on them while they play.'

We followed her through the archway onto a small patio area where a smaller table and metal chairs competed for space amongst straggly foliage trailing out from stone built beds.

'They were so tidy at the start of spring,' sighed Nina, 'but we went back to the Netherlands for a visit and when we came back they were so overgrown. The grass in the orchard alone takes forever. It grows back as quickly as it's mown.'

Beyond the patio the orchard stretched out for a good fifty metres to the far end of the land. I spotted a couple of apple trees, but it seemed that the rest were all cherries, heavily laden with fruit, with more, pecked by the birds, all over the ground.

'Wow!' I exclaimed. 'Aren't you lucky! A cherry orchard all of your own!'

'No,' laughed Marcus, 'We are not lucky. There is a story behind them. Nina will tell.'

Nina giggled. 'Last spring, Marcus said, "we still have room for more trees, Nina – we'll go to the market and you can choose." We went to Monterroso, maybe it was the time we saw you? They had everything – apples, pears, plums, nectarines… I told Marcus that cherries were my favourite. We bought seven cherry trees and planted them in the spaces. At the end of March the other trees began to blossom. You wouldn't believe it, apart from two apple trees all the rest were cherries too.'

'Seventeen,' added Marcus. 'And we had planted another seven. Now we have twenty four cherry trees and don't know what to do.'

'You'll take some, of course,' said Nina.

'Yes, please,' I grinned.

'What's this?' asked Gary, pointing to a small metal dome sticking out of the ground.

'It gets rid of moles,' said Marcus. 'It is brilliant. One hundred per cent effective. You have my word.'

'Hmm,' I grimaced. 'Not like the one that Gary bought a couple of years back, then. That was a waste of bloody money. It's still there now, gathering moss under the fig tree. It was neither use nor ornament – it hasn't trapped a single mole to this day.'

'Neither has this,' said Marcus solemnly.

I stared at him. Hadn't he just told us his gadget was completely effective? Something must have been lost in translation; perhaps Marcus wasn't so fluent in English after all.

'But you just said it was brilliant,' frowned Gary.

'I did,' Marcus nodded.

Gary frowned even harder. 'I don't understand.'

Marcus was grinning mischievously. I suspected this wasn't a language problem after all.

'Right, Marcus,' I said. 'I've missed something somewhere. I'll repeat what you've told us and you can stop me if I get it wrong.'

Marcus nodded, then winked at Nina. There was no doubt about it, he was having fun.

'Right,' I began. 'It's a hundred percent effective?'

'Yes.'

'But you've never caught a single mole?'

'Correct.'

I looked at Gary, who shrugged his shoulders. 'And you haven't found any dead ones?'

'Correct again.'

I looked at Nina, then back at Marcus. Something was definitely going on. 'Okay. I give up. You've lost me. Fill us in.'

'It is not a trap,' said Marcus.

'But you said…'

'Actually, I didn't – *you* did. It is a repellent. It gives off a signal and the moles run away.'

'Seriously?' said Gary.

'Yes,' nodded Nina. 'He's telling you the truth.'

I was mesmerised. 'So you stick it in the lawn and all the moles leg it? Just like that?'

'Leg it?' frowned Marcus.

'Yes,' I grinned. 'Skedaddle, scarper, run off.'

He winked at Gary. 'Liza's English is very bad.'

'It doesn't happen overnight,' explained Nina, helpfully. 'It gives out a signal that vibrates in the soil and drives the moles away. It takes a couple of weeks, but they don't come back.'

Gary looked at me expectantly.

'Don't even think about it,' I glared. 'You'd be throwing good money after bad.'

'It wasn't so expensive,' said Nina. 'Maybe, erm, ten or…'

We never did find out the cost of the miraculous mole repellent; at that moment a commotion broke out at the far end of the orchard. There was a barrage of barking, followed by a pitiful whimper and a deep growl.

'They're fighting!' cried Nina.

Seconds later, Lulu came running towards us but Lenda was nowhere to be seen.

'Shit,' I mumbled, and hurried off through the orchard. The reason for the skirmish soon became clear; at the foot of the furthest cherry tree, Lenda was burying a bone. Once she was satisfied that the bone was hidden she came running up to me, looking triumphant.

'Oh, Lenda,' I laughed. 'That was very bad manners. Come on, you monkey, let's go and see if you can make amends.'

Lulu hunkered down as we approached the patio, but Lenda ignored her. By the time I'd sat down and rolled a cigarette, the pair were cavorting again.

'Who's hungry?' asked Nina, once it was clear that their quarrel had been forgotten.

'We all are,' said Marcus. 'You should fetch the lunch.'

Ten minutes later, Marcus, Gary and I were back in the courtyard, sitting around the table. Even with an ensemble of builder's buckets, cement bags and a hosepipe in the corner, the setting was just as lovely as a photo in *Casa y Campo* magazine.

'It's such a pretty space,' I said.

'It needs a lot of work,' frowned Marcus. 'But it will do for now.'

Eventually Nina returned, carrying a trio of large serving bowls on a metal tray. She set it down on the table. There was boiled rice and a green salad and something deliciously fragrant that looked like minced meat.

'It's Indonesian spicy beef,' she told us. 'My Mum calls it *bieftuk pedas*. Go on, eat while it's warm.'

Marcus began to heap rice onto his plate and Nina passed me the beef. Gary looked on longingly as he lifted lettuce from the salad bowl with a fork. The aroma wafting from my plate was irresistible and I was overcome with the urge to dig in. Remembering my manners I hung on until everyone else was ready. The *bieftuk pedas* was rich and tasty and certainly well worth the wait.

'It's wonderful,' I enthused. 'I could eat like this every day.'

'So could I,' laughed Marcus. 'But she only makes it when we have visitors. The rest of the time we eat Dutch food. Meat and potatoes – it is very plain.'

'What's in it?' I asked. 'I can taste chilli, cinnamon, anis, tamarind…'

'Very good,' nodded Nina. 'And lime leaves, lemon grass, powdered shrimp…'

'Powdered *shrimp*?' said Gary. 'As in, prawns?'

'Yes. We call it *trasi*. It's used in lots of our recipes. I'll give you some to take home.'

It was the perfect meal in a perfect setting. The sun beamed like a beacon above us, yet we were bathed in the shadows cast by the walls. For the next half hour we munched and chatted, issuing occasional warnings to the canine opportunists as they snuffled around our feet.

When she was sure we'd finished, Nina began to collect the plates.

'A short rest before dessert,' declared Marcus. 'We need time to smoke.'

My eyes widened. 'I'm not sure I can manage a...'

'Don't worry,' smiled Nina. 'It's not a proper dessert. It's Indonesian spice cake. We call it *kek lapis*. I thought we could have it with ice cream.'

'Cake *and* ice cream?' I echoed, standing up to help her. 'Oh heck.'

'I might struggle,' grinned Gary. 'But I'll do my best.'

Leaving the men to their cigarettes, Nina and I went round to the kitchen. It was laid out like José Val's, those of our neighbours and almost every rural home in Galicia. In the middle was a range, surrounded on three sides by marble surfaces with long wooden benches beneath. Beneath the window, an aluminium sink had replaced the original one of stone. Against one wall was a wooden dresser. A butane cooker and fridge freezer served as a reminder that time had moved on.

'Before I forget,' said Nina, 'I'll get you some *trasi* to take home.'

'It's very kind of you,' I smiled. 'But I don't want to leave you short.'

'You won't. I've plenty in here. I always stock up when I go home. I bring *trasi*, tamarind, peanut butter...'

'Peanut butter?'

'Yes, for the satay. It costs a fortune in Lidl.'

'Tell me about it,' I frowned.

Nina opened the door of the freezer and brought out a zip-lock bag. Inside was a cardboard box filled with small plastic sachets. She handed me one and instinctively I sniffed. I regretted it instantly, recoiling in utter disbelief.

'My *God*!'

Nina laughed. 'I know what you're thinking. It smells disgusting. That's why Marcus insists I keep it in the freezer. I used to keep it in the dresser but he said the whole kitchen smelled like something had gone off.'

'Gone off?' I grimaced. 'It smells like a long lost pair of dirty knickers abandoned at the bottom of a laundry basket.'

Nina shrieked with delight. When she'd finally stopped laughing she wrapped a handful of sachets in foil and popped them into another zip-lock bag.

'Be sure to only use a little,' she told me. 'And remind me *never* to offer to wash your clothes.'

This time we both fell into fits of giggles. We were only beginning to gather ourselves when Gary appeared at the door.

'Alright in here? Which way's the loo?'

'To your left,' said Nina. 'You need to move the door handle upwards, not downwards. When you've finished you can give us a hand.' She turned to me as she walked over to the dresser. 'You'll be impressed when you see the cake.'

She brought out a serving plate, but the cake remained a mystery, concealed under a plastic mesh dome. She set it down on the marble surface.

'Go on,' she said. 'Take off the lid.'

As I reached for the loop at the top of the cover my sense of anticipation surprised me. What on earth could be so exciting about a cake? I lifted it slowly and gaped in amazement. The cake was made up of at least a dozen layers.

'Crikey!' I exclaimed. 'It must have taken you *ages*!'

'Not me,' laughed Nina. 'My Mum. She sends me back with two or three and I keep them in the freezer for special occasions. It's made up of twelve layers. Each layer is cooked separately. It takes her over two hours.'

I imagined a little Indonesian lady, an older version of Nina, pouring cake mix into a dozen baking trays. I had to admit; it did look enticing, but I wasn't convinced that a cake could be worth so much work.

'Couldn't she just bake two or three cakes and slice them thinly?'

Nina frowned. 'Oh no, they have to be baked separately or you wouldn't see the layers.'

I peered hard at the cake but couldn't see what difference it would make. There were a dozen thin layers of sponge, alternated with even thinner layers of something russet-brown. Despite my unsettling experience with the *trasi*, my olfactory curiosity got the better of me. I leaned forward and inhaled deeply. This time I didn't recoil. There was cinnamon, anis and, was that a hint of nutmeg? All the fragrances of Christmas were there in a stripy sponge.

'It smells gorgeous,' I said. 'What's the brown filling?'

'That's not a filling,' replied Nina. 'It's the top of the sponge.'

The *kek lapis* was a culinary enigma. I couldn't for the life of me see why it didn't fall apart.

Nina must have sensed my confusion. 'The dark layers are the top of each cake,' she explained. 'When the first layer is cooked, you pour the mixture on top and put it back in the oven. You carry on like that until there's no more mixture left. It doesn't burn because you cook it on a very low oven and the bottom layers stay lovely and moist.'

The *kek lapis* was delicious; even with a generous blob of ice cream, Gary and I both managed to find room.

When Marcus had polished off a second helping he sat back and gave a contented sigh. 'I will never say a bad word about my mother-in-law,' he smiled, 'as long as she keeps sending the cake.'

'Perhaps Liza will bake one for you, Gary,' said Nina.

It was a nice bit of cake, granted, but I didn't fancy wasting a whole morning just to serve up a half-decent sponge. Gary seemed to have warmed to the idea, but I knew exactly how to knock his enthusiasm on the head.

'I suppose I could,' I said slyly. 'How long was it baked for Nina? Over two hours, I think you said?'

'Two hours?' frowned Gary. 'It'd cost us a fortune in butane. P'raps you could leave it 'til winter. I bet it'd cook lovely in the range.'

I was slipping Lenda's lead on when Nina came up with a carrier bag.

'Don't go without the cherries,' she reminded me. 'And I've put the bag of shrimp powder on top.'

'Lovely,' I smiled. 'I'm ever so grateful.' I wasn't lying; I was pleased with the cherries, after all.

That evening I emptied a sachet of the dirty-knickers powder into a mug of hot water. I wanted to see what wonders its rehydration would bring. After ten minutes the water was grey and there were lumps of something vile floating in the miasma. As far as I was concerned the origin of the *trasi* was all too clear. This putrid concoction didn't have its origins in succulent prawn flesh; I'd have bet my bottom dollar it was the stuff they chucked out when the prawn was deveined. I poured it down the sink and tossed the rest of the sachets in with the rubbish. I was still looking forward to making *bieftuk pedas*, but I wouldn't be adding *trasi* to *my* spicy beef.

Sunday Afternoon
(to the tune of 'Sunny Afternoon' by The Kinks)[1]

Weekend's here, a time to roam;
Take a trip away from home,
Driving on a Sunday afternoon.
Gary's temper's way too hot,
Patience he sure hasn't got,
Driving on a Sunday afternoon.

Save me, save me, save me, someone please;
I got an angry husband cursing, please believe.
And I'd love him to drive pleasantly;
Laugh and sing and joke with me,
Driving on a Sunday afternoon.
In the countryside…
In the countryside…
In the countryside…

Pass a couple in a car,
Happier than us by far;
See how jolly country drives can be?
Now, alas, I'm sitting here,
Wishing I could disappear,
Driving on a Sunday afternoon.

Help him, help him, help him please, I pray;
Put a smile upon his face and make my day;
'Cause I'd love him to drive pleasantly,
Laugh and sing and joke with me,
Driving on a Sunday afternoon
In the countryside…
In the countryside…
In the countryside…

---

[1] The Kinks. 'Sunny Afternoon'. *Face to Face.* Pye, 1966

Liza Grantham

Save me, save me, save me, someone please;
I got an angry husband cursing, please believe.
And I'd love him to drive pleasantly,
Laugh and sing and joke with me,
Driving on a Sunday afternoon,
In the countryside...
In the countryside...
In the countryside...

Chapter 4

Up in the Air

On Monday morning I awoke to a familiar pattering against the window. It was far pleasanter than a cat in a litter tray, scratching like a skiffler on a washboard, and it was a sound for which I'd come to be grateful; the quality of our lifestyle was heavily dependent on that blessèd Galician rain.

An hour later I stepped out into the drizzle. It was lighter than I'd expected and I tossed my umbrella unopened onto the bench. It was almost a fortnight since the last of the blossom had fallen from the apple trees. All that remained were the wispy filaments, and beneath them the tiny green swellings that would grow and ripen into sweet russet fruits. Beneath the fig tree, the soft pink mauve of the dead nettles and the brilliant blue of lungwort dappled the melange of myriad greens. In the veg plot the pea nets were jewelled with glistening raindrops and the blackbirds busied themselves under the bean sticks, pecking out grubs for themselves and their young.

It wasn't only the birds' nests that would be full of new life this morning. It was thirty one days since Doe had paid Buck a visit; her gestation was as reliable as any calendar and I had no doubts that her babies had arrived. Over in Warren Place I opened the door into the escape run and stepped over the divider into Doe's pen. We'd had the rabbits for over a year now, but I could clearly remember the battle I'd had convincing Gary that as well as their hutches, both rabbits would need their own run. He'd griped about costs, but I'd dug my heels in. When he'd finally come round to my way of thinking he'd surpassed himself with the finished result. The pens were spacious and, after some tweaking, were finally escape proof. The hutches were perfect from day one. Each had a large side-opening door which could be swung open for cleaning, and a smaller pull-down door which served as a ramp. Every morning both rabbits would be waiting impatiently for their breakfast; Buck would be thumping and Doe would be scraping, reminding me it was time to release them into their runs.

I knelt in front of Doe's hutch and lowered the ramp with due deliberation. I wasn't expecting a full-blown nativity scene; the new-borns would be hidden under a blanket of fur. As Doe bounded out on a mission to find her breakfast, I was taken aback to see two wrinkled grey new-borns squirming on the bare wooden floor. Up until now, Doe had been meticulous about leaving the babies well-hidden; there had to be a reason she'd singled these out from the rest. For a moment I was thrown into confusion. I'd heard that touching the young would cause the mother to eat them, and there was every chance she'd eat the rest of her litter too. The babies were tiny and vulnerable; they wouldn't be able to maintain their body temperature and would perish quickly away from the nest. I glanced over at Doe, who was munching heartily. She'd be oblivious if I leaned in and moved them now.

I took a deep breath. Every second counted and I had to act fast. I slunk out of the pen and pulled a couple of leaves from the fig tree. Back in the run, I used them to scoop up the babies and deposit them gently on top of the fur. I could only hope Doe wouldn't sense my intrusion; I was counting on Mother Nature to save them now.

With both rabbits fed and watered, I made my way down to the chooks' pen. I squelched over the damp grass, avoiding the giant black slugs and their treacherous slime. I sighed when I spotted Waynetta scratching around the feeder; the warmer, lighter mornings were tempting her early descent from the tree. Her wayward behaviour was a worry and I feared I might lose her; if she flew down too early the fox might still be out on the prowl. Springtime was always a medley of swings and roundabouts; new life was in abundance and predators were out in force.

'Crikey,' yawned Gary as he came into the kitchen. 'Have you remembered to check the mouse traps? Something in here doesn't half pong.'

'It's the *trasi*,' I laughed, as I passed him his cuppa. 'Don't worry, it's out in the barn with the rubbish. I doubt it'll linger for long.'

'I'm glad I'll be out shopping – at least Día doesn't stink.'

'Trust you. It'll smell gorgeous in here by lunchtime – I'm going to turn Nina's cherries into pies. Oh, that reminds me, you're getting the veg plants this morning, aren't you? I fancy a bit of variety – can you grow us a pumpkin this year?'

'A pumpkin?'

'Yes. You know – large, round, orange? Like a space hopper but without the horns.'

'There's no need to be sarcastic. Don't forget we'll have courgettes and marrows and squashes.'

'I want a pumpkin. It'll be just the job in the autumn. I'll make pies and soups for the freezer, and we'll have a lovely big lantern for Halloween.'

'You're like a big kid sometimes. Go on then – I'll see what I can do.'

It was almost lunchtime when Gary returned with the shopping. I'd half expected him to forget my pumpkin, so when he passed me the flimsy black plant pot it came as a lovely surprise. The plantlet itself seemed so small and fragile, the thought of it bearing a huge sturdy pumpkin was hard to conceive.

'Thank you,' I smiled.

'Anything to stop you sulking. I've bought you some strawberry plants as well.'

'Really? That's amazing! I was planning on making a fruit bed this year.'

'I know. I *do* listen… most of the time.'

I wrapped my free arm round his waist and was about to kiss him, when he spoke again.

'I called in to see Ángel at the garage to book the van in for its MOT.'

My brow furrowed. Trust Gary to spoil the moment. Yesterday's outing was still fresh in my memory; the last thing I wanted to hear about was the wretched van.

'It's next Tuesday,' he continued, ignoring my expression. 'I told him he won't need to take it in for me. I know all the parts in Spanish and I'm sure I can manage on my own.'

My face softened and my heart swelled with pride. Only eight years ago he'd left England with barely a word of Spanish. I couldn't help but admire him. Maybe he deserved that kiss after all.

By teatime, the strawberry plants were aligned in their freshly dug border, and the frail little pumpkin sprig was nestled in a bucket where it would strengthen and thrive. In the meantime, Gary had been busy with the rest of the veg plants. The raised beds were arrayed with beetroots and brassicas, while aubergines, peppers, tomatoes and cucurbits flopped bravely against canes in the ground.

An afternoon on the garden, though pleasant, had been tiring. After Lenda's walk, all that remained was to shut away the livestock; I was looking forward to a shower and a beer. Down in the chicken run, I could see neither hide nor feather of Waynetta. I assumed she'd flapped her way further up the tree. Over in Warren Place, Doe had tossed the two babies from the nest a second time. I didn't bother with the fig leaves; they were dead on the floor of the run.

When Gary came back from Rose's on Tuesday it was way past his tea-time. He looked decidedly cheerful when he got out of the van.

'Crikey,' I said. 'I bet you're starving. You don't look as tired as you did last week. Was it an easier day?'

'I wouldn't say *easier*, but it was surprising. I had an unexpected workmate – Pete was there.'

'Pete? Never. Well, I'll be blowed.'

Rose's husband Pete was still working in England, although Rose had been living on and off in Galicia for the past two years. When they'd bought their ruinous house they'd planned to move out together when the repairs were completed, but Rose was so impulsive she'd decided not to wait.

'You didn't say Pete was coming over.'

'That's because I didn't know. Neither did he, as it happens. Rose had one of her madcap whims and booked him a flight for Saturday morning. He's going back tomorrow. She thought it'd do him good to have a long weekend.'

'So Pete didn't mind then?'

'Oh no. He'd been thinking about making a visit anyway. He wanted to see what she's been spending the money on. He confided in me when we were building the greenhouse. He said, "Between you, me and the gatepost…"'

'Whoa! Hold on! The *green*house? You didn't mention *that* last week.'

'It's not a greenhouse as such. It's one of those… oh, what do they call them? The long plastic things with a curved roof.'

'A polytunnel.'

'That's it. It was delivered on Thursday apparently, not long after I'd set off for home.'

'Ah,' I smiled wryly. 'I see.'

It wasn't hard to imagine the scenario. Rose had probably been expecting the delivery on Thursday morning and hoped that Gary would be able to assemble the polytunnel in the afternoon. The chances were, when it turned up late she was disappointed she'd have to wait until Tuesday to see it in all its glory. What was the betting she'd booked a last-minute flight for Pete so he could rig it up over the weekend?

'She hasn't half got a cheek,' grinned Gary. 'She was saying how she'd asked the delivery blokes if they'd stay and put it up for her. She laid it on really thick, telling them how bad her back was and that nobody ever dropped by.'

I giggled. 'That sounds like Rose, bless her. So how come Pete didn't see to it on Sunday?'

'He said it was a two-man job, much to Rose's annoyance. He wasn't kidding – we had quite a battle with it. It's nearly as long as this kitchen and about half as wide. It's impressive at first glance but close up it looks a bit flimsy. It certainly wasn't worth two hundred quid.'

'Two hundred quid? For a plastic marquee? She's bonkers – look what happened to the tent!'

'Crikey, I'd forgotten about that. I'm surprised she didn't think of it. You're right though – if a fierce wind can tear through canvas it'd have no trouble shredding an over-sized plastic bag.'

'Oh well, on her head be it. I doubt we'll have any more storms now 'til autumn – it should be okay 'til then.'

When we settled down with our beers that evening Gary was looking pensive.

'Penny for 'em?' I ventured. 'You look as though there's something on your mind.'

'I was thinking about the polytunnel. I reckon we ought to have one. Driving around the countryside I've noticed loads in people's *fincas* – their popularity seems to be on the rise. It'd be great for starting the seeds off and it might protect the tomatoes from blight.'

I couldn't believe what I was hearing. I only had to *mention* animal feed or chicken wire and Gary's blood pressure was through the ceiling. Now he was thinking of investing in some fancy housing just for the veg.

I looked at him. 'I can't see the point to be honest. You said yourself they're a rip-off and you're always reminding me we can barely make ends meet.'

'I wasn't suggesting we *buy* one. I'm sure I could knock one together quite cheaply, but it wouldn't be a dome. It'd have to be like a traditional greenhouse, but instead of glass I'd use polythene, and for the framework I'd use wood.'

Two years ago we'd made it our rule of thumb to follow whatever the neighbours did. None of *them* had a polytunnel, or a greenhouse or any other mollycoddle-your-plants type constructions. Seeds were broadcast onto the soil and plantlets were stuffed into furrows; it was as simple as that. I was about to point this out but decided to say nothing. The veg was Gary's responsibility; if he wanted a jerry-built polyhouse it was up to him.

'Sounds good,' I lied. 'Where will it go?'

'I thought I'd put it at the end of the veg plot, under the chestnut tree. It's a massive space and it's a shame to waste it. We can't grow veg there because of the roots.'

The very idea was preposterous. The canopy of the chestnut tree would be sure to block out the sun. If that wasn't enough, come autumn the top would be bombarded by prickly chestnut cases and the plastic would be sure to split.

'So,' Gary continued, 'what do you think?'

I feigned a look of approval. 'That'll be great.'

On Wednesday Gary was up bright and early. He was like a kid waiting for Christmas, keen to be at the woodyard when they opened at ten. Alas, I was far too preoccupied to share in his excitement. I'd been playing hunt the chicken since daybreak. Waynetta had disappeared.

'Gone?' he yawned, as I passed him his cuppa. 'She can't have, don't be daft.'

'Believe me, she has. I've looked everywhere. I haven't found so much as a feather. The fox must have had her. Oh, Gary – it's all my fault.'

'Of course it isn't. Nobody forced her to sleep in the damson tree. If the fox *has* had her then she's only got herself to blame.'

As sorry as I was, I couldn't help smiling; I imagined Waynetta chiding herself as she dangled helplessly from the fox's jaws.

When Gary came back from the woodyard I was feeling much brighter. Every time I thought of Waynetta I couldn't resist a smile.

'You're looking cheerful,' said Gary. 'Have you got news?'

'I have, as it happens. Waynetta's still missing and there's lasagne for lunch.'

'Oh well, bad news and good news then. Do you want to see the wood?'

'Not really. I want to get the laundry out before lunchtime. You can astound me later when I've done.'

I was wringing out the last of the towels when Gary came into the kitchen.

'Your lunch isn't ready – it's in the oven. I'm still on the laundry, but I won't be long.'

'Don't worry, that's not what I've come for. I've got a surprise for you under the apple tree. It'll only take a minute – I think you'll be pleased.'

I froze. I couldn't have cared less about the polyhouse, but if he thought he was sticking it under the apple trees he could think again. I turned the oven down and wiped my hands on the tea-towel.

'Right then,' I sighed. 'Let's go.'

As we crossed the threshing floor I looked over towards the apple trees. I breathed a sigh of relief when I saw that the grass beneath them was undisturbed. I began to walk over, but Gary was already striding off down the lawn.

'Liza, where are you going? I don't mean *those* apple trees. We need to go down to the chicken run, come on.'

Now I was baffled. The only trees in the chooks' pen were the chestnut and the damsons. I feared his poly-mania was affecting his mind. I followed him into the enclosure and he stopped by the henhouse.

'There, look,' he said, pointing through the wire fencing. 'See the big apple tree on Paul's land?'

'Right,' I nodded. 'Now I've got you. I can only see the tree though, where's my surprise?'

'You'll need to get behind the henhouse. We won't both fit – squeeze round and then I'll tell you what to do.'

Filled with curiosity I stepped past him and inched my way into the narrow gap between the house and the crumbling stone wall. 'Now what?'

'Position yourself to the left of the tree trunk.'

I leaned sideways. It was a tight fit.

'Are you there yet?'

'Just about.'

'Right, now look closely at the bottom of the trunk.'

I stared hard at the base of the tree but saw nothing but a large stone amongst the sodden brown leaves that had been there since autumn. As I clutched at the wall the stone moved. I leaned forward and the stone moved again.

'Waynetta!' I exclaimed. 'Oh, Gary, it's Waynetta! You're an absolute hero! You've made my day!'

Half an hour later, Waynetta was sitting on her ten secret eggs, on a deep nest of straw in the maternity house. Mrs Brown clucked and fretted over her ten week old chicks who were scratching about with the big chooks out in the run.

When I went up to take the rubbish, Maruja's back door was open. I could see her in the passage, nodding and frowning into the phone. I waved and she raised her hand in greeting. Whoever the caller was, her expression suggested they were bringing bad news.

On my way back she was standing on the doorstep.

'*Hola*, Elisa,' she said, as I wandered over. 'I've been on the phone to my sister. She lost a dozen hens yesterday. The fox got through a hole in the fence, and it happened during the day.'

'Oh dear,' I frowned. 'That sounds like a vixen. I've had a narrow escape this morning. I thought I'd lost one of mine.'

When I told her about Waynetta's exploits her face broke into a smile.

'That happened with one of ours in April. José Manuel found her in the *cuadra* opposite Alfonso's. He'd gone down to fix the door, because that's where we shut Luna when she's in season. The hen was under some boxes – she was sitting on eighteen eggs. We took some away and let her sit twelve altogether. They all hatched. The chicks are in the farmyard now – they'll be coming up for three weeks old.'

'That's amazing. I had no idea they could sit so many. Has Luna's season finished now?'

'Oh, yes. It lasted about three weeks altogether. Pastor's too old to show any interest, but Res was a problem – it was a battle trying to keep them apart.'

I nodded. Res, their large white shepherd, was a working cow dog. He was young, powerful and virile and I could imagine it would be a nightmare to keep him restrained.

'You'll have to watch Lenda,' said Maruja. 'She's not a puppy anymore. Her season will be due soon.'

Maruja was right. Lenda was ten months old; her first oestrus was imminent. I couldn't help wondering if Pastora had been in season too. I hadn't seen her for ages and I missed her, but I didn't miss seeing the blue ticks hanging in clusters from her neck or the way her skin pulled taut against her rib bones when she moved.

'I hope Pastora isn't pregnant,' I sighed. 'It upset me last year, she was so painfully thin.'

'Pastora won't be having any more puppies, Elisa. She's dead.'

The news hit me like a sledgehammer and my eyes filled with tears.

'No,' I stammered. 'Not Pastora? She *can't* be. Oh God, no.'

I sank down onto the wooden bench, between an empty bucket and a length of chain. I put my face in my hands and my shoulders trembled as the tears fell.

'Oh, Elisa,' said Maruja kindly. 'You were fond of her, weren't you? Try not to let it upset you. She's in a better place now.'

'What happened?' I sniffed eventually, wiping my eyes with my hand.

'I don't know, but I doubt she'd have suffered. Tonito told Javier she'd been fine on the Sunday. On the Monday he found her dead in the field.'

As I trudged back down the lane I thought about Pastora. She'd been such a happy, lively little pup when we'd met her that first summer before we'd moved in. During that month she'd spent so much time with us that I'd almost come to think of her as ours. When we'd returned to the *aldea* at Christmas she was no longer a puppy and Tonito was training her to work with the cows. Anxo had adored her and they'd soon become playmates. I hoped that somewhere over the Rainbow Bridge they'd be playing together now.

When the day of the MOT came round, Gary rose early – again. Once again he was restless, but unlike the previous week he showed no signs of enthusiasm. Gone was the kiddie at Christmas; he was the cat on a hot tin roof. When he'd finished his cuppa, he reached for the Spanish dictionary. There was a lot of tutting and sighing as he began to thumb through. I couldn't see the point of his eleventh hour cramming; as far as I was concerned the outcome was doomed.

'I don't know why you're bothering,' I frowned. 'It won't matter how good your Spanish is – it won't alter the fact that it's a shit van.'

At nine thirty Gary set off for Lalín. I blew him a kiss and waved from the doorstep. I regretted my earlier cynicism and it was the least I could do to make amends.

As the van screeched through the village I took Lenda out to the garden. It was only a week since I'd put in the plantlets but already my strawberries had grown. Despite my misgivings, Gary had made a good job of the polyhouse. The framework was lightweight yet sturdy, with a panel at the front that rolled up like a blind. Inside, the tomato plants seemed to be thriving, along with my cherished little pumpkin, which wasn't *quite* ready to be planted outside.

By eleven thirty there was no sign of the van *or* Gary. I was beginning to wonder if the van had been deemed too dangerous to be driven home. It was just after midday when a banshee's howl rang out through the village. The van hadn't been impounded; Gary was home. When he came into the kitchen he was grinning.

'Put the kettle on – I've got news.'

'Let me guess. It had a rare moment of mechanical compliance, disguised the fact that it's ready for the scrap heap and passed the MOT.'

'Eh?'

'The van.'

'Oh, right. Yes, it passed, but that's not the surprise.'

'I can assure you it's a surprise as far as *I'm* concerned.'

'There's no need to be sarky. Do you want the news or not?'

'Sorry. Go on then, don't keep me in suspense.'

'Paul's back.'

'Rubbish. He can't be – he'd have been round for his key.'

'Alright then, Miss Fussy-Britches. Paul's *coming* back. He's on his way.'

'Right. Why didn't you say so? Did you pass him coming through the *aldea*? Has he parked up at the church?'

'If I can get a word in edgeways I'll tell you. Now are you putting the kettle on or not?'

Five minutes later we were sitting in the kitchen with our coffees. Once Gary had rolled himself a ciggie he was ready to spill the beans.

'I was driving out of Lalín when I spotted him. He was sitting at a table outside a café. I was in a line of traffic so I couldn't pull over or sound the horn.'

'You were imagining things. Probably still in shock from passing the MOT. I can see how it might have sent you delusional. Don't worry, you'll soon come round.'

'I'm telling you, Liza, it was Paul, for definite. He said he was coming back in May, didn't he? I wasn't mistaken – he was drinking red wine.'

After lunch I took Lenda out to the garden. I was closing the gate when I heard someone calling '*Hola*' from the top of the lane. I waved when I recognised the figure walking towards me; hunched under the weight of a bulging rucksack was Paul.

'Hey up,' I grinned. 'Gary said he'd seen you in Lalín and I didn't believe him. I couldn't imagine why you'd take the long way round.'

'Lidl,' he grinned reaching behind him and patting his rucksack. 'Had to go to Lidl. Cheddar and proper sausages. I've stocked up.'

On Sunday it was Maruja's birthday and I wanted to surprise her. The cherry pie I'd defrosted looked scrumptious; Gary's face was a picture when I told him it wasn't for him.

As I drew near to the farmhouse I could hear the telly blaring inside the kitchen. Even on her birthday Maruja would be busy; she'd either be making cheese or preparing the lunch.

I rang the bell and waited. Maruja worked slowly and deliberately; it always took a few minutes for her to answer the door. Eventually I saw her through the glass, wiping her hands on her pinny. The door opened and Flea-pelt shot out, yapping and twirling manically around my feet.

'*Hola*, Maruja,' I grinned. '*Feliz cumpleaños.*'

Maruja beamed. 'Elisa! I can't believe you've remembered! It smells nice, is it a *tarta*? I'll get a plate for it, come on in.'

Maruja's kitchen was like a sauna. A huge pan of kale and potatoes was bubbling away on top of the range.

'Have you seen Paul yet?' I asked, as she lifted a plate from the dresser.

'I have,' she nodded. 'He was out in the lane in his *bóxers* and it's not even summer. He won't be doing that next week, they've given rain. I wish he spoke Castilian – there's a *refrán* that's ideal for him. He wouldn't understand me if I told him – it's a shame.'

I knew that the Spanish, especially the *galegos*, had lots of proverbs and sayings relating to the weather. I didn't recall having heard any about wearing boxer shorts in spring. I looked at Maruja quizzically, knowing she'd fill me in.

'*Hasta el cuarenta de mayo no te quites el sayo.*'

I repeated it slowly. Something about the *refrán* didn't quite make sense. Perhaps I'd heard it wrongly? I translated it mentally word for word. 'Until the fortieth of May, don't take off your *sayo*.' A *sayo* was a smock, an old-fashioned overall – that wasn't the problem. Of course; the *fortieth* of May. Proverbs carry a moral or message, but not all of them are meant to be taken literally; there's often a metaphor or exaggeration involved. What the *refrán* really meant was, 'Don't go anywhere without your coat until we're well into June.' As a smile of enlightenment spread over my face, Maruja began to smile with me, pleased that I'd understood.

'It's clever,' I nodded. 'I'll tell Gary – he'll like it. I don't think it's worth telling Paul.'

That afternoon I repeated the proverb to Gary over coffee.

'It doesn't make sense,' he frowned. 'Are you sure she didn't say *catorce* – the fourteenth?'

'No,' I said. 'She said the fortieth. You don't have to take it literally – let's call it poetic licence. *Now* does it make sense?'

He paused for a moment. Eventually the penny dropped.

'Aha! *Now* I get it! You're best to wait 'til May's over and done with. You're not home and dry until June.'

'Exactly. That's a good way of putting it actually – when you say it like that it's pretty much the same as the one we have in English, "Never cast a clout 'til May's out."'

'Crikey, I'd forgotten about that one. I remember my Gran used to say it. In England it was bloody good advice.'

'Maruja wanted to recite it to Paul.'

'That's not a bad idea, but it'd need some adjusting. Forget the *sayo* – "don't take *all* your clothes off" would be nearer the mark.'

A week passed and there was no change in the weather. I was beginning to think Maruja had been mistaken; on Monday morning there wasn't a cloud in the sky.

Over in Warren Place, Bravo Buck was thumping impatiently but Doe, with nine babies, deserved priority and it wouldn't hurt him to wait. Since she'd ousted the pair of new-borns, Doe had reverted to being the perfect mother. I could only assume that she'd deemed eleven babies a definite 'no'.

Once the rabbits were all munching, I made my way down to the chooks' pen. As I neared the entrance I heard a spinechilling keening; if I wasn't mistaken, one of my birds was in pain. Dumping my bucket by the feeder, I hurried across to the henhouse. From amidst the scuffling and squawking there came a pitiful strangled crow. I took a deep breath and steeled myself for the heartache; something was terribly wrong with Wayne. When I opened the door, the hens flapped and jostled their way into the sunshine and Wayne strutted out behind them without a care in the world. As I stared in confusion the smallest of the young cockerels flew down from the perch and paused on the doorstep. He arched his head back proudly and warbled a strained 'cock-a-doooo'. I couldn't contain my laughter; it sounded for all the world as if he'd forgotten his words. Nevertheless, it was a sterling effort; with a little more practise he'd soon find his 'doodle' too.

When Gary came back with the shopping he had news.

'We've had a message. You won't be happy. We need to call in at the bank this week.'

'Oh, that's a nuisance. Whatever for?'

'Something to do with security. They want to see your passport. It won't be anything to worry about. I'm sure it's just routine.'

'It'll be a round robin, I'll probably ignore it. Did you bring the phone in with you? I'll know when I read the text.'

'There wasn't a text.'

'They rang you? Crikey! P'raps it *is* important after all.'

'They didn't ring.'

I stared at him. He was grinning. I still had the lunch to cook and I was keen to get out in the garden. I was in no mood for his fooling around.

'Gary. You're not being funny or clever – just tell me how you know.'

'The woman in the fag shop told me.'

I gaped at him. 'No.'

'On my life. I walked up to the counter and instead of asking what I wanted she said, "Are you the *inglés* from Cutián?" I nodded and she gabbled something about my *mujer*. She'd lost me for a second but then it dawned on me – she meant you.'

'Charming.'

'Anyway, it turns out the cashier's a friend of hers. She'd tried to ring us from the bank but we were always *sin cobertura*. She knew that we lived near Antas so she asked her mate in the fag shop to pass the message on.'

'But how did she know that we use the fag shop? If you'd said Bar Farelo or the *ferretería* I could understand it. Come to think of it, how did she even know we smoke?'

Twenty minutes later we'd run through all sorts of possibilities, but none of the ideas we came up with seemed to make any sense. I was no stranger to the infamous rural grapevine; if I wasn't mistaken it had been working its magic again.

When I went into the chooks' pen on Tuesday morning there was no mistaking the high pitched peeping coming from the nursery. I released the marauding hordes into the sunshine and when they were pecking around the feeder I made my way over to the maternity wing. I opened the door to the house and Waynetta squawked in disapproval. Heeding her warning, I knelt down on the damp earth and peered through the wire. I waited until my knees ached and my legs felt leaden, but my patience was finally rewarded when a tiny head popped out from beneath the straw.

On Thursday morning, Waynetta was out of the nest when I opened the house up. To my delight, seven tiny chicks were hopping and pecking amongst the corn. The other three eggs hadn't hatched and I reached in to remove them. Waynetta jabbed at me fiercely; there was no doubt about it, she was going to be a great mum. I would have been happy to stay there all morning watching Waynetta with her babies but, alas, we were off to Palas; there was a bank job to be done.

In Palas the locals were going about their business and groups of pilgrims were hiking along the main street while others were gathered in huddles around the square. The air felt warm and clammy, and the sky was marbled in ominous hues of graphite and steel. Inside the bank, the cashier smiled when she saw us. It was the perfect opportunity to solve the jungle drums mystery, but I was in no mood for small talk; I wanted to get home to my chicks. I handed over my passport and ten minutes later we were back in the van. As we drove out of Palas the floodgates opened. The thunder rolled in the distance and the first fork of lightning streaked across the sky.

'Can you drive a bit quicker?' I mumbled.

'I can't go any faster, Liza. Look at it, for God's sake. I can barely see the road as it is.'

Gary was right. The wipers were whizzing ten to the dozen across the windscreen, and all I could see of the car in front were blurred taillights through a curtain of rain.

I sunk back in my seat and sighed.

'What's the matter?'

'I'm worried. The chicks are only three days old. They're ever so tiny. If this rain keeps up they'll be drowned.'

'They won't be drowned. The first sign of a raindrop and they'll dive under Waynetta. They'll all be tucked under her by the time we get home.'

I sighed a second time and stared out of the passenger window. Water was coursing along the gutters and pouring from downpipes onto the street. It was sure to be raining in the *aldea*; the chooks' run would be a quagmire and the dust-bath hollows would be pools. I screwed my eyes shut and pictured the maternity wing. Was it built on an incline or would the nest be submerged by the time we were home?

I was trembling with panic by the time we drove into the *aldea*. Gary had long since lost patience and said I was over-reacting; only that morning I'd told him Waynetta was a fabulous mum.

Inside the passage I dumped my bag on the floor and gave Lenda a half-hearted greeting before grabbing my dustbin-lid brolly and dashing back out through the door. Down in the chooks' pen most of the flock were sheltering in the henhouse. A couple of stalwarts were lingering on the threshold and Wayne crowed out above the sound of the torrents as if to rally them in. I waded through the mud and over to the nursery. Waynetta was perched in the house, but there was no sign of the chicks. As I stared through the wire, I winced at the work of the downpour. The soil had been washed away leaving a hollow under the house. I closed the door shut and eased the house backwards; five tiny limp bodies lay dead in the mud. Ignoring the corpses, I glanced round about me; if I acted quickly I might still save the two missing chicks. For almost an hour I tramped round the chooks' pen, using my brolly to poke through the mud and damp leaves. When my clothes were sodden and my feet were freezing it was time to face up to reality. I wouldn't find any survivors; all seven babies had been lost to the storm.

By bedtime the torrents had dwindled to a steady drizzle, but the wind had gathered momentum and was gusting in fiercely from the south. The storm had claimed fatalities but there was no point in brooding; it wasn't the first time I'd lost livestock and it wouldn't be the last. Tonight the rabbits were secured in their hutches and Waynetta was back in the henhouse where all were safely on the roost. I snuggled down deeper under the duvet, content to drift off into Dreamland. I'd battened down all the hatches; now the weather could do its worst.

Liza Grantham

Waynetta

Waynetta the wayward young bantam
Was given to throwing a tantrum;
Our birds of a feather
Would all stick together,
But she sought her own inner sanctum.

The hen house did not suit Waynetta,
That awkward hen thought she knew better;
She slept in the tree,
Disregarding my plea,
And I had no choice but to let her.

We thought that she must have skedaddled,
But on her ten eggs she was straddled,
We tried hard to calm her
And did not alarm her,
For fear that the eggs would be addled.

We made her a place much more fitting,
And now on her treasures she's sitting;
There's no need to roam,
She'll be safer at home,
And from now on we'll have no more flitting.

Chapter 5

Lock Up Your Daughters

In the early hours of Friday morning I was jolted abruptly from the Land of Nod. I propped myself onto my elbow and listened in the darkness. The door to the terrace was banging persistently; the repetitive, resonant slamming was enough to wake the dead. Sighing in exasperation, I eased my way out from under the duvet, trying not to disturb the slumbering Scholes and Fred.

In the half-light of the living room I paused to look through the window. Outside the wind was howling like a banshee; the cable of the streetlight was swinging ominously and I wondered how many tiles would be missing from the roof of the barn. I padded through the dining room and fastened the bolt on the door to the terrace. It was no wonder it had been banging; a fierce draught was coming up from the passage, gusting up the staircase and blowing the length of the house.

Down in the passage, Lenda was shaking. Her tail gave a wag, but her body was all of a quiver.

'Oh, Lenda,' I whispered. 'You're scared.'

I bent down to fuss her and she pushed her head firmly against me.

'You softie,' I smiled. 'It's the wind. No wonder it woke us – it's making a heck of a noise.'

I went through to the kitchen and filled the kettle. Lenda gruffed crossly as something clattered about in the lane outside. I rolled myself a cigarette and resigned myself to an early start to the morning. I wouldn't be able to sleep while the gale was howling and as long as I was with her, Lenda would stay calm.

It was almost three hours later when Gary came into the kitchen. The years were certainly taking their toll on his hearing; against all the odds he'd managed to sleep through the squall.

'Morning,' I said, as I passed him his cuppa. 'There hasn't half been a racket. I'm surprised you could sleep.'

'Tell me,' he yawned. 'I don't know why you got up so early. I've not slept a wink since I heard you banging that door.'

'Don't talk such rubbish – you were dead to the world. And I *didn't* bang the door, I got up *because* it was banging. Whoever was last in the bathroom forgot to slide the bolt.'

'And that'd be me, would it?'

'I didn't say it was you – I said "whoever". Your trouble is you always…'

'Shh!'

'Don't you *dare* shush me. I…'

'Listen! Can't you hear it? What the *hell* is that noise?'

I fell silent. Somewhere outside there was a fearful groaning and creaking. It seemed to be coming from the garden. Gary began to say something when he was rudely interrupted by the most almighty crash.

'Shit,' he frowned. 'That was a tree.'

'I think you're right. I bet it's that apple tree of Carmen's – the one that's overhanging our lawn.'

'I hope not. Go on then – you're nearest to the window. Have a look.'

I went over to the sink and opened the curtains. As I hoisted myself onto the drainer, Gary tutted and shook his head.

I tutted back. 'Do you want to know about the tree or don't you? I can't see bugger all through the frosted glass.'

I stood upright and peered through the clear panes at the top. 'No. We're alright. It's not Carmen's apple tree. The big branch is bowing and swaying, but it hasn't come down yet. The chestnuts haven't budged and that eyesore of a conifer's still with us. That's your lot really – I can't see the rest for the barn.'

'Well it won't be the fig tree – it's stumpy. And it won't be our apple trees – they're as wide as they are tall. Do you know what I reckon?'

'What?'

'It'll be one of Paul's.'

'You could be right. I tell you what, I'll see to the chooks and rabbits and then I'll take Lenda. Instead of going down the track, I'll take a detour. I'll go round the back way and have a stroll across Paul's land.'

'I'm not sure that's a good idea.'

'Why not? He won't be up for hours yet – he never surfaces 'til lunchtime. Do you want to know what made that noise or not?'

Out in the garden the wind showed no signs of abating but just as Gary had predicted, the fig and apple trees had stood firm. The threshing floor was strewn with fragments of tiles from Carmen's roof, yet those on Warren Place remained in situ, thanks to the windbreak provided by the barn. The overhanging branch of Carmen's apple tree was creaking mournfully and I feared it was only a matter of time before it crashed down onto our lawn. At first glance there appeared to be no damage in the *huerta*; the bean sticks were still standing and the pea nets were flapping but not torn. Nevertheless, something seemed different but I wasn't prepared to linger. The wind was doing its damnedest to shove me across the garden; Gary would have to look later when the gale had calmed.

As I neared the end of the garden I realised what was wrong with the veg plot. I was used to hens flying out of the chooks' pen, but this morning something decidedly bigger had flown in. I stared at the chestnut tree and the wire that formed the escape proof perimeter of the enclosure. It was nothing short of a miracle that the polyhouse had blown over in one piece.

When I came back into the kitchen, Gary was making his second cuppa.

'You're not going to believe this,' I began.

He lifted the teabag from his mug, dribbling a trail over the dresser. 'Go on.'

'The polyhouse is in the chooks' pen.'

'You're having a laugh.'

'I wish I was. It looks as though the wind's lifted it up and carried it clean over the fence. It's a stroke of luck that you sawed the lower branches from the chestnut tree; they'd have ripped straight through the plastic. It seems to have missed everything sharp or spiky. You'll never believe this – it looks completely unharmed.'

'You're right, I don't believe it. I'm going to have to go and look.'

'Finish your cuppa. It's dangerous down in the chooks' pen; Paul's trees are creaking like the dining room floor. You're better to wait 'til I come back with Lenda. I'll help you to lift it back over the wire after break.'

Whether through cowardice or integrity, I opted for a third mug of coffee before I set out on the dog walk. A blustery day was one thing, but a full-on gale was a different matter entirely; Lenda was easily daunted and I wondered how she'd go on.

Despite Gary's misgivings, I opted for the impromptu diversion across Paul's overgrown land. As soon as we reached his threshing floor I spotted the tree that had fallen. An old oak trunk had come down by the perimeter, missing by inches the standing stone wall. The tree, though dead, wasn't rotten; with a day's graft and a chainsaw it would yield enough logs to burn for a month.

As we set off through Paul's wilderness, Lenda was restless. She was ready to charge off into the bracken, but until we reached the fields I was determined to keep her safely on her lead. When we came out onto the track which wove through the woodland, the noises around us were chilling. The winds conspired with the leaves in a whisper, as if in callous mockery of the painful groans of the trees. I picked my way over fallen branches and twisted bramble, stumbling over rocks and into potholes while Lenda tugged forwards, desperate to be free of her lead.

Out in the open, Lenda's enthusiasm soon diminished. She ventured a short distance across the first field then scampered back in confusion, looking behind her as if trying to make sense of the wind.

Up in the fourth field the wind took on a scarily different dimension. It circled above and around us like a taunting, invisible sprite. The swirls were picking up strength and ahead of us the steep slope of the fifth field was looming. The birch at the entrance was swaying portentously; it made sense to cut our losses and head for home. As we dropped back down into the third field the wind was howling through the pine woods and I was staggered by its force. My oversized waterproof flapped and billowed and I feared I'd be lifted upwards like an unwilling human kite. I hunched over with my chin on my chest and tucked my arms in close to my body. Seconds later, a giant gust thrust me sideways and sent me plummeting to the ground. As I eased myself onto my knees, my palms were stinging and my hip was throbbing with pain. If I stood up now I risked being bowled over again, yet somehow I had to reach the safety of the second field. I looked at Lenda who was moving like a hunting dog, with her belly lowered and her nose to the ground. She was finding it hard to forge forwards but, unlike me, she wasn't at risk of being whipped up into the air. She was compact with a smaller surface area and her centre of gravity was close to the ground. The best thing I could do was imitate her; if the low-level, four-legged posture was working for Lenda there was no reason why it shouldn't do the same for me. Thankful that I was wearing the waterproof trousers I eased myself down onto my knees. I leaned forwards, taking my weight on my elbows, then shuffled along as if I was crawling under a cargo net in the way that I'd seen on TV. Under normal circumstances I'd have covered the distance in a couple of minutes, but it seemed a heck of a lot longer crawling like a pantomime tortoise all the way to the opposite side.

At breaktime I was filling the kettle for our coffees when the kitchen light went out. It didn't seem long since we'd changed the fluorescent tube, and it normally juddered for days before finally dying with a buzz. I'd have to send Gary into Antas, and I knew he wouldn't be happy. I plonked the kettle on the draining board and went out into the garden to give him the unwelcome news. Much to my surprise, the polyhouse was back under the chestnut tree and Gary was securing a fluttering pea net with twine.

'Crikey,' I said. 'You've moved it all ready. Don't you think you've been a bit hasty? I'd have thought you'd have waited 'til the wind had died down.'

'I'm not daft you know. I've pegged it down with some of the rods from the old telly aerial. It'll take a hurricane to shift it now.'

I grinned at him. 'Don't tempt Fate.' I paced round the polyhouse and gave it the once over. 'It looks perfect – you'd never know it'd moved.'

'I know. It's a miracle really. I thought it'd be ripped underneath where it landed, but there was only a tiny tear that I've mended with a squirt of glue.'

'I'm glad you've finished. I've got a job for you. I need you to go into Antas after break.'

'You're *joking*. It'll be the third time this week I've had the car out. It's costing us a fortune in petrol. No wonder we can barely make ends meet.'

'Hark at you. You're such a tightarse. It's a twelve-kilometre-round journey. It'll probably cost you two quid.'

'It all adds up. What is it that's so urgent it can't wait?'

'The fluorescent tube's died. I'm sorry I didn't see it coming – remiss of me, I know. I can manage in the day, but tonight we'll be buggered. We haven't got any candles left either – we can hardly sit playing scrabble in the dark.'

He put the twine down and sighed. 'Alright then. You can make us a brew while I change out of my work boots. And while the kettle's on, take the tube out. You know what they're like in the *ferreteria* – if I don't take it with me I'll end up with the wrong size.'

A thought struck me. I *didn't* know what they were like in the *ferreteria*; I'd probably been in twice in the last three years. If the truth be told, I was morphing into a typical rural *galega*. I tended the poultry and rabbits. I cooked and laundered and cleaned. In the afternoons I worked in the garden from spring through 'til autumn and kept the fire burning in the kitchen through the bitter winter months. My feet were always in wellies or work boots; I wore a village pinny; I talked about the egg count and the price of feed. Apart from my walks with Lenda, I rarely left the village and up until now I hadn't given it a second thought. I was happy that way, but what about Gary? I'd assumed he was as contented as I was. He'd never commented, but should I be making more of an effort? He must have thought me a boring old frump of a wife.

I turned to him and smiled. 'Why don't I come with you? If we go now, we can stop for a coffee while we're in Antas. We don't often go out together – it'll make a nice change.'

So much for him feeling neglected; he looked at me as if I'd suggested a trip to the moon.

As we drove out of the *aldea*, we could see the extent of the damage caused by the storm. Along the main road, a scattering of branches and pinecones bore testament to the ferocity of the wind. Gary cursed as a carrier bag blew across the bonnet and I wondered how many miles it had travelled on the wind. Unlike our polyhouse, the little tin bus-stop was still standing, and only an insider would notice that the poster for last year's fiesta had gone. When we came to the farm at Penela, three German shepherds leapt up from the doorstep, barking crossly as we gave way to Suso, the farmer, turning his tractor into the yard.

Ten minutes later, as we neared the approach road into Antas, we were hailed by a man with a 'Stop' sign. A flat-bed lorry, stacked high with pine trunks, was turning round on the crossroads up ahead. Bored by the hold-up, I looked over at the stately Pazo de Vilane, set back in its formal gardens edged with precisely spaced pines. There was something not quite perfect about the array of trees this morning; the one on the corner was missing and the wall had fallen down.

By the time we drove into Antas I was ready for a coffee. 'Let's go to Farelo's first,' I suggested. 'It's way past our time for a brew.'

Nodding his agreement he turned off the main street and pulled up outside the café. It was almost half past eleven yet there were no lights on inside.

'Shit,' groaned Gary. 'It's closed.'

'No it isn't,' I said. 'There're folks inside.' I pushed my face up against the window. 'Look, the waiter's clearing a table, and there's a group of old blokes playing cards.'

As we came through the door the waiter bid us 'Good morning'. He was a blubbery fellow with a morbidly pallid complexion; I couldn't begin to imagine him hoeing around his kale. 'There's no coffee,' he told us. 'We've had a power cut. There's beer, wine, spirits, juices... you can have what you like as long as it's cold.'

I turned to Gary. 'Bugger that for a game of soldiers. Come on, let's go home.'

Out on the street I made a bee line for the van, while Gary strode off in the opposite direction.

'Where're you going?' I called. 'You can forget the *ferretería*. I didn't know there was a power cut – the tube in the kitchen will be fine.'

As we drove off along the main road I began to giggle. Gary looked at me as if I was bonkers. 'Well?' he frowned. 'Go on.'

'It's nothing much. I was just thinking – it's a good job the cooker runs on butane. You'd have been having carpaccio for lunch.'

'You're never going to let me forget that, are you?'

'No way. It was hilarious. Nice restaurant too, as I remember – trust you to lower the tone. When the waitress put it in front of you, your face was a picture. You gaped like a goldfish and said, "It's raw!" Thank God for doggy bags, at least it didn't go to waste.'

'Scholes loved it. *He* didn't call me a philistine. If I'd been a know-all like you he wouldn't have enjoyed a treat.'

As we drove down into the *aldea*, the light was on in the farmhouse kitchen. Maruja would be scooping out curds from a bucket while Javier's dinner sat bubbling on top of the range. I'd been out of the village for an hour and had achieved nothing. There was something to be said for being a typical *galega* after all.

By the following weekend, the weather had done a complete U turn; on Saturday morning there wasn't a cloud in the sky. Out on the bench, I listened to the call of the cuckoo ringing out from the oak wood and the good-natured rumpus coming from number fifteen. I was rolling a second ciggie when I heard whistling and Másimo strolled past the corner. He waved in greeting and I did likewise. Instead of bounding over to greet him, Lenda barely gave him a second glance.

After lunch I went out to tend to my borders. The strawberry plants had grown quickly, but so had the weeds. Scholes and Fred were dozing in the shade beneath the fig tree, where the wildflowers were amass with butterflies and bees. High above, a hawk was hovering on the thermals, and the sun shone brightly in the cloudless blue sky. The afternoon heat was surprising and I paused to take off my cardi. Maruja's *refrán* was uncanny; today was the ninth of June.

Summer's long-awaited arrival had brought with it a newfound vitality amongst the livestock. Doe's five-week-old babies were thriving and it would soon be time to move some to the Death Row overflow pens in the barn.

Since the fateful storm, Waynetta hadn't returned to her damson tree and knowing she was safe in the hen house at night was a weight off my mind. Only this morning she'd accepted Wayne's amorous attentions, and it was only a matter of time before she'd be laying again.

Unlike the rest of the menagerie, Lenda was quieter than normal. She didn't want to play 'tuggy' and was happy to relinquish her ball. I hoped against hope there was no need to worry; it was a scorching hot day after all.

On Sunday morning, Lenda still seemed under the weather. When Gary came into the kitchen I voiced my concerns.

'I'm worried,' I said as I passed him his cuppa.

'Really?' he yawned. 'What about?'

'Lenda. She seems… tired. I can't put my finger on it – she's just not herself.'

'Did she eat her breakfast?'

I nodded.

'Well then, she's fine.'

I was about to protest, but Gary continued.

'You're over-protective, that's your trouble. Don't get me wrong – you're bound to be after losing Anxo, but sometimes you can be over the top. You bring her in when it rains and you lie awake listening for her when it thunders. You were even worried about taking her out in the wind.'

'I don't think that's over-protective. I think it's sensible. I don't want her to end up ill.'

I looked at Lenda. Her eyes were bright and her coat was shiny. She looked as fit as a fiddle; perhaps Gary was right after all.

Monday was shopping day and I was expecting ructions; Lenda had picked at her breakfast so I'd made an addition to the list.

'Liver?'

'Yes, Gary, liver. It's for Lenda, not you. It's probably just the heat, but she *is* low in energy. The extra iron should give her a boost.'

Over the next two days I kept a close eye on Lenda. Her appetite had definitely dwindled and she was reluctant to leave my side.

On Wednesday morning I was thrown into panic; Lenda wasn't waiting in the passage to greet me when I came down the stairs. When I went into the kitchen, she was lying on her back by the dresser with her legs in the air. A knot formed in my stomach and I thought at once of Anxo. I cursed myself for listening to Gary. I should have followed my instincts and rung the vet. I lowered myself onto the tiles and knelt down beside her.

'Oh, Lenda,' I whispered. 'Whatever's wrong?'

Much to my surprise, Lenda rolled onto her side and wagged her tail. It was then that I noticed the droplets of blood on the floor. I was appalled by my own stupidity; Lenda hadn't been poorly after all.

I leaned over and gave her belly a gentle rub. 'Poor Lenda,' I smiled. 'Have you got tummy ache? It's nothing to worry about, I promise. Mum'll take care of you – you'll be fine.'

As I filled the kettle I thought about Lenda's predicament. It was only a matter of time before dogs began to queue up outside. Pastor was old now, and Flea-pelt was too small to be a danger. Res, however, was a different matter entirely. He was strong, well-muscled and feisty. I was going to need eyes in the back of my head.

'Morning,' yawned Gary when he came into the kitchen. 'Crikey. What's up with Lenda? Why is she upside down?'

'Nothing's up with her,' I said, as I passed him his cuppa. 'I think she's trying not to get blood on the floor.'

'She's bleeding?' He stared at Lenda, then looked at me awkwardly. 'You don't mean... Is she...'

I smiled inwardly. For all his cussing and lack of decorum, Gary could be quite prudish at times.

'You *can* say it, Gary. It's her season. She's in oestrus. Her body's making eggs.'

He frowned as he reached for his bacca. 'Will she need to see a vet?'

'Don't be daft. Does a woman go to the doctor when she...'

'Alright, alright. I was only asking. How long will it last?'

'A fortnight if we're lucky, but it could be more. Whatever happens we'll need to be extra vigilant. You know what a game Maruja has with Luna. It won't be long before we've got randy dogs queuing up at the door.'

After I'd let out the chooks and the rabbits, I stood on the doorstep with Lenda. I'd expected all of the dogs in the parish to be waiting, but strangely enough there wasn't a single mutt in sight.

There were still no suitors waiting when I opened the back door on Thursday morning. Fighting the urge for a ciggie, I nipped out to see to the livestock. Our luck wouldn't hold forever; it made sense to walk Lenda while the coast was still clear.

Out in the fields, I looked all around us. When I was sure we hadn't been followed I let Lenda off her lead. I watched in amazement as she zigzagged in and out of the bracken and darted about like a mad thing from tree to tree. If she'd been listless in the house she was a different dog in the *campo*. Perhaps it was down to the liver, but there was no hint of lethargy today.

Half an hour later we were on our way homewards. We hadn't been out as long as usual but it made sense to make tracks while the going was good. As I strode back across the fields I was feeling uplifted. Lenda was bright and alert and healthy. In a couple of weeks life would be back to normal; her season would be over and she'd be able to be spayed. I was drawn from my musings by a growl and a high-pitched yelping. Something was rustling about in the bracken up ahead. Lenda ran to my side, but her tail was wagging. I breathed a sigh of relief when Flea-pelt and Res emerged into the field. If the dogs had been strangers, I'd have been nervous for Lenda, but these two were different; she knew them and I was sure I'd have no trouble in coaxing her safely home. I was about to slip on her lead when she dodged sideways and darted ahead. I stared in disbelief as she sashayed over to the intruders, before turning her back end towards them with her tail in the air. There was no doubt about it she was flirting. When Res began to sniff her I'd seen enough.

'Bugger off!' I shouted. 'Bugger off the pair of you! *Vamos*! Go on!'

Flea-pelt, wimp that he was, skedaddled back into the bracken. Res was a different kettle of fish entirely; he stood stock still and looked me straight in the eye.

'Right!' I snarled in the fiercest voice I could muster. '*Vamos*, Res! Clear off!'

The look he gave me was priceless; it was the canine equivalent of a 'screw you' scowl. If that wasn't enough, he seemed determined to drive his point home. In an act of doggy defiance he turned to the nearest gorse bush and cocked his leg.

I slipped Lenda's lead on and set off towards the eucalyptus wood. It was a relief to know that in ten minutes we'd be home and dry. We hadn't been walking a minute when Lenda stopped and looked round. Much to my annoyance we were leading a convoy; Flea-pelt and Res were only metres behind. I tugged on the lead but Lenda was behaving like a prize bimbo. While I yelled and cursed at the gigolos, Lenda did her utmost to tempt them. Thanks to her encouragement they stalked us all the way home.

When we finally arrived on the doorstep I was cross and frustrated. We'd wasted half an hour on what should have been a ten minute jaunt. We couldn't carry on like that for the next fortnight; I was going to have to change the routine. Walks would be off the agenda, and Lenda would be exercised out in the garden. I'd throw the ball and tussle with the tuggy and we'd have plenty of games of chase.

When I called Gary in for coffee he was frowning.

'You don't look happy,' I said. 'What's wrong?'

'I've just found Res in the garden.'

'You're joking! How the hell did he manage *that*?'

'He must have jumped over the wall from Paul's side. He was cocking his leg right, left and centre and he didn't look happy when I shooed him out through the gate.'

'The crafty beggar. He was waiting for Lenda. You know what this means? You're going to have to extend the fence.'

Avoiding his gaze, I reached for my tobacco. The f-word was guaranteed to spark a row. I started to roll my ciggie and waited for the explosion. The silence seemed to go on forever. Eventually he heaved a sigh.

'I'll finish my coffee and then I'll drive over to the woodyard. It's going to cost us a fortune but the last thing we want is a litter of pups.'

When Gary set off for the woodyard, I went out to the garden to check that Res hadn't returned. Lenda was safely indoors, but I still had the livestock to think of; I didn't want him skulking about near the rabbits and the hens. There was no sign of Res, but the Eau de Bimbo was really working its magic; a wiry little dog with sand-coloured hair was snuffling about on the lawn. I scooted him out through the gate and he scurried away past the barn. On the corner, Flea-pelt and Res had been joined by a German shepherd. If I wasn't mistaken it was one of the trio from Suso's farm.

By Friday lunchtime the fence was finished. Haste had overridden elegance and in places the palings were doing a Mexican wave. Whilst lacking in aesthetics, it was sturdy and durable. It was the creative approach to canine contraception; the barrier method had arrived in Cutián.

On Saturday morning I took Lenda out to the garden at daybreak; as soon as she'd finished her business I nipped her straight back indoors. After a coffee and a ciggie I went out to see to the livestock. The shepherd and his sandy sidekick were back on the corner, and Res and Flea-pelt were making their way down the lane. I wasn't overly worried about Lenda's admirers; thanks to our impenetrable perimeter I was sure she'd be safe when I put her outside.

I was filling the kettle for breaktime when I heard Gary yelling in the garden. Hoping he wasn't shouting at Carmen I dashed out through the back door to see what was wrong. I didn't know whether to laugh or cry when I saw the cause of the commotion. Gary, with a face the colour of beetroot, was shooing the shepherd and the sandy dog out into the lane.

'Come on,' I said. 'it's time for your coffee. Think of your blood pressure. You need to calm down.'

Back in the kitchen I made him a coffee and rolled him a ciggie. When his colour had returned to normal I assumed it was safe to speak.

'So how did they get in?' I asked him. 'Surely they didn't clear the new fence?'

'Don't be daft – it'd keep a tribe of Vikings out. They came in under the apple trees. They must've clambered up from the track. Now I think about it, it'll be easy to fix. I've got some wood left over so I'll put a post in and make a barrier from the corner where the peppers are to the side of Warren Place.'

For the next three days I stayed with Lenda whenever she was out in the garden. If I couldn't guarantee her my undivided attention I made sure she was shut safely away indoors. By Wednesday there had been no further breeches of security and, satisfied that we were finally invader-proof, I decided it would be safe to leave her outside on her own. Gary was pleased that I'd decided to relinquish what he'd deemed my obsessive behaviour; if Lenda needed a round-the-clock minder then his efforts with wood and wire had been a complete waste of time.

Shortly before lunchtime I went out to peg out the laundry. Lenda wasn't lying in her usual place by the gate. I wasn't unduly worried; thanks to her recent lack of athleticism, and the latest addition to the fencing, I was confident she hadn't escaped. I glanced round the garden and spotted movement down by the chooks' pen. Sure enough, it was Lenda, but much to my horror, she wasn't alone. Her latest Romeo an ill-favoured specimen with a stocky black body and short bandy legs. He had the flat face of a boxer and tusks that curled up from his protruding lower jaw. He was the last dog in the world I'd have chosen as a husband for Lenda; she deserved a lot better than a bonsaied *jabalí*.

Ten minutes later my floozy was sulking in the kitchen while her toothy admirer was pining outside the back door. I returned to the garden, eager to discover where Toothy had found a way in. I peered over into Carmen's and saw that her gate was open. Toothy must have snuck in and scrambled his way over the wall. Poor Toothy. He wasn't much of a looker but I admired his tenacity; he'd come so close to succeeding where all of his rivals had failed. The trouble was, I couldn't be sure that he *hadn't* succeeded. I wracked my brains, but there was no way of knowing how long they'd been left alone.

'Well,' said Gary, as he polished off the last of his omelettes. 'At least you caught them in time.'

'I *think* I did. I can't be a hundred per cent certain, but even if I didn't, they definitely wouldn't have had time to tie.'

'Tie?'

'Yes. You know – when they sort of stick together after mating. They don't have to tie for the bitch to get pregnant but it improves the chance.'

'So you're saying she *could* be pregnant?'

'In theory, yes, but we'd have to be bloody unlucky. It's too late for worrying – only time will tell.'

For the next nine days the lovelorn lotharios continued to wait on the corner. Shep and Sandy would be there soon after daybreak, whilst Flea-pelt and Res would join them once Javier was up and about with the cows. The four of them spent the days in a cycle of fruitless activity: dozing and mooching; fighting and pacing; spraying and licking their balls. Throughout the shenanigans only Toothy maintained his decorum. His devotion to Lenda was unerring, and he wooed her daily, with doggy determination, through the bars of the gate.

There wasn't a dog in sight when I looked out into the lane on Friday morning and I thanked my lucky stars that Lenda's season had finally come to an end. So much for Toothy's undying devotion: the chances were he would never come calling again.

Sophie looked half her size when she snuck in through the cat-hole later that morning. She made straight for the food bowl and dug in as if she was eating for ten. Somewhere in the village she was nursing a litter of new-borns. I could only hope that, come September, Lenda wouldn't be doing the same.

Dogs on the Corner

The dogs lie in wait on the corner;
There are two, maybe three, maybe four.
I can't go out walking with Lenda:
I daren't step outside the back door.

The dogs lie in wait on the corner;
There are three, maybe four, maybe five.
If I go out walking with Lenda
I'm sure to be eaten alive.

The dogs lie in wait on the corner;
There are four, maybe five, maybe six,
And each of them's waiting for Lenda,
Oh goodness, we are in a fix!

The dogs lie in wait on the corner;
There are five, maybe six, maybe seven.
If I go out walking with Lenda
Her suitors will think they're in heaven!

The dogs lie in wait on the corner;
There are six, maybe seven, maybe eight.
I want to go walking with Lenda
But fear for our possible fate.

The dogs lie in wait on the corner;
There are seven, maybe eight, maybe nine.
I'm desperate to go out with Lenda
But sadly the choice isn't mine.

The dogs lie in wait on the corner;
There are eight, maybe nine, maybe ten.
Oh when will her season be over
So we can go walking again?

Chapter 6

Ghost Stories

On the first of July we were off to the ex-pats' get-together. Thanks to the storm, it was almost two months since we'd seen Nina and Marcus; it was hard to believe how quickly the time had sped by. Since the day of the power cut, I hadn't stopped thinking about my hermitic existence. Gary had never mentioned it, but that didn't mean he wouldn't enjoy having a social life again. I thought back to the previous year, when we'd had friends to visit and hosted a couple of barbecues. Gary had been the life and soul of the party; he fancied himself as a comedian and was in his element when he had people to entertain. I'd decided to make more of an effort to compromise; I'd be outgoing, spontaneous and fun. When Gary came down the stairs I was brimming with excitement. Once I'd furnished him with his cuppa I announced my plan. I hadn't been expecting him to do cartwheels, but even at that time of the morning I'd been counting on more than just 'Hmm.'

I looked at him, incredulous. The least I'd hoped for was a glimmer of enthusiasm; I was dragging myself from my comfort zone purely for him.

'*Hmm*? Is that all you can say? I thought you'd be pleased or excited or... I thought you'd be over the moon.'

'I'm not bothered one way or the other to be honest. I thought you were happy with things the way they are.'

'I am. It's you I was thinking of. When we're with friends you're the life and soul of the party. I thought you'd enjoy the change.'

'I might, I s'pose, but it won't happen. You don't like leaving the village and you're obsessed with your daily routine.'

I swallowed hard and reached for my bacca. I'd been right. He hadn't said anything but he'd noticed the change in me. Tears of indignation pricked at the back of my eyes.

'That's not fair. I'm *not* obsessed. I have a lot to juggle and I like things to run smoothly. You've said yourself you can't believe how much I manage to do. Anyway, you'll see that I mean it. I'll turn over a new leaf, starting this morning. By the end of the month our social calendar will be full.'

As we neared Monterroso, we joined the queue of market day traffic. Gary was already tutting and twitching; his Irritable Driver Syndrome was about to kick in. There was something I needed to say before my words were lost in his fug of expletives. I tugged on his arm.

'Whatever you do, don't mention the *trasi*.'

'What?'

'The *trasi*. You know, the stuff that...'

'What the fuck is he *doing*?'

The van screeched to a halt at the traffic lights where an old man with a carrier bag was dithering about at the kerb.

'Look at him! Just *go* if you're going to! I *hate* driving through town on market days. I don't know why we come!'

Once the poor fellow was safely across the road I tried again. 'The stuff that Nina gave me. Whatever you do, don't...'

'Now what's *that* arsehole doing? I swear some of these idiots have never been taught to drive.'

I sighed and stared out through the window. IDS was a brutal affliction. It was the partners that suffered. Perhaps one day there might be a cure.

Twenty minutes later we arrived at the Hotel Río Ulla. Gary was all smiles once he was out of the van. Nina and Marcus were already outside with their coffees. Lulu was as lively as ever, and I was surprised to see how much she'd grown.

'Crikey,' I laughed. 'She's almost as big as Lenda.'

'Yes,' agreed Marcus. 'But I think she is stronger. And she will remember that Lenda stole her bone.'

'Did you make the spicy beef yet?' asked Nina.

'I did,' I nodded. 'It was nice. I think it needed more chillies. It wasn't as tasty as yours.'

'You missed the prawn stuff out,' said Gary.

I shot him a warning look but the cat was out of the bag.

'The *trasi*?' asked Nina. 'Oh no!'

'Oh yes,' he continued. 'She chucked it away.'

I felt myself colour and reached for my tobacco. As I struggled to think of excuses, Nina began to giggle and Marcus gave a hearty guffaw.

'I told you!' he laughed. 'I *told* you!'

'You did,' giggled Nina. 'Marcus said, "Liza will not want it in her kitchen. She will put it straight in the bin."'

I was groping for a defence when I spotted a familiar figure coming along the pavement.

'Ooh, look,' I beamed. 'There's Rose.'

I watched as she ambled her way up to the terrace, weighed down by an assortment of bags.

'Hiya!' she grinned as she came, breathless, up to our table.

'You are late,' frowned Marcus. His eyes were twinkling. 'You have missed the joke.'

'A joke?' she grinned. 'I could do with some merriment. There's a war on in Vilabeira. I've had trouble with the neighbour from Hell.'

I smiled inwardly; trust Rose. She'd been courting disaster ever since she'd arrived in Galicia. Some things would never change.

She turned to me. 'On a brighter note, Pete's flying over on Friday. I'd ask you both over for lunch, but you're always busy. I know that going out isn't really your sort of thing.'

My face coloured a second time. Was I *really* so predictable? It wasn't only Gary that thought so; other people had noticed it too.

'On the contrary,' I said airily, 'I'm always up for a spot of diversion. Lunch sounds a great idea.'

'Right,' beamed Rose. 'Let's say this Sunday. If Gary's out on Friday… Oops! I haven't asked you yet, Gary – silly me!'

'Asked me what?' he frowned.

'Verna wondered if you were free this Friday. She can give you a day's work.'

I was pleased with myself. We'd only been at the hotel for ten minutes and already we had a lunch date and a day's work for Gary as well.

Over the next couple of hours, people came and went at their leisure. Some dropped by for a coffee before going on to the market, whilst others arrived later, ready to head off en masse for the *menú del día* lunch. Most of the faces were familiar and it was fun to catch up with the news. We heard about holidays and road-trips and stray dogs and snake bites. The story of Lenda and her suitors went down a storm. Eventually people began to drift back to their cars, and we were thinking of making tracks when Gary nudged me and pointed to a couple coming along the street.

'Is that the Poo Woman we met a few months back?'

I shielded my eyes and watched as they drew nearer. Sure enough it was Helen, who'd regaled us with the benefits of humanure.

'It is,' I nodded. 'Fancy you remembering. Her name's Helen. Damn, she gave me her number – I completely forgot to call. It'll look rude if we leave now they're arriving. We'll have to stick around for a while.'

'Hi!' I called, as they strolled onto the terrace.

'Hello,' smiled Helen. 'You've not met my partner, have you? This is Paul.'

The pony-tailed man beside her stepped forward. 'Hi,' he grinned. 'We're always late for things, but we're not usually this bad. It looks like everyone's leaving now we've arrived.'

When we'd finished our greetings the men went inside to fetch coffees. Alone with Helen, now was my chance to make amends.

'I'm ever so sorry,' I told her. 'You must think I'm awful. I promised I'd ring and I didn't. I can't offer any excuses – the months seem to roll into one.'

'Don't worry,' laughed Helen. 'I know what it's like. I've been teaching six days a week since Easter. I'm on holiday now 'til September. Just ring me when you've got time.'

The market was all but over when we finally drove back through Monterroso. A few last-minute shoppers straggled along the pavement but the road through the centre was virtually clear. In contrast to our earlier journey, Gary was pleasantly chipper. His good mood couldn't be solely down to the stress-free driving. Perhaps he was starting to trust my gregarious intentions after all.

'There you go,' I said proudly. 'I told you I'd do it. Three events for the calendar already – that's a great start.'

'Three?'

'Well, potentially. Lunch at Rose's, a day's work at Verna's…'

'That's hardly a social call.'

'It's similar. You'll get a fabulous lunch and have a good chinwag. If it wasn't for Lenda I'd tag along.'

'And the third?'

'Helen and Paul. I've told her I'll give her a ring.'

'Well make sure you do. Paul was interesting. He's from Belfast you know, and he loves Irish music. He plays the concertina and he's completely self-taught.'

'Crikey, that's handy. If we go over you can take your bodhran. They're lovely folks and this time I *will* keep my promise. I'll call them next week and we'll sort something out.'

Gary had already left for Verna's when I came home with Lenda on Friday morning. It was sure to be scorching in the south of the province and he'd been keen to set off while the sun was still low in the sky. After a quick cool shower, the bright summer's day lay ahead of me. With no need to spend time on cooking for Gary, I was going to make excellent use of the time.

Over in Warren Place, Doe's run had become overcrowded. The first job on my list was to move four of the youngsters into the overflow pen in the barn. At the end of August, all nine would be ready for the freezer, and in the meantime Doe would be mated again.

Down in the chooks' pen, there was already a small, pointy egg in the nest box. Only five weeks since her chicks had been lost to the rainstorm, Waynetta was laying again. Since that fateful day, she'd been happy to roost with the big hens; I only hoped that her newfound fertility wouldn't cause her to abscond again.

With the livestock taken care of, I was ready to fetch water from the *rio*. The tank in the *huerta* had to be replenished ready for the evening's watering. It was a gruelling task but shared between two of us it was workable. Alas, it would have to be a one-woman effort today.

It was after eleven when I made the final trip back from the *rio*. Though only a short distance down the track, the return trek was steeply uphill. After fourteen shuttles with full buckets, my muscles were screaming, but I'd poured well over a hundred litres into the tank.

As I closed the gate to the *huerta*, I heard Carmen stumbling about in her garden. Taking care not to tread on the strawberries, I crept through the fruit bed and peeped over the wall. Much to my horror she was swaying fitfully. There was something wrong with her balance and it seemed she was going to fall. I was about to call out, when I spotted the reason for her predicament. She was balanced precariously on an upturned wheelbarrow, her neck craned as she leaned forward, peering through the trees into Paul's field. Whatever had caught her interest was clearly worth breaking a limb for; it seemed only reasonable that I should witness it too. To find out what was happening, I'd have to shin up the wall down by the chooks' pen. Carmen would be sure to see me and know that I was as nosy as her. For a moment I was flummoxed. There was no way I could see what was happening without being rumbled by Carmen. There was only one solution; I'd go round and pay our neighbour a call.

As I crossed Paul's threshing floor I heard a strange thudding and scraping. There was movement in the area he'd marked out for a pétanque court at the edge of his land. I strode along the half-hidden path, skirting overhanging branches and obtruding clumps of bracken and broom. Paul was standing up to his waist in a trench and digging for all he was worth. The project would be an enormous undertaking and I'd doubted that he'd really go through with it. I'd obviously misjudged him; it seemed that it was going ahead as planned.

'Hi, Paul,' I called cheerily. 'I thought I'd drop by and see how you're getting on.'

'It's nice to see you,' he smiled. 'You're always so busy. It can't be healthy. You need to slow down.'

'Aha,' I grinned. 'That was the old me. I've made a pledge to get out and about more. I've turned over a new leaf.'

'Glad to hear it,' he smiled. 'You'll be able to come round for a game of pétanque when it's done.'

'I'd like that,' I lied. 'I bet it'll look quite impressive. There's a big area to go at – does it need to be quite so deep?'

'Oh, yes,' he said earnestly. 'I need to get all the roots out. They'll make cracks in the surface if they push up from underneath.'

I looked at the pile of gorse roots heaped beside him; not only was he making good headway, he was doing an admirably thorough job.

'You're doing well,' I said. 'But it's going to take ages. When do you think you'll be done?'

'A couple of months, three at the latest. I've got plenty of time now I'm living here. It'll be done by October. I'm having a party for the end of the world.'

Each time I thought Paul could no longer surprise me he managed to come up trumps.

'The end of the world?'

'They're saying the world's going to end in October. It's been in the news.'

I chuckled. 'I always said you were bonkers. What a load of old guff.' I studied him briefly. 'You don't *really* believe that, do you?'

He smiled wryly. 'It *might* be true.'

'And then again it might not. If you listened to all these theories, the world would be ending every week. You'd spend your whole life partying if you paid them all heed. Still, it's as good an excuse as any I s'pose.'

I hovered for a while, but Paul resumed digging. No doubt he was keen to hold a few tournaments and time was running out. I couldn't help thinking he'd have been better off digging himself a veg plot. Even in July he could grow a few lettuces, or maybe plant winter cabbages or Galician kale. I wasn't about to say so; I was used to Paul and his foibles. He had his own way of going about things and he wasn't one for taking advice.

'I'll leave you to it,' I smiled eventually. 'I really ought to be doing some weeding of my own.'

'Dig deep,' he grinned as he emerged from the hole with another shovelful. 'That's the secret, you see – you should always dig deep.'

I was closing Paul's gate when Carmen came up behind me. If the end of the world was coming, she'd be sure to know all about it; was she about to deliver a prophecy or was she eager to pick my brains for an update on the garden of number ten?

'*Hola*, Carmen,' I smiled. '*Qué tal?*'

'*Hola*, Elisa,' she half-whispered. 'Have you been to see the Englishman? Isn't he working hard? He's digging down ever so deep and taking all the weeds out.

If he gets some manure from Maruja he'll have a good harvest next year.'

Poor Carmen. Her eyes shone with admiration. I hadn't the heart to explain that Paul wasn't creating a crumbly, fertile bed in which to nurture his plants. In the fullness of time she'd learn the true reason for his labours. She might even enjoy chucking a few balls about with him now and again.

When Gary came back from Verna's he looked surprisingly clean and unflustered. If he hadn't been wearing his work clothes, I'd have said he'd been on a social call.

'Crikey,' I laughed. 'You look like you've been on a jolly. You're not mucky or sweaty. What jobs did you do?'

'I was working inside, thank God. It's been scorching down there; I reckon it's five degrees higher once you get past the Miño valley. I've been making furniture with a chap called Adey. It's not been a bad way to earn eighty euros. It's been quite a fun afternoon.'

I was puzzled. Gary had made a decent job of some shelving and flooring, but he certainly wasn't a carpenter. By his own admission he was a great bodger who got by on a wing and a prayer.

'*You've* been making furniture?'

'Alright then, assembling a flatpack wardrobe.'

'And it's taken two of you all day?'

'More or less. There were three boxes of it, and there were drawers and hanging rails and all sorts of bits. We didn't start 'til eleven because Verna made coffee and Adey was telling us hilarious stories. No sooner had we unpacked all the boxes than it was time for lunch.'

'What was it like?'

'Fantastic. Fried chicken with chips and salad. Cherries and ice cream for pud.'

'I meant the wardrobe, but never mind. So, what was he like, this Adey?'

'Great fun. He's a natural comedian – like me, I s'pose.'

'Really? Hmm.'

'What do you mean, "hmm"? Everybody except you finds me funny. You've got no sense of humour, that's your trouble. I'd have been great on the stage.'

I rolled my eyes skywards. 'Anyway – Adey.'

'Ah, yes. He's quite a character. He can't half tell a good story. Some of the things he comes out with are unbelievable. He's been working in a house near Taboada that's got a ghost.'

I rolled my eyes again. 'A ghost. Right. He's seen it has he?'

'He hasn't seen it, but he's felt it. It was there with him in the room.'

'He's *felt* it? Honestly, Gary. You don't believe it do you?'

'I'm not sure to be honest. There was something about the way he said it that made me think he was telling the truth.'

'So what did it do then, this… ghost?'

'It chucked stuff at him.'

'*Chucked* stuff at him? What *stuff*?'

'Stones.'

'That's ridiculous. It sounds like you've been working with a nutcase all afternoon.'

'He said he's been working on the ceilings. Something's been pelting him with stones when he hammers into the beams.'

'That'd be bits falling out of the ceiling.'

'That's what I said, but he reckons they've been flying across the room.'

'Get away.'

'I know what you're thinking, but honestly, he was trembling. It wasn't just that though, there's more.'

'Go on.'

'According to the neighbours the house has got some creepy history to it.' He took a swallow of coffee. 'I don't know if I should tell you this.'

'For God's sake, Gary, I don't need protecting. Are you going to tell me or not?'

'If I do, I don't want you having nightmares. You're a nuisance when you yell and lash out in your sleep.'

I giggled shamelessly. I'd woken up howling and flailing on many occasions. The first time it had happened I'd given Gary quite a scare.

'I won't, I promise. Go on.'

'Okay then.' He cleared his throat. 'Many moons ago the house was the laying out parlour for the village.'

'Crikey. Now that I *can* believe. The thing is, Gary, it makes Adey's story even *less* believable if you think about it. The house must've held dozens of corpses, and yet it's only got one ghost.'

'I hadn't thought of that. I see what you mean. Well, keep your fingers crossed – I might get to find out before long.'

'What do you mean?'

'I might have some work there. The owners only come over once in a blue moon, so Adey sees to the garden. The trouble is, he's struggling to fit it in because of his carpentry. He reckons there's been a real upturn in ex-pats in the south of the province. Half of them don't speak Spanish, so English tradesmen are in big demand. He asked if I'd be interested in taking it on.'

'Did you say yes?'

''Course I did. It's only one day a month, but it's eighty euros. He's going to give them a ring and see if they mind me taking it on.'

'That's brilliant. Good old Adey. It'd make a big difference – we'll need spending money now we're planning on getting out and about.'

'That reminds me – there's a big fiesta in Monterroso today. It's San Cristobo according to the posters. There's a stage up where they usually have the market. I had to drive all through the back streets to get through the town.'

During the summer, fiestas are held throughout the whole of Galicia. From the grandest of cities to the humblest of villages, each locality celebrates its own dedicated festival in reverence of its time-honoured patron saint. The greater the population, the louder and longer the occasion, and in some towns the revels continue non-stop for three days. Out in the *aldea* there was no such extravaganza. We were blessed with a poster, three masses, a few fireworks and a jaunt round the churchyard with an over-sized doll.

'It's a pity we didn't know earlier,' he continued. 'It might have been fun.'

I grimaced. If the big stage was up, there would be an *orquesta*; a pop group belting out songs from the seventies and eighties like lycra-clad Osmonds on speed. Even with the wildest of imaginations it couldn't have been described as fun.

'You're right,' I lied. 'Never mind. There's bound to be another before the summer's over. We'll keep an eye out for posters and we'll go next time.'

Gary was still dead to the world when I set off with Lenda on Saturday morning. It was well after ten when we came back from the *campo*, but he was only just making his brew.

'You're late,' I grinned. 'You slept through my nightmares then, did you?'

'I must have done,' he yawned. 'A pity I can't say the same about the racket next door.'

'You don't mean the family? I love to hear them. It's like a real-life soap opera – The Ouros at Number Fifteen.'

'If you say so. But this wasn't their usual noises. Masi's been playing the drum.'

When I called Gary in at breaktime he was chuckling.

'Let me guess,' I grinned, as I passed him his coffee. 'It's either Carmen or Paul.'

'Eh?'

'The reason you're smiling. It's got to be one or the other. I can tell by the look on your face that something's amused you. They're equally bonkers, so I'm hedging my bets.'

'Actually you're wrong – it's Masi. He's been drumming again. He wants me to go round tonight for a jam.'

'You're not thinking of going, surely?'

'I am.'

'But you called it a racket earlier.'

'That was different. I was cross 'cos it woke me up. I've had chance to listen properly since then and I must say he's good. I went round and told him so, and he couldn't stop smiling. I reckon I've made his day.'

'Aah, good for you. It's nice to be neighbourly. Will you take the guitar?'

'Don't be daft. You know I can't play it. We'll be doing percussion – I'm taking the bodhran.'

By a quarter to nine that evening we were still only half-way through the watering, but what was a year's worth of sustenance when there was drumming to be done?

'You'd best make tracks,' I grinned. 'You'll need to change out of your wellies and we can't have you turning up late for your gig.'

'If you're sure you don't mind.'

''Course I don't. I won't need to do it all with the watering can. I'll save time by sloshing the bucket over the peas and beans.'

While Gary set off up the garden, I carried on watering the peppers. Fred was lying on his back beneath the foliage, kicking his back legs up at a dangling piece of twine. At almost a year old, he was still such a rascally kitten. It didn't seem five minutes since he'd first walked into our lives.

As dusk descended, a lingering warmth hung over the *huerta*, and the garden was bathed in a balmy stillness, broken only by the drumming from number fifteen. I could clearly make out the rasping military trill of the snare drum, interspersed with the softer thudding of the bodhran. Gary had been right when he'd said that Masi was a competent drummer; I could quite imagine him marching along with a band. When I'd finished the last of the watering, I decided to nip round. I was making my way up the garden when I heard footsteps and Gary appeared at the gate.

'Crikey,' I said. 'That didn't take long. I wasn't expecting you back so soon.'

'Solina put her foot down,' he chuckled. 'She couldn't hear the telly, so she came out and called time.'

'That's a shame. I was enjoying it. In fact, I was thinking about coming round.'

'I'm glad you said that. You can have a repeat performance. I've asked him round here next week.'

For a split second the impromptu announcement threw me off balance. I was about to protest when I remembered my promise.

'Brilliant. We'll ask Paul and...'

'Paul? You can't be serious? He doesn't play an instrument – he'd be bored.'

'Not Pétanque Paul. I was about to say Paul and Helen. He can bring his concertina. The world's going to end in October – we might as well go out with a bang.'

On Sunday morning I awoke with a sense of anticipation. I had a feeling that lunch at Rose's was going to be fun. It was two years since I'd paid her a visit at her home in Vilabeira. Back then, the place had been little more than a ruin. A house tour had been impossible; it hadn't been safe to step inside because of the falling-down walls. Gary had since been over a few times to work on the garden. He'd given me progress updates and I was dying to see how the place had come on.

It was just before two when we arrived at Rose's. It had been warm in the van and I'd dozed for most of the journey, missing out on the views of the Ribeira Sacra valley and the majestic River Miño meandering far below. As we climbed out of the van, Rose and Pete waved us over to where they were sitting. They'd opened a bottle of wine and were chomping on bread and cheese, perched on lawn chairs on the grass in front of the house. Behind them I could see an array of raised beds and the overpriced polytunnel. It seemed an inappropriate backdrop for the *déjeuner sur l'herbe.*

'Hiya!' grinned Rose. 'You didn't mind us starting without you? It's only bread and cheese, I'm on a very strict budget. Pete, have we got some more of that decent wine?'

For the next half hour we munched on our butties and listened to Rose as she waxed lyrical about her plans for the garden. Now and again, Pete rolled his eyes and shook his head despairingly. Rose's ideas were not only ambitious but extremely costly. It was no wonder poor Pete couldn't wait to retire.

Our picnic complete, it was time for the house tour. This time it was safe to venture over the threshold; the builders had magicked the piles of fallen boulders into sturdy inner walls. Rose pointed out where she'd be having the lounge, the kitchen, a downstairs bedroom and a shower room. Once the staircase was built and the floors were replaced, there would be four en suite bedrooms upstairs.

As we walked back through to the entrance, Pete pointed to a window in the adjacent wall.

'You wouldn't believe how much trouble *that's* caused us. Rose is adamant it's staying, but for two pins I'd have it filled in.'

I stared at the opening. The lintel looked solid, and there was no sign of bowing or cracks in the wall. 'I don't understand,' I said puzzled. 'It looks fine to me.'

'It is,' frowned Rose, 'but the neighbour from Hell thinks otherwise. He's a complete and utter shit.'

'So what's his problem?' asked Gary. 'It's not as if it overlooks his land.'

'Ah, but it does,' said Pete. 'Well, half of it anyway. Come on, let's go back out and walk round the side. It'll be easier to show you what I mean.'

Pete led us out through the entrance and back down the side of the house through a straggly stretch of field. Smack, bang in the middle was a rectangular patch of kale.

'There's the problem,' said Pete, nodding towards the veg plot. 'He owns that little bit of a garden. If you stand in the middle of his greens you're directly opposite half of the window. That's the bone of contention – he's saying his property's overlooked.'

Gary and I nodded. To the uninitiated it would have seemed trivial, but out in rural Galicia such things could trigger a war.

'What he *actually* said,' added Rose. 'Is that it's going to "molest" him. As if.'

I smiled despite her predicament. In Spanish, *molestar* means to bother or to be a nuisance, but because of the obvious connotations the English couldn't resist translating it as 'molest'.

'How often is he here?' asked Gary.

'Well that's just it,' Rose continued. 'He only turns up once in a blue moon.'

'And when he does,' added Pete, 'he only hoes around his cabbage-things. It's not as if we'll be lining up at the window to gawp.'

'And I told him so,' said Rose. 'But he was adamant he'll report us if we don't get the problem resolved.'

'So what does he want you to do?' asked Gary.

'Well,' sniggered Rose, 'we can either board the window up halfway or – you're going to love this one – we can put in frosted glass.'

'Never!' I gasped.

'Ridiculous!' laughed Gary. 'It's s'posed to stop folks looking *in*!'

'Tell me,' said Rose. 'I've tried my best to be pleasant, but he's taken against me. If you ask me, he's barking mad.'

'Talking of which,' I grinned, 'what about this chap that's been working for Verna? Gary got on with him like a house on fire, so that's a sure sign he's bonkers. He reckons he's seen a ghost.'

'Adey,' nodded Rose. 'He hasn't seen it, he's felt it. It waits until he's up the ladder, then it pelts him with stones.'

Gary looked at me. 'There you go.'

I studied Rose's expression. There wasn't a trace of a smile on her lips, nor the hint of a twinkle in her eyes.

'You believe him.' It wasn't a question, but a statement of incredulity. First Gary, now Rose. I was stunned.

Rose looked at me directly. 'Don't get me wrong, Adey's got the gift of the gab and he tells a great story. I'm not saying he hasn't embellished the details, but I don't doubt for a moment he's telling the truth.'

'Why?'

'Because he might be a great comedian, but he's certainly no actor. I saw the fear in his eyes when he told me and it wasn't put on.'

I turned to Pete, who shrugged his shoulders. Gary was nodding his agreement and I knew the argument couldn't be won.

'There's another reason,' Rose added, 'and you'll probably think *I'm* bonkers…'

'I do anyway,' I grinned. 'Sorry, carry on.'

'I've had one too.'

I frowned. 'What?'

'A visit from a ghost.'

I glanced across at the ruin. 'What, here?'

'No, at Verna's.'

This time even Gary looked sceptical. 'Get away,' he smiled. 'You're having us on.'

'I knew you'd say that, but I'm not joking. I swear on my life it's true.'

My curiosity overrode my cynicism. 'Go on then, fill us in.'

'I go over a couple of nights a week for some company. We have a good natter and I sleep over so I can have a drink.'

I nodded. 'Go on.'

'Well, the first night I was drifting off and I had the strangest feeling that there was somebody else in the room. I lay still and listened and I sensed somebody creeping across the floor and back again. It happened every time I slept over until I finally plucked up the courage to tell Verna. She said she'd have a word with it and it's never been back since.'

After a tour of the garden, the orchard and the site of the yet-to-be-planted food forest, time was ticking on.

'We'd better be making tracks,' said Gary eventually. 'We have to get back for Lenda – she's not used to being left for so long.'

'You will come again?' asked Rose. 'Pete's off back to England at the weekend, and I get so bored on my own.'

'We'd like to,' I sighed, 'but it's hard, what with Lenda and the livestock. Here's an idea though – why not drive over to us? We're busy next weekend, but how about the week after? Come over at six on Saturday and stop the night.'

Rose liked to party and she didn't need asking a second time. 'Okay then,' she grinned. 'I will.'

On Monday, Adey sent Gary a message. The haunted house owners would be over from Málaga at the weekend. They wanted to meet him on Saturday teatime to discuss the job. There was also a reply from Helen, accepting our invitation. They'd be over to join us at seven with instruments, beers and Pepe the dog.

The Undertaker's Ghost

Young Adey was a carpenter
Who lived near Taboada;
You'd often find him sawing wood
Or climbing up a ladder.

He started work inside a house,
Where once an undertaker
Had laid out all the local folks
Who'd gone to meet their maker.

As Adey hammered on the beams,
He had the strangest feeling
That bits of roof were raining down,
Each time he banged the ceiling.

But as he stared above his head
He saw no fragments falling;
The bits came from across the room,
All heading straight towards him!

He stood there, troubled and confused;
There was no explanation;
Someone was pelting him with stones;
Oh what a weird sensation!

Poor Adey didn't know back then
About the old mortician,
Or that the house was haunted by
His restless apparition.

Next day a neighbour, passing by,
Asked how the work was going;
So Adey told him all about
The pelting and the throwing.

Liza Grantham

'Aha,' the neighbour said at once,
'I don't mean to alarm ya,
But this old house is haunted by
The ghost of the embalmer.'

Poor Adey didn't sleep that night,
So hard the shock had hit him;
Next day he rang his boss and said,
'Forget the job – I'm quitting!'

Chapter 7

The Food of Love

When Saturday came round, Gary had much to look forward to. With a job interview *and* a shindig ahead of him, he should have been wild with excitement. As it happened, he wasn't. He spent the whole of the morning fretting about Helen's dog.

'What were you thinking of?' he moaned when he came in at breaktime. 'I still can't believe you told her she could bring the dog.'

'Gary, I've already told you – I *didn't*. I was just as surprised as you were. Anyway, it'll be company for Lenda. What harm can it do?'

'It'll ruin the whole evening. Have you forgotten how mad she was with Lulu? I'm surprised you've not asked Maruja and told her to bring *her* dogs as well.'

When he came in for lunch he was still harping on.

'We're s'posed to be making music and it's going to be out and out chaos. Can't you send her a message and tell her to leave it at home?'

I dried my hands on the tea towel and reached for my tobacco. I couldn't stand it any longer; enough was enough.

'For God's sake Gary, I'm sick of you whingeing. If it bothers you that much *you* can ring her on the way to your meet-up. Find some excuse but try to be tactful. The number's in the phone.'

It was well after six when Gary came back from the Ghost House. Much to my relief, he hadn't rung Helen. He'd also been offered the job.

'Fantastic,' I smiled. 'Put the van away and we'll celebrate with a beer in the garden. You can tell me all about it. We've got plenty of time before folks arrive.'

The new bosses were an English couple called Matt and Debbie who lived and worked on the Costa del Sol. They'd asked him to do a full day towards the end of every month and they'd pay his wages directly into the bank. He'd be mowing the grass in the orchard and weeding the gravel paths that ran between the vines. There was also the chance of earning a generous bonus if he could clear a heap of household junk from the outbuildings and take them over to the *punto limpio* in the van.

'That's brilliant,' I beamed. 'It sounds as if the job was made for you – are you pleased?'

''Course I am. You and your silly questions. Oh, and they've given me a key so I can use the bathroom and make myself a cuppa. They told me I can use the toaster and the CD player as well.'

A shiver of excitement ran through me; if he was going to spend time alone in the house he might get to meet the ghost. I wondered if he'd managed to find out any more.

'Did you ask them about the ghost?'
'What?'

'The ghost. Did you ask Matt and Debbie if they've seen it or felt it or... well, whatever it's s'posed to do?'

'No.'

'*No?*'

'I completely forgot.'

'*Gary*! You're hopeless!' I grabbed the bodhran beater and made booing and hissing noises as I poked him repeatedly in the ribs.

Within seconds, Lenda leapt up and started to bark loudly. Irish Paul, with a tote bag slung over his shoulder and a box-shaped case under his arm, was watching us from the gate. There was no sign of the gate-crashing pooch, nor Helen for that matter. A look of relief was already spreading on Gary's face.

'Evening, Paul,' he called cheerily. 'Ignore the wife, she's mad.'

'Human xylophone,' I grinned. 'It's all the rage. Come on through, Lenda won't hurt you. Where's Helen? Did she change her mind?'

'She'll be here in a minute. An old lady stopped her to say hello.'

'That'll be Carmen,' grinned Gary. 'She'd talk the hind legs off a donkey. Helen could be there all night.'

As Paul came through the gate, there were footsteps behind him. It was Helen, with her plus-one on the end of an extendable lead.

'Hello,' she smiled. 'This is Pepe. Thanks for letting us bring her. She gets stressed if we leave her too long.'

'Poor Pepe,' I said. 'Come and meet Lenda. She'll be excited at first, but she'll soon calm down.'

Lenda dashed over, her tail wagging, but Pepe gave her a growl. Lenda faltered for a moment, as if weighing up her visitor. I could imagine what she was thinking. This stranger was nothing like Lulu; she was older, smaller, hairier and she *wasn't* going to play.

While Gary nipped round to fetch Masi, Paul took a tin whistle from his bag.

'I fancy a warm-up,' he said. 'I'll start with a reel.'

As his fingers moved deftly over the holes, I started to tap my feet but Lenda began to tremble and pressed her head against my legs.

'She's shaking,' said Helen. 'Do you think it's because of Pepe?'

I shook my head. 'I think it's the whistle. She might be better with the concertina. I'm ever so sorry, Paul. Do you mind?'

As Paul took the concertina from its case, Gary and Másimo appeared at the gate. Masi's face lit up when he saw our visitors. '*Mas instrumentos,*' he beamed. '*Muy bien.*'

'I'll play something calmer,' said Paul. 'Let's try "Women of Ireland". It's one of my favourite airs.'

The air was slow and soothing, but Lenda didn't think so. Within seconds she was trembling again. If she was frightened now, Heaven only knew what she'd be like when the drumming started. It made sense to cut our losses and take her indoors.

Lenda stopped shaking as soon as we were in the kitchen. To show her she wasn't in trouble I gave her some ham.

'Poor Lenda,' I sighed. 'First Pepe and now the music. I think you'll be happier in here.'

Back in the garden, Masi was growing impatient. His sticks were poised at the ready, as if willing the song to speed up. When the air came to an end he stepped forward and took control.

'*Bien,*' he nodded. 'But now something faster. A *muiñeira* – can you play one of those?'

I smiled in recognition. It was pipe music that had first brought us over to Galicia for the Festival do Mundo Celto in Ortigueira four years before. We'd spent the weekend listening to the bands of *gaiteros* piping *muiñeiras* as they marched through the town.

'I wish I could,' sighed Paul. 'I love them, they sound so Irish. I could learn one I suppose, but I'd need time to practise – I couldn't play one off the top of my head.'

I thought for a moment. Paul was right when he'd said the *muiñeiras* sounded Irish. Galicia's musical roots were deeply embedded in the Celtic tradition, not least because the Celts had populated the northwest corner of the Spanish peninsula way back in the years before Christ. *Muiñeiras* were popular lively dance tunes with a circular, six-eight rhythm reminiscent of an Irish jig.

I turned to him eagerly. 'Can you play any jigs?'

He looked at me curiously. 'A few, why?'

'Because they're just like *muiñeiras*, aren't they? They've both got that la-la-la, la-la-la, rhythm and...'

'I've got you,' Paul nodded. 'Let's give it a try.'

Másimo looked at me expectantly. 'What did he say?'

'He said "yes",' I fibbed. 'He knows some *muiñeiras*. He'll play one now.'

'Okay,' said Paul. 'This is "The Rakes of Kildare".'

As he struck up the tune, the notes rang out from the bellows in twirling triplets and Másimo's face broke into a smile.

'That's it!' he beamed. 'That's a *muiñeira*! *Si, eso es*!'

He picked up his sticks and began to drill out the rhythm, while Gary added the pulse on the bodhran.

I listened, transfixed, as the rhythm and melody blended to create a pleasingly passable sound. I winked at Helen and she gave me the thumbs up. The jig was a roaring success.

For almost an hour we clapped our hands and stamped our feet to the makeshift *galego* dance band.

Our *gaitas* were a squeezebox, our *tamboril* a snare drum and our *bombo* was the trusty bodhran.

When the sun was sinking behind the house and Paul had all but exhausted his repertoire, Masi declared it was time for him to go up to the farmhouse to join Javier for a drink.

'Right,' said Gary, as our maestro disappeared around the corner. 'I think more beers.'

'Good idea,' I agreed. 'But it's turning chilly. I've got goosebumps and Helen looks frozen. Let's go inside and relax upstairs.'

'Is it alright to bring Pepe?' asked Helen. 'We can't really leave her out here.'

'She could stay in the kitchen with Lenda…' I began.

'That won't work,' frowned Gary. 'Look how she growled at Lenda earlier. We can't leave them together unsupervised – what if they started to fight?'

'Well,' I faltered, 'She could come upstairs, I suppose, but what about Scholes and Fred?'

'She doesn't mind cats,' said Helen. 'If anything she's scared of them. She tends to ignore them or walk away.'

'That's it then,' I smiled, before Gary could answer. 'Lenda can stay where she's comfy and Pepe can join us upstairs.'

Up in the living room, Scholes was asleep on the sofa. When he saw Pepe he glared at her crossly, before strolling off to the bedroom to resume his slumber in peace. We were just settling down with our beers when I heard a soft thud from the staircase. Seconds later, Fred appeared at the top of the stairs. He froze in terror when he spotted our visitors, but when he saw Pepe he turned on his heels and fled.

'Oh dear,' said Helen. 'He didn't like Pepe. I'm ever so sorry. Poor little chap.'

'Don't worry,' I smiled. 'He's still a bit wary of Lenda. He'll walk past her when she's out in the garden, but he soon darts off if she goes up for a sniff. He'll be back later when the coast's clear. He'll be fine.'

It was approaching midnight when we said our goodbyes to Paul and Helen. When we'd waved them off up the lane I hovered about on the doorstep.

'What are you doing?' asked Gary. 'Come on, I'm ready for bed.'

'You go up,' I said. 'I won't be far behind you. I thought I'd have a quick look for Fred.'

'Don't be so daft – he's got his cat-hole. He'll come home when he's ready. Come on upstairs to bed.'

When I woke on Sunday morning, the first thing I thought of was Fred. I reached out through the half-darkness but there were no cats on top of the duvet. For a moment I was gripped by panic, but a tell-tale crunching from the living room assured me he was home. I crept across the bedroom and peered through the open doorway. My heart sank when my eyes came to rest on the food bowl. Scholes was having his breakfast, but he was eating alone.

Down in the passage, Lenda was waiting to greet me. Was it my imagination, or did she seem slightly subdued? Her humans had had a great night, but it had been awful for Lenda. She'd been growled at by Pepe and scared by the music, then left in the kitchen when we were upstairs having fun. I set the kettle to boil and mused on the night's proceedings. Thanks to our revelry, I'd neglected Lenda and Fred had absconded and still wasn't home. How I regretted my promise to Gary; what had possessed me to make changes to our peaceful, self-contained life?

When I went out to see to the livestock I cast my eyes over the garden. Fred was a creature of habit and I was fully expecting to see him going about his business without a care in the world. At this time of the morning he'd either be having a poo in the *huerta* or stalking the blackbirds as they grubbed and pecked on the lawn. Once in a while he'd be up in the fig tree or mousing down in the chooks' pen. It was very mysterious; he was in none of those places today.

I was making a second cup of coffee when Gary came into the kitchen. There was a good chance that while I'd been mooching about in the garden, Fred had slipped in through the cat-hole and was happily munching upstairs.

'Morning,' I smiled. 'Your cuppa won't be a minute. Is Fred up there?'

'I've not seen him,' he yawned. 'He was in earlier, wasn't he? I heard him eating when you got up.'

'That was Scholes. I've looked all round the garden and there's no sign of him. I'd have thought he'd be home by now.'

'I wouldn't worry. He probably came in while we were sleeping. He won't have gone all night without grub.'

In the afternoon I went round to see Solina. Cats could be petulant creatures; Fred might have returned, in a sulk, to his original home.

'I've not seen him,' she said, when I explained my predicament. 'I've been here all morning so I wouldn't have missed him. The other one's been in though. She had kittens a couple of weeks ago. If he doesn't come back you could always have one of those.'

I smiled and thanked her. There was no point in explaining. It wasn't a kitten I wanted. It was Fred.

On Monday morning I was feeling uneasy; Fred still hadn't come home. Although concerned, I was sure we were going to find him. Perhaps I'd misjudged the impact of his encounter with Pepe and he was still lying low. Up until now my search had been limited to a scout round the garden and a trip to number fifteen. This morning it was time to start searching in earnest; I was going to do everything in my power to bring Fred home.

When Gary set off for Monterroso, I went through to the animal pen. I shone my torch into the darkest corners and scuffed at the lumps in the earthen floor. Next came the barn. Gary had assured me he'd scoured every inch of both storeys but I had to be certain. After half an hour, I emerged covered in cobwebs and wished I'd trusted his word. I searched the annexe, the abandoned stable with the overhang and the courtyard next to the kitchen. When I'd exhausted all possibilities, I traipsed back to the kitchen, saddened and perplexed. I was filling the kettle when I heard the familiar screech of the van.

'Any joy?' asked Gary, when he came in with the shopping.

'Not yet. I've looked in all of our buildings, the *cuadra* and the courtyard. After lunch I'll go and ask Javier to look round the farm. There are all sorts of outbuildings he might have wandered into. I think there's a good chance he's been locked in.'

After lunch I made my way up to the farmhouse. Luna and Pastor were asleep on the doorstep. 'Hey, Luna; Pastor,' I said half-heartedly, as I reached over and rang the bell.

Eventually I heard footsteps in the passage. The heat from the kitchen hit me as soon as Maruja opened the door.

'*Hola*, Elisa,' she smiled. 'Isn't it hot?'

All that spared me from laughter was my overriding concern for Fred.

'*Hola*, Maruja. I've got a problem. I don't want to be a nuisance…'

'Elisa,' she smiled. 'Come in.'

I followed her through to the kitchen where pans of green beans and potatoes were bubbling on top of the range. A tray on the marble surface was piled with enough chops to feed an army. Flea-pelt was yapping and running in circles around the floor while a smiling woman on the telly was pointing to a huge map of Spain. 'Next week the temperatures will soar into the thirties in the north and…' She was interrupted by voices in the passage. Javier and José Manuel had arrived for lunch.

While the men ate and Maruja scrubbed at the oven tray, I explained my concerns for poor Fred.

'He's gone looking for *chicas*,' said José Manuel sagely.

Maruja shook her head. 'He hasn't. He's castrated, isn't he Elisa? He's had *antiparásito* treatments as well.'

It didn't surprise me that Maruja had remembered. She'd been incredulous when I'd told her of Fred's operation. 'You're wasting your money,' she'd said.

'You've had its *cojones* chopped off?' laughed Javier. 'No wonder it's run away.'

Although I was hurting I wasn't offended. Javier was a farmer and I was used to his mindset when it came to small animals. Cows were at the top of the hierarchy and somewhere at the bottom, not far above vermin, were cats. I managed to smile politely, but inside I felt such a fool. Asking him to check the outbuildings and the cowshed would be futile. I asked him to keep an eye out instead.

Back in the kitchen I sobbed into my tissue. For once Gary didn't accuse me of overreacting. When I passed him his coffee I was sure there were tears in his eyes. It was going to be hard on both of us, but we had to accept it; it was looking unlikely that Fred would return.

On Saturday morning I couldn't have felt less like company. I hated to poop on the party, but I was going to have to cancel the evening's plans. Over the course of the week, I'd sunk deeper into despondency. My heart ached for my lovable, overgrown kitten, and worse still, Scholes was missing his devoted friend. Throughout the week, Gary had done his utmost to raise my spirits. He'd even promised to see to the cooking so that I could relax with Rose.

I took a deep breath as he came into the kitchen, summoning up the courage to let him down.

'Morning,' I sighed as I passed him his cuppa.

'Morning,' he yawned. 'Try not to be sad. You'll feel better later. I'm donning the chef's hat and you'll enjoy seeing Rose.'

I smiled weakly. It was too early in the morning to put up any resistance. I resolved to tell him at breaktime. After a good walk and a shower to shake off the cobwebs, I'd have summoned up courage to renege.

At breaktime Gary didn't appear when I called him in for his coffee. I waited a couple of minutes then went out to the barn. Up on the top storey he was emptying a dustpan into a feed sack. When he looked up and saw me he grinned.

'What do you think? I told you I'd have it all shipshape. The barbecue's scrubbed and after lunch I'll pick salad stuff fresh from the *huerta*. You won't have to do a thing.'

By half past six there was no sign of Rose, and Gary was starting to chunter. Second only to incompetent drivers, hunger was always guaranteed to put him in a bad mood.

'I'm starving,' he grumbled. 'If she's not here on time, we'll start without her. I've lit the charcoal and the meat can go on at seven. It's tough if she's still not here when it's done.'

'Oh, Gary,' I sighed. 'Don't be like that. It's meant to be a cheer-me-up night, remember? I'm sure she'll have a good reason. I'll nip up to the church if you like and see if she's rung.'

I set off up the lane but paused when I reached the corner. Carmen was hovering by her doorstep and there were voices and laughter coming from the end of the path.

'*Hola*, Elisa,' she half-whispered. 'There's a woman in the Englishman's garden. I think she might be English too.'

It didn't take a genius to work out what had happened to our errant *invitada*. I had to get Rose out of there. Soon.

When I walked through the gate I was surprised to see that neither Paul nor Rose were imbibing. They were standing at the edge of the threshing floor, staring at the area of overgrown grass that Paul referred to as his lawn. My urgency was replaced by curiosity. 'Hello,' I said. 'What's going on?'

'Hiya!' giggled Rose. 'I was accosted by your neighbour. I've been hearing all about the leisure complex. Paul's been telling me his plans.' She turned to him. 'It was lovely to see you, but I'd better be going. Good luck with the pool.'

Up in the top of the barn, we plonked ourselves down at the table. As I reached for my tobacco, my stool wobbled alarmingly on the uneven wooden floor.

'Careful,' grinned Rose, as she pulled a scrunched up piece of knitting from her handbag. 'You don't mind, do you? I can knit while we're talking. I'm making Verna a shawl.'

I was admiring her handiwork when Gary came in and passed us each a can of chilled lager. 'Evening, Rose,' he nodded. 'Better late than never. I'll talk to you later – I need to turn the meat.'

'Wow,' laughed Rose, once he was out of earshot. 'You've been working on him. Either that or he's got a guilty conscience. He wasn't as well-trained last year.'

'Actually,' I sighed. 'It's neither. I've been in pieces all week and I almost rang you to cancel. We've lost Fred.'

'Oh no! I wish you'd said sooner. What happened – was he hit by a car?'

'No. He's not dead. At least, I hope not. He went missing last Saturday. I've looked everywhere I can think of. I've checked the animal pens and the outbuildings and I've asked all the neighbours to keep an eye out. I don't understand it. It's as if he's vanished off the face of the earth.'

Despite being blithe and impulsive, Rose was also empathic and caring. She went quiet for a moment, then groped in her bag.

'Here,' she said gently, passing me a tissue. 'You have a good cry, then I'll tell you my plan.'

All of a sudden I didn't feel weepy. I was about to be regaled with another of Rose's harebrained schemes.

'I'm fine,' I assured her. 'Go on.'

'Right,' she said firmly. 'You need a distraction. Something therapeutic. I have the perfect solution. I'm going to teach you to knit.'

I looked at her in surprise. 'Really? I'd love that. I learned once, when I was little. I've always regretted not keeping it up.'

She rummaged about in her bag and brought out a small pair of wooden-looking needles and a half-used ball of blue yarn. 'You can keep these,' she told me. 'They came free with a magazine. They're bamboo, and I can't get on with them. They'll do for starting you off, but you can buy some proper ones later and move your work onto those.'

It sounded straightforward enough and I smiled my appreciation.

'Okay,' Rose continued. 'I'll cast on twenty stitches, then I'll talk you through the first couple of rows. After that, all you have to do is keep knitting – row after row after row.'

I nodded eagerly. I could remember doing the same with my Granny when I was seven. I thought at the time that it was the first step on the ladder to being a great knitter. My debut piece never grew to more than a few inches long.

'Your stitches will be messy at first,' Rose added. 'But you'll have to be patient. They'll improve over time when you get the hang of the tension. You'll drop loads, and you'll probably make some. When it happens don't worry about trying to correct it. Just keep knitting to the end of the row.'

I watched as Rose cast on the stitches and began to knit. In a matter of seconds the first two rows were done.

'Here,' she said, passing me the needles, before picking up her own. 'Hold them like this…'

I positioned my fingers just as she'd shown me.

'Good,' she nodded. 'You're ready to go.'

I looked at the needles and the memory came back to me. 'I don't believe it,' I gasped. 'I think I can remember what to do.'

I poked the right hand needle up into the first stitch and wound the yarn around the point. I stared at it for a moment, then slid the stitch off the end. 'Oops,' I grinned. 'That wasn't quite right, was it? Now I've only got nineteen.'

'Pass it here,' giggled Rose. 'I'll make another stitch and show you what to do.'

She took the needles from me and performed a nifty manoeuvre. 'There,' she said. 'Done.' She passed me the needles and I repositioned my fingers. 'Right,' I nodded. 'Go on.'

'Do exactly what you did before, but after you've wound the yarn round, poke the right hand needle back through… no, into the space between the two stitches. That's it, now slide it off. Ta-da!'

'Hey!' I beamed. 'It's easy! Let me do it again.'

I knitted the second stitch, then the third. Once Rose was satisfied I could manage she picked up her shawl. We sat for a while in silence, save for the sound of the needles. Rose clicked away expertly whilst I fumbled along. Now and again, I'd curse and Rose would giggle, and then we'd fall silent again. After two rows I stopped to admire my progress. The work was bumpy and gappy but I was pleased with my efforts and decided to stop for a fag. I dropped the knitting onto my lap and reached over for my tobacco. As I leaned forward the stool wobbled and my knitting fell to the floor.

'Shit,' I mumbled.

'Don't worry,' laughed Rose. 'There's probably no harm done. Just be careful how you pick it up.'

I bent down and lifted the needles up carefully. It was nothing short of a miracle that I hadn't lost a single stitch.

'Phew!' I sighed. No sooner had I said it than I dropped the needles again. This time I wasn't so lucky. When I picked up the knitting, half of my stitches had gone.

By the time Monday morning came round I was exhausted; my life as a rustic socialite had really taken its toll. This week I had no plans to leave the *aldea* and I'd be visitor-free until the weekend. I planned to relax in the garden with my knitting and try not to think about Fred.

'Needles?' said Gary as he vetted the shopping list. 'There're some in the drawer.'

'Not *that* sort,' I frowned. 'Knitting needles. Here, let me write it down properly. I shall need a size four.'

'Will they have them in the shit shop?'

'More than likely, but I want them from the wool shop on the high street. If I'm going to knit like my Granny l want the proper kit.'

When Gary came back with the shopping he looked shifty.

'Here're your needles. Two pairs of fours, look – long ones and shorter ones. And to be on the safe side I bought threes and fives as well.'

Less than three hours ago the needles had been the ultimate inconvenience. There had to be a reason I'd ended up with four pairs; he must have been to the shit shop after all. He passed me my goodies. Sure enough, the name of the yarn store was printed on the bag.

'Thank you,' I smiled. 'How thoughtful.' Perhaps I'd misjudged him after all.

'And here's a coincidence,' he continued. 'There's a poster in the window for a percussion workshop at the library. It's next Saturday and it's only fifteen euros. You can sign up for it in the shop.'

'I'm surprised you didn't. That sounds right up your street.'

'I thought you'd say that, so I rang Paul and asked him if he fancied going. I've booked us two places. Do you mind?'

The heatwave began with a vengeance on Tuesday morning. Out in the *campo* the air was heavy and humid and beads of transpiration stuck to the remaining blades of grass. Lenda was panting and my tee shirt clung to my body. The flies buzzed around us like dirty kids in a comic strip and it wasn't my idea of fun. By the time we came back along the track I was itchy, sticky and desperate for a cold shower. I was also in a decidedly crotchety mood.

As we neared the corner of the barn, Lenda charged off ahead of me. When she reached the corner she stopped dead in her tracks and growled. As I came up behind her I was quick to spot the cause of her consternation; two bulging backpacks had been left outside on the bench. Lenda went over to sniff them and I stared at them crossly, wondering who the perpetrators of this untimely intrusion could be.

As I opened the door I was sure I could hear Gary speaking in English. I dismissed it as my heat-addled imagination. It seemed unlikely that any of the ex-pats crowd would pay us a visit unannounced.

Inside the kitchen, Gary was leaning on the door jamb talking to a young man and woman as they sat drinking tea. He gave me a barely perceptible shrug of the shoulders as I fixed him with a look that said, 'You'd better explain.'

'This is Rudi and Sandra,' he breezed. 'They've walked all the way down from the Farelito. They're from Madrid.'

'Hello,' I smiled, in an effort to hide my annoyance.

'Hi,' they chorused, as Lenda ran over to them, wagging her tail.

Her greeting was rewarded with a fuss and affectionate laughter.

'She's lovely,' said Rudi, in English. 'Gary was telling us about her. Hello, Lenda. Good girl.'

Despite the unwanted intrusion. I found myself warming to our visitors.

'I'm sorry to hear about your cat,' said Sandra. 'Don't give up hope. I worked for an animal protection centre and there was a case where a cat came home after almost a year.'

I suddenly felt guilty for my earlier misgivings. Rudi and Sandra were instantly likeable. I could quite understand why Gary had invited them in.

'So where are you heading?' I asked them. If they were walking the Camino de Santiago they'd wandered miles out of their way.

'We're staying in an *aldea* near Antas,' said Rudi. 'My Grandfather was *galego*. His house is empty, so we come over every summer. We love the region so much we've decided to move here. We've set up a charity to preserve the environment and plant more indigenous trees.'

'Good for you,' I said. 'That's fantastic. It sounds like the National Trust.'[2]

'The National Trust?' echoed Sandra. 'What's that?'

'It's a UK charity,' I explained. 'They conserve the habitats of native plants and animals and they create nature reserves to protect endangered species.'

'They look after historical buildings as well,' added Gary. 'They hold big classical concerts outdoors. People take picnics and there's a big finale with fireworks. It's good fun.'

'What a coincidence,' said Rudi. 'We hold classical concerts too.'

'Never!' I gasped.

'It's true,' he continued. 'I'm a violinist. I play for the symphony orchestra in Madrid. Every summer I put on a programme of chamber music to raise money for our group.'

'We're having a concert in August,' said Sandra. 'It's in Antas. You should come.'

I was about to say yes but remembered our budget. Concerts could be pricy and we already struggled to make ends meet.

---

[2] https://www.nationaltrust.org.uk

'We'd love to,' I sighed. 'But I have to be honest, we're very short of cash.'

Rudi smiled. 'That's not a problem. Our concerts are free. We ask for donations, but it isn't compulsory. Some might give fifty euros; others might give two.'

I looked at Gary and he nodded.

'That's great,' I beamed. 'We'll come.'

'It's the first Saturday in August,' said Rudi. 'We'll be putting the posters up this weekend.'

'We have a website as well,' added Sandra. 'You can find out about all our projects. Quercus Sonora[3] – that's the name of our group.'

'Quercus,' I said. 'That's an oak tree, isn't it?'

'Yes,' nodded Sandra.

'I like it,' I smiled. 'The musical oak.'

It was almost mid-day when I finally went up for my shower. The water was cool and refreshing, but I didn't dare linger. The water pressure would be sure to dwindle eventually; we'd already resorted to bucket washes by this time last year.

When Gary came in at lunchtime he was breathing heavily.

'You're panting,' I frowned. 'Are you okay?'

'I'll be alright when I've eaten. I feel a bit drained, that's all.'

'Oh dear,' I frowned. 'I've only done you a salad. Still, there's cheese, hard boiled eggs and ham with it, so it should fill you up.'

'That'll be fine,' he nodded. 'I couldn't have managed anything hot today.'

Ten minutes later Gary pushed his plate away. He'd left most of the cheese and salad and one of the hard boiled eggs.

---

[3] https://www.quercussonora.es

'Crikey,' I frowned. 'That's not like you. You've barely touched it. Are you okay?'

'I'm not sure. I *thought* I was starving, but once I started eating I wasn't. My stomach feels weird.'

'Well, leave it if you don't want it. You might feel like it later. If not it'll do for your tea. Do you want me to make you a cuppa instead?'

'No thanks. I'm going to sit in the barn and read the football paper. Do you mind?'

''Course I don't. I'll finish fetching the water from the *río* and then I'll pick the courgettes and beans.'

After a couple of trips to the *río* I could quite understand how Gary had come over all flaky. With the sun beating down on my head and neck I was soon feeling queasy myself.

When we sat down with our beers that evening, Gary was unusually quiet and subdued. I tried to make idle chitchat in an effort to lighten his mood.

'Lovely folks, weren't they, Rudi and Sandra?'

'Who?'

'Rudi and Sandra – the couple that came this morning. I'm looking forward to the concert. I think we should ask Rose.'

'Eh?'

'The concert. I think we should ask Rose.'

'Yes. Yes, good idea. Look, I'm sorry – do you mind if we give Scrabble a miss tonight? I know you enjoy it but I wouldn't be much competition. To be honest, I'm feeling a bit strange.'

I studied him for a second. In the afternoon he'd looked drawn and sallow; now his face was an unnatural shade of red.

'Listen,' I said gently. 'Why not finish your beer and go to bed? You've not been right all day and you look exhausted. After a good night's sleep you'll feel as right as rain.'

Where's Fred?

Hey, Scholes, have you seen little Fred?
'Cos he hasn't come home to be fed;
I'm starting to panic,
It's driving me manic
To think the poor lad might have fled.

Hey, Scholes, you must know what to do,
You're a cat; he shares secrets with you.
You've known him since summer;
Would Fred do a runner?
Without him I'm feeling so blue.

Hey, Scholes, do you think he'll come home?
I wonder what's caused him to roam?
I'm all of a dither,
When will he come hither?
He's out there somewhere all alone.

Hey, Scholes, if you see him pass by,
Tell him 'Mum has done nothing but cry.'
Please say I adore him,
And I'm pining for him;
Oh, where has he gone, Scholes, and why?

Hey, Scholes, you're my true number one,
But Fred brings such laughter and fun,
I'm totally smitten
With our ginger kitten;
Wherever has poor Freddie gone?

Chapter 8

Jekyll and Hyde

Gary looked as right as ninepence when he surfaced on Wednesday morning.

'Morning,' I smiled as I passed him his cuppa. 'How are you today?'

'Fine,' he yawned. 'I'm ready for some breakfast. I hardly ate anything yesterday. I fancy some eggs.'

'I'm pleased to hear it. Don't overdo it though, you're having your favourite for lunch.'

'Spaghetti bolognese? Just what the doctor ordered. You're not such a bad wife after all.'

'Don't go thinking I was worried about you. You're starting your new job on Friday. We can't afford for you to be ill.'

Although I'd made light of it, I was relieved that Gary was feeling better. Last night he'd looked like he was running a fever by the time he went to bed. It struck me how easy it was to take one another for granted. He could be tightarsed and impatient, but he was still a good husband; in spite of his foibles, I loved him to bits.

When lunchtime came round Gary didn't looked nearly as well as he had at breakfast. I could hear his stomach gurgling as he dragged his fork around his plate.

'Is it alright?' I asked him.

'What?'

'Your spaghetti.'

'Yes, it's lovely. It's not the food, it's me. I've got that weird feeling again in my stomach. I can't tell if I'm empty or full.'

'Are you in pain?'

'No, it's not hurting. I feel hollow. I'll have a drink of water and finish this off for my tea.'

He spent most of the afternoon asleep on the bench in the barn. By evening his face was scarlet. For the second night running we abandoned Scrabble and he took himself off to bed.

On Thursday I was expecting Gary to wake up cheerful. I was also expecting him to deteriorate as the day wore on. For the last two days he'd been fine in the mornings; the problems had started when he'd picked at his lunch. If he could eat a full meal, he might not feel jaded in the evening. I'd played my ace with the spag bol but there *had* to be something more I could do. I wracked my brains for a treat that might tempt him. He loved curries and chillies, stir-fries and pizzas, but when it came to the crunch he was an Englishman; egg and chips smothered in ketchup would be sure to come up trumps.

That afternoon I tossed a pile of cold chips into the chooks' pen. The eggs weren't quite as fresh as they'd been that morning. I hoped the poor hens wouldn't take offence.

As the sun went down, I sent Gary up to the living room to relax while I did the watering. Two hours later I came in sweating and aching. Gary was down in the kitchen, eating bread and serrano ham.

'Brilliant,' I beamed. 'Your appetite's back. I'll go up for my shower then I'll thrash you at Scrabble. I'm so glad you're on the mend.'

When I came out of the shower, Gary was back in the living room. The Scrabble box was on the coffee table and he was eating cheese with his wine.

'Are you fetching yourself a beer?' he asked, as I hung my towel over the balustrade.

'Oh, didn't you bring me one? Never mind, you can set the Scrabble up while I'm gone.'

'Bring me the rest of the ham will you, while you're at the fridge?'

The absence of a 'please' grated, but I decided not to push it. His face was flushed and ruddy but, in contrast, his eyes were narrow and cold.

When I returned to the living room the Scrabble was ready but Gary was yawning. I sat on the sofa and passed him his ham.

'You look shattered,' I said. 'Do you still want to play?'

'I've set the board up, haven't I? Don't make such a fuss.' He stuffed the ham into his mouth and took a letter from the bag of tiles.

We began to play, and the atmosphere returned to normal. A triple letter score put a smug smile on his face and shunted him well into the lead. Competitive by nature, he was happy while he was winning; as long as I didn't out-point him all would be well. Ten minutes later I was faced with a dilemma; with the tiles on my rack I could make ANGERED or DERANGE. Using all seven letters would give me a fifty-point bonus but then I'd risk Gary growing angry again. Both words struck a chord and I hoped it wasn't portentous. In the end I settled for DANGER and prayed I wasn't tempting fate.

As I reached into the bag for more letters I noticed that he was yawning again.

'Why don't you give Matt's a miss tomorrow?' I suggested. 'You might feel more like it next week.'

'Don't be ridiculous. You won't let up, will you? For God's sake, just play the game!'

'I'm sorry. I was only trying to be helpful. You're really lacking in energy and if you fainted or fell...'

He slammed the bag down onto the coffee table. The Scrabble board juddered, causing the tiles to jolt out of place. Some fell from the table and scattered across the floor.

'Why can't you fucking shut up about it? I'm sick of hearing you nagging. You can forget Scrabble. I'm off to bed.'

Before I had chance to answer, he stormed off to the bedroom. I stared at the floor in stunned disbelief. There was a thud, then another, as he pulled off his loafers, then the crash of his belt buckle as his jeans hit the floor. I had no intention of following until I was certain he was sleeping. As soon as I heard the bedsprings creak, I crept down the stairs.

Down in the kitchen I made myself a coffee and tried to make sense of the tantrum. I'd gone out of my way to be supportive and I certainly hadn't nagged. I'd done the lion's share of the *río* trips and watered the veg singlehanded. I'd sweated over the chip pan and hadn't so much as murmured when he'd wasted half his lunch. I'd only had his welfare at heart when I'd suggested he postpone his stint at Matt's. I still believed it was a bad idea, but if he wanted to go, let him. If I was on my own, I wouldn't fall foul of his temper; after the way he'd been tonight, it would be a relief. On the downside, how would he behave in the evening? He might be worse than ever after a day spent working in the heat.

Gary was sweetness and light when he surfaced on Friday morning. He was either completely audacious or he'd forgotten that something was wrong. If the latter was true, then his condition was more of a worry than ever. My fears were allayed when he'd finished his second brew.

'I'm sorry for last night. I shouldn't have shouted – I know you were worried. I'll still go to Matt's but I'll take my time and I won't overdo it. Are *you* going to be okay?'

His expression was sincere and I gave him a half-hearted smile.

'I'll be fine. I'll be so busy I won't have time to think about it. There's the water to fetch, the veg to pick, then there's the blanching and freezing. Look, I'm not being rude, but I'm going to take Lenda. It'll be hell if I leave it much longer – the flies are a nightmare over the fields. Your pack-up's in the fridge – try to eat it all, won't you? You have a good day, and I shall want to hear all about the ghost when you get home.'

It was well after five when Gary came home that evening. His shirt was drenched and his face was the colour of a beetroot when he climbed out of the van.

'I'm sweating like a glassblower's arsehole,' he cursed. 'I need a beer.'

I tutted my disapproval. 'Can't you say, "sweating like a pig"?'

As he opened the fridge he glared at me. 'What the hell's wrong with you? Do you have to be so stuck up?'

My eyes widened. The venom in his voice had hit me like a bolt from the blue. I was about to retort, but my lip trembled and my eyes filled with tears. It wasn't like me to cry so easily, but I was physically and emotionally drained. I'd worked like a trooper in the searing heat and was still struggling to come to terms with losing Fred. If I'd been hoping for a kind word or a hug, I'd have been disappointed. He opened his lager and looked at me with disdain.

Later that evening we watered the veg plot in silence. I hadn't dared offer to relieve him of the burden. When I came to the peppers I stared at the dangling twine. I'd lost my beloved Fred and now something awful was happening to Gary. Whatever was plaguing him was more than an artisan's rear-end affliction; he'd never spoken to me so coldly before.

I was on tenterhooks when I heard Gary stirring on Saturday morning. The previous day's unpleasantness had left me all of a dither and I wondered how he'd react when he came down the stairs. As it turned out, I needn't have worried; he was Doctor Jekyll again.

'Morning,' he smiled as I passed him his cuppa. 'Don't I get a kiss?'

Thankful that, at least for now, he was back to normal, I leaned down and gave him a reluctant peck on the head. Despite the upturn in his demeanour, the events of the last few days could no longer go unchallenged. Something was ailing him and we needed to get it fixed. Good mood or no, now wasn't the time to broach the subject. This morning he was off to the percussion workshop and I didn't want to spoil his day.

'I've made you a pack-up,' I said. 'Cheese and onion butties and some cherry tomatoes. Will that be enough?'

'Plenty,' he nodded. 'Look, I'm really...'

I was in no mood for another apology. I looked at him coolly. 'Just leave it, okay?'

When I came back from the fields with Lenda, Gary had already left for the workshop. Though it saddened me to admit it, for the second day running I was glad of the time on my own. For the next few hours I could push my problems aside and throw myself into my workload. The temperature would be touching the thirties by mid-morning and I was keen to complete my trips to the *río* before the sun was too high in the sky.

The hot summer months could be cruel to the countryside and its inhabitants, but as far as hand laundering was concerned, the relentless heat was a blessing in disguise. By lunchtime, three thick, fleecy throwovers were hanging on the clothesline which sagged disconcertingly under their drenched weight. The rugs from the terrace lay on the threshing floor, the soapy water drying the second it seeped onto the hot stones. Pleased with my efforts, I was sitting on the lawn rolling a cigarette and listening to the distant jingling of cowbells, when I heard voices coming from over the standing stone wall. I crept over to the herb bed and peered through the gap into Carmen's overgrown garden. Through the dense foliage I could see her peering over the wall into Paul's. Paul was smiling and nodding, but Carmen was shaking her head and waving her arms. I strained to listen to what they were saying above the birdsong and the buzzing of flies.

'*No necesitas un pozo*,' said Carmen.

'A pothole?' Paul frowned. 'No, deeper than a pothole. Much deeper. *Muy* deep.'

'*Hay agua ahí*,' Carmen insisted, pointing over the wall, somewhere beyond Paul's threshing floor. '*Ahí*.'

'*Si*,' nodded Paul, pointing downwards. '*Agua. Muy bien*.'

Carmen shrugged impatiently and shuffled off through the foliage. She disappeared out of eyeshot and I heard the clang of the gate. Seconds later there was a second clang and she reappeared in Paul's garden. I stared, transfixed, as she scurried past him and up to his trough. Unlike the one in our garden, Paul's trough was enormous. It was easily the size of three bathtubs, and the sides were a good three feet high. Paul's mouth fell open as she clambered up over the rim and stood in the middle, pointing to the tap.

'*Agua!*' she announced, as she turned on the tap. '*No tienes que hacerlo – hay agua aquí.*'

'Yes,' Paul nodded, smiling broadly. '*Agua, muy bien.*'

Satisfied that she'd saved him digging down until he struck water, Carmen clambered out of the trough and scurried back through the gate. Ten minutes later, she came down the lane with a mattock over her shoulder. I waited until she'd turned round the corner of the barn before setting off up to Paul's to find out what was going on. When I walked through the gate I was surprised to see him shovelling earth from a *very* deep hole in his 'lawn'.

'Hello,' I grinned. 'I've come round to be nosy. I was watching over the wall when Carmen was doing her nifty manoeuvres in and out of your trough.'

'Hmm,' he frowned. 'I couldn't quite make out what she was up to. I think she was making sure I'd have enough water to fill the hole.'

I chuckled. 'She wasn't. She was showing you why you *don't* need to be digging a hole.'

He leaned on his shovel and frowned.

'It really is time you learned Spanish. She was saying "*pozo*" not "pothole". She thought you were digging a well.'

'Never! I thought she was asking me if I was going to put water in it. You can see how easy it was to misunderstand her. She'd have been right, you see – it's a pool.'

'A pool?' I was baffled. Hadn't he told me the world would end in October? If he was digging a swimming pool he'd be at it from now until kingdom come. I glanced around me, trying to fathom out which direction the pool might be extended. It would have to reach all the way up to the track through the woodlands if it was going to be long enough for Paul to have a swim. He'd always referred to the threshing floor as his 'patio' and he'd even tried to tart it up with some plastic solar lights stuck into the border around the edge. That was the explanation. It was going to be a pond.

'Ah,' I smiled. 'You mean a pond.'

'No,' he insisted. 'I mean a pool. For when I'm sunbathing. If I want to cool off I'll be able to take a dip.'

The idea was absurd, but it didn't surprise me. I wondered what Carmen would make of it all. As if nude sunbathing wasn't enough, he'd soon be adding skinny-dipping to his outdoor pursuits.

'I've got you,' I nodded. 'A plunge pool. Poor Carmen, you aren't half confusing her with all this digging. She thinks the pétanque court's for growing veg. That's a point, how's it coming on?'

'Slowly but surely. I've decided to make it bigger. I googled it when I went into Antas. It needs to be double the size. It should be ready for the concrete by September. Do you want to come and look?'

'I'd love to,' I lied, 'but I've got so much work on. I want to make the most of the time while Gary's away.'

'Away?'

'In Monterroso. He's at a percussion workshop with Irish Paul.'

'Ah, a lads' day out is it? And you don't mind holding the fort?'

'Not at all. He's been a bit under the weather this week. I'm hoping it might perk him up.'

'What's been the matter?'

'It's hard to explain. He's fine when he gets up in the morning, but towards lunchtime he changes. He says he's starving but then he doesn't eat his dinner. He feels exhausted and spends the whole afternoon lying down in the barn.'

'It could be the weather. It *has* been very hot.'

'It's possible, I s'pose, but there're other things too…' I faltered. I was certain Gary couldn't help the way he'd been behaving and I didn't want to speak out of turn. 'Look, d'you promise you won't say anything if I tell you?'

'Of course.'

'It's his temper. By evening it's unbearable – it's so out of character. He's snapped at me for no reason and his face goes bright red.'

'Oh dear. That doesn't sound like Gary. He's usually good fun. Look, if you're worried, why don't you get him to go to the doctor?'

'I wish I could. I've been thinking about it, but I'm scared to. He'll get really angry and say I'm just making a fuss.'

'Why don't you talk to him when he comes home from the workshop? He's bound to be in a good mood if he's been out for the day with Paul. Make hay while the sun shines – it's got to be worth a try.'

'You're right,' I smiled. 'I'll do that. I hope you didn't mind me offloading – I feel better for sharing. If I can persuade him to see the doctor it'll be a weight off my mind.'

As the afternoon wore on my resolve began to dwindle. Talking to Paul had left me feeling much brighter, but by teatime I was dreading going through with my plan. The fact that Gary had left in high spirits brought little consolation; there was a pattern to his condition and there was no guarantee he'd still be in a good mood when he came home. On top of that, I'd begun to feel guilty; had I been disloyal to Gary by sharing the events of the previous night? Whatever my doubts, at some point in the evening I'd have to broach the subject of the doctor's appointment. The flare-ups had been unprovoked and unacceptable; it was time for Gary to admit that he wasn't well.

By six o'clock I was starting to panic; Gary still wasn't home. If he'd had another of his turns, Irish Paul would have sent me a message. I was debating going up to the church when I heard the familiar screeching of brakes at the top of the lane.

When Gary got out of the van he looked as fit as a fiddle and as chipper as he'd been in the morning.

'Well?' I smiled. 'How did it go?'

'Excellent, thanks, it was worth every penny. Get me a beer out, will you, while I put the van away? I can't wait to tell you how I got on.'

Once we were out on the bench with our beers, Gary didn't need any prompting. For his enthusiasm alone it was fifteen euros well spent.

'The bloke was called José. I bet he was only in his thirties. He started off with an introduction in *galego* about the traditional instruments and why percussion's such an important part of Galician music.'

'And you understood him?'

'Not everything, but he was very lively, waving his arms about and pulling faces, so I got the gist. Anyway, the generally accepted reason's simple. It's to get people to dance.'

I nodded. 'That makes sense.'

'Well, that might be the case now, but it's not how it started.'

'No?'

'No. The tradition goes way back to when the Celts invaded. The drumming encouraged them to get a spurt on when they rampaged from place to place, because they had short stubby legs.'

I looked at him. His expression was perfectly serious. The man had obviously been joking, yet it seemed that Gary had believed him. Not only that, his understanding of *galego* must have been far better than I'd thought. Suddenly his face broke into a smile.

'He didn't say that really. I was joking. I had you going though didn't I? It's not like you to be so naïve.'

I was about to protest but remembered the awkward mission that lay ahead of me. Letting him feel victorious would help to keep him sweet.

'You were very convincing, I must admit. To be fair, it seemed a reasonable explanation. In all the time we've been here I've never seen a Galician, man or woman, who's taller than me. So, what really happened?'

'After the introduction he came round with a box of little wooden plaques. He told us to take two each. He said they were *tejoletas*. Most of the folks seemed to know what they were and started clicking them together. I couldn't believe it. I looked at Paul and said, "he's having a laugh, surely? We've paid fifteen euros for *this*?"'

'Oh dear.'

'But then he gave us a demonstration and we were spellbound. You wouldn't believe how many different sounds you can make with two little bits of wood.'

'Really? How little? Come on, I want to know what they were like.'

'Well, they were about so long...' He spread his thumb and index finger about four inches apart. 'And a couple of inches wide. They were about as thick as a piece of cardboard and they each had a dent in one side.'

'Where you put your fingers?'

'Yes. You have to clack them together in your hand, like castanets I s'pose. We were hopeless at first, 'cos we were trying to move them with our fingers. There's a knack to it and it's quite tricky. The movement has to come from your wrist.'

'Wow.'

'And this is interesting. Ours were made of oak, but originally they were made of broken ceramic tiles. Little tiles, you see, that's what *tejoletas* means.'

I nodded. I knew what it meant, but I wasn't going to say so. It was fantastic to hear Gary's enthusiasm; he was really on a roll.

'And after the *tejoletas*, it was the *charrasco*...'

'A *churrasco*? As in – a barbecue? Bloody hell! So you did get your fifteen euros worth after all.'

'I didn't say "chu", I said "cha" – *charrasco*. It's a shaking stick. We saw them in Ortigueira – a cross between a broomstick and a tambourine.'

'Now I'm with you. The mini telegraph poles with little metal discs on that jingle when they bash them on the ground.'

'They're the ones. The discs are called *ferreñas*. They don't just bash them though – they hit them with a stick as well. There's quite an art to it if you watch closely. The tapping and beating produce different sounds and you can use all sorts of combinations to create amazing effects.'

'Crikey. You sound quite the expert. Were you any good?'

'I was actually. The bloke said I was a natural. He could tell I'd played percussion before.'

'You've found your niche then. You'll be wanting one next.'

'You're right, and I'm going to have one. Don't look like that, it won't cost a *céntimo* – I'm going to make it myself.'

When we went up to the living room that evening I was plucking up the courage to voice my concerns. Gary was flushed and tired, but he was still upbeat from his workshop. I trod carefully to begin with; there was always the chance he might turn.

'So how have you been today?' I ventured. 'I don't mean the workshop – I mean your health.'

'No different really. I ate all my butties but I still felt hollow. When we were leaving, Paul said I looked red.'

'You still do. I don't want you to get cross with me, but I think you might have high blood pressure. I've been saying it for years now, but you always ignore me. You go like a beetroot when you're angry or hot.'

He went quiet for a moment and I wondered if I'd overstepped the mark. When I looked at his face he wasn't cross, he was pensive. Eventually he spoke.

'So going red's one of the signs, is it?'

'It can be. It's a symptom of lots of other things too, though – there's no way of really knowing unless you get it checked out.'

'By a doctor, you mean?'

'Unless you'd prefer a vet.'

I regretted the words the second they left my mouth. How could I even *think* of joking when we were discussing something so grave? I bit my lip and waited for the backlash, but when Gary chuckled I knew I'd won through.

'The doctor it is then,' he grinned. 'I'll make an appointment on Monday – just for you.'

Gary was as good as his word on Monday. When he came back from shopping he had a doctor's appointment for Wednesday. He had other news as well.

'There's a poster in Farelo's window for Rudi's concert. Eight-thirty this Saturday at the Casa de Cultura. Do you still want to go?'

'I'd love to. Did it say what they're playing?'

'It did. I knew you'd ask and I knew I wouldn't remember...'

I sighed.

'...so I wrote it down.' He pulled a crumpled serviette from his pocket. 'Here y'are.'

'Tchaikovsky. Serenade for Strings in C Major. Splendid.'

'Oh, do you know it?'

'No, but that doesn't matter. It'll be something new.'

He looked at me fondly. 'It's good to see you smiling. I've been a bastard lately, haven't I? Roll on Wednesday, we'll soon get it sorted out.'

If a cure was on the horizon, there was still a fly in the ointment. He had other less welcome news.

'There was another poster as well. Remember how we said we'd go to the next fiesta?'

Of course I remembered. I remembered being confident that there wouldn't be another until next year. My answer was guarded. 'Ye-es.'

'Well, there's one in Santa Mariña this Saturday. It's a big one – a stage and a group and everything. We could pop over in the afternoon if you want to, and still go to Rudi's concert at night.'

For a moment I was speechless. Santa Mariña was such a quaint little picturesque village. It was the last place I would have imagined holding a full-blown rumbustious bash. It was going to be a rush and it really wasn't my cup of tea, but Gary looked so enthusiastic and it might just do him the power of good. Suddenly, I didn't care if the group wore spangly shirts and made a racket. I wouldn't just grin and bear it, I'd go with a smile on my face.

'Brilliant,' I smiled. 'We should go.'

'I knew you'd be pleased. We'll set off straight after lunch and be back in plenty of time for Rose.'

'Rose?'

'Yes. You were going to ask her over for Rudi's concert, weren't you?'

'I was, but I thought... well, you know, with your illness and everything...'

'Liza, listen. I'd love Rose to come with us. You could ask Nina and Marcus as well.'

When Gary came home from the doctor's on Wednesday, his face was ashen and his expression was grim. He hadn't looked so solemn since we'd lost Anxo and I could only assume the prognosis was bad. He was about to speak, but I shushed him and squeezed his arm.

'Wait,' I said gently. 'Put the van away and I'll stick the kettle on. Whatever's the matter, I'm here for you. You can tell me all about it over a fag and a brew.'

Once we were sat in the kitchen with cigarettes and coffees, I was ready. I took a deep breath and swallowed. 'Okay,' I whispered. 'What did the doctor say?'

'She didn't seem concerned about my stomach – she thought it might be a bug. She's referred me to the hospital just to be on the safe side. I might have to wait a few weeks.'

'That's good news then, isn't it? I thought you were going to tell me something was terribly wrong.'

'That's not all. She sent me through to the nurse to give blood for analysis. I've got to go back for the results in a week.'

'Okay,' I nodded, sensing there was more to come.

'You were right about my blood pressure. She's put me on tablets – it's way too high.'

The news didn't surprise me, but it wasn't too worrying either. Once the tablets kicked in, he'd be fine. I was about to say so when he leaned forward and looked at me earnestly. If I wasn't mistaken there were tears in his eyes.

'It's not just high, you see – it's serious.'

My stomach knotted and my mind began to reel. High blood pressure could cause strokes or heart attacks. In some cases it could also lead to dementia. Perhaps his mood swings were only the beginning. If he was really losing his marbles I wasn't sure I could cope.

'How serious? You could have a stroke? A heart attack?' I couldn't bring myself to say dementia. 'Shit, Gary – what did she actually say?'

'She said it's *crónico*.'

'*Crónico*. Okay. And what else?'

'Nothing, that's it. "*Es crónico*" – they were her exact words. It's chronic, Liza. I'm scared.'

Poor Gary. He'd misunderstood her completely. A wave of relief washed over me and I smiled.

'Liza! Didn't you hear me? It's chronic. It's severe. It could be fatal. I don't want to die.'

'Gary,' I said, calmly. 'There's nothing to worry about. You've got the wrong end of the stick.'

'But…'

'Listen. In English you hear people say "chronic" to mean terrible or serious. But they're using it wrongly – it's slang. The true meaning is ongoing or long-lasting. In the medical sense it means persistent. It can be managed with the tablets, but it sounds like you'll be on them for the rest of your life.'

He looked at me, childlike and hopeful. 'Are you sure?'

'I'm certain. Trust me, Gary – as long as you keep taking your tablets you're going to be fine.'

The next two days saw an upturn in Gary's condition; it was a sure sign the blood pressure tablets were kicking in. He shuttled backwards and forwards to the *río* in the mornings and joined me at sunset to water the veg. He continued to nap after lunch and still felt exhausted by evening, but he wasn't as flushed or bad tempered and he was keen to play Scrabble again. Whilst his mood had improved, his stomach remained a conundrum. He picked at his meals at lunchtime then ate like a gannet at nights. I was intrigued to see how he'd be by Sunday evening; with the fiesta *and* a concert ahead of him, it was going to be a *very* tiring weekend.

Liza Grantham

Heat Rage

(A parody on Sonnet 18 by William Shakespeare)

Shall I compare thee to a July day?
Thou art hot-headed, rash, and obdurate:
Such temper, soothing winds shall not allay,
Apollo's fiery curse has sealed thy fate:
If e'er the eye of heav'n refused to shine,
Or by a gauzy veil his glare be dimmed:
Perchance your fury would, awhile, decline,
And let your heart with joy be overbrimm'd:
But his infernal ardour shall not fade.
Nor ebbs the anger that thou oft bestow'st,
Nor shall thy ire be tamed by mercy's shade,
And kinder, vernal times thou shalt not know'st,
Thy breath is stifled, eyes too hot to see,
While summer's heatwave rages, so shalt thee.

Chapter 9

What A Performance

Two thirds of the summer were already behind us and it had hardly been the season of mirth and merriment we'd known in previous years. June and July had brought little but doom and disorder, thanks to Lenda's season, Fred's disappearance and Gary's malaise. Nevertheless, on Saturday morning I awoke with renewed positivity; August lay ahead of us and life was looking up once again. Although Fred had been missing for three weeks, deep down inside I was clinging to the hope that he'd come home. For a while I'd wondered if Toothy had accomplished his mission with Lenda, but by mid-July there were no signs of pregnancy and I'd thanked my lucky stars that I'd discovered them in time. Most importantly, Gary's illness, though still concerning, wasn't a matter of life and death, at least for now. Knowing that things were back on an even keel had rekindled my trademark optimism and I was determined to enjoy what was left of the summer before the dark nights and colder weather set in.

Over in Warren Place, I coaxed Doe into paying Buck a romantic visit and down in the chooks' pen, Mrs Brown was broody again. My strawberry plants were still yielding plump, juicy fruits and my single pumpkin was already the size of a football. The beans, now covered in black fly, were almost over and I was secretly relieved. I still had to find room for nine rabbits and two cockerels in the freezer and there was no joy to be found in working in a kitchen full of steam.

As I came back across the threshing floor, I heard a loud mewing. It wasn't the wailing sound that Scholes made when he was hungry, or the miaow he gave when he had an announcement to make. I stood still and listened. The noise was a melodious chirrup and it was coming from somewhere down the lane. As I opened the gate I caught sight of Sophie slinking out of the corner field. When she reached the annexe, she paused and chirruped again. I was certain she was calling her babies and knew I'd be sure to see them if I waited by the gate. Seconds later, I gasped in delight as two tiny kittens emerged from the undergrowth. The first was ginger and fluffy, while the second was tortoiseshell and white with short fur. Sophie chirruped a third time and the happy trio trotted off in the direction of Solina's gate.

When I came back into the kitchen Gary was drinking his cuppa. The tablets really *were* working; he'd made me a coffee as well.

'Morning,' I chimed. 'You'll never guess? I've seen Sophie with her kittens. There's a tortoiseshell and white one – that'll be a female, and a longhaired ginger one which I suppose is a boy. Now, talking of babies, Mrs Brown's broody so I've moved her and the eggs to the maternity house. I've put Doe in with Buck, so the youngsters are going to need killing within the next fortnight, and the two cockerels are five months now, so…'

'Whoa! Slow down! You're rambling away like a mad thing! Can't a man have his cuppa in peace?' He reached for his tobacco and gave me a knowing grin. 'I know what's brought this on – you're excited about the fiesta, aren't you? I knew you would be – what time shall we leave?'

'We'll go straight after lunch and be there before two. Most people will go on from the one o'clock mass, so things will just be getting off the ground.'

When we arrived in Santa Mariña, the place was heaving. Either the crowds had opted for one of the earlier masses or they were planning to leave it until Sunday in the hopes they'd have more to confess. On our previous visits, the village had struck me as quaint and bijou; the *pazo*, stone houses and the *hórreos* were typically Galician, yet there was a hint of Englishness in the tiny pub with its hanging sign, overlooking the village green. Today the green was hidden beneath a giant juggernaut which would serve as a stage for the pop group, and the Águila Negra was dwarfed by an enormous canvas-sheltered bar. From toddlers to octogenarians, everyone had smiles on their faces and all were dressed up to the nines. There was nothing remotely English about this full-blown fiesta: Santa Mariña was quintessentially Spanish this afternoon.

'I won't have a beer,' said Gary. 'If we're going for a drink before the concert I'd better have a coke.'

'I think I'll join you,' I nodded. 'I'd be glad of the ice.'

'Come on. We'll nip over to the Águila Negra. If we can grab a table we'll still be able to see the stage from there.'

As we sat sipping our cokes, I noticed a poster in the pub's window. The *orquesta* would be coming on at two.

'Orchestra?' said Gary. 'I thought they always had one of those glitzy pop groups – four guys, four girls, that sort of thing.'

'They do. That's what they call it in Spanish. Trust me, you won't be getting your classical fix 'til tonight.'

'It's ten to two – we won't have to wait long. Let's people-watch and see if we can spot anybody we know.'

As Gary began to scan the crowds I heard my phone beeping.

'Did you hear that?' I asked. 'I think we've had a text.' I reached into my bag and pulled out my phone. Adjusting myself to avoid the glare of the sun I squinted at the screen.

'I s'pose it's Rose,' said Gary. 'It wouldn't surprise me if she's crying off, you know what she's like.'

'Actually it's from Helen. Hold on…' I shifted further out of the sun. 'She says there's a Horse Fair in Vilar de Donas tomorrow. They're going in the morning but the racing's on all day. It sounds interesting, but it's very short notice. What do you think?'

'Racing? Are you kidding? If there's a racetrack, there might be a bookies. We should go.'

I frowned. After a fiesta *and* a classical concert I knew I'd be ready for a restful Sunday. Apart from that, there was Gary's condition to consider. He'd improved enormously since he'd been taking the tablets, but I didn't want him to burn himself out and end up back at square one. I needed to dissuade him without sounding like a killjoy. The answer came to me in a flash. 'Vilar de Donas is near Palas, isn't it?'

'Yes, why?'

'I've seen it in the guidebooks, it's got a famous church or monastery or something. I've never read anything about a racetrack though, and if there *was* one, surely it would have been mentioned in the books.'

'Not necessarily. It might have been built recently. Those books upstairs must be twenty years old.'

I sighed inwardly. He was right and I was out of excuses. I'd have to bite the bullet and go.

'Okay. We'll go after lunch then. Rose is sleeping over tonight so she might want to come as well.'

'Good. Let's hope I can put a bet on. Oh, hey up, it looks like the music's starting. There's the group look. Bloody hell!'

We stared as six men in black jumpsuits and two women in pink lycra hotpants danced onto the stage. Something told me the *orquesta* were going to be even worse than I'd imagined and I turned my attention to the audience instead. Couples that were as old as Solina and Másimo were spinning each other round and clapping their arms above their heads. By the looks on their faces, they were in their element and I felt like a square peg in a round hole. Gary was more of a spectacle person than I was; he loved all the pomp and showmanship. I looked across, expecting to see him smiling, but his brow was furrowed and in the glare of the afternoon sunshine his face looked an angry shade of red. A wave of panic shot through me; was he having another of his turns? I didn't understand it; he'd not made so much as a frown since Thursday, yet there was no doubt about it; something was wrong. I said nothing, for fear he might have a tantrum and make a scene. I sat quietly and looked at the *orquesta*, as the two curvy women strutted their stuff at the front of the stage. How people turned out in their droves to witness such a spectacle was beyond me.

I glanced back at Gary. He was no longer frowning but his shoulders sagged and he let out a sigh.

'Are you okay?' I asked him.

He nodded. 'I'm alright.'

I knew that he wasn't. 'Is it your stomach?' I ventured. 'You're looking pained.'

'I am, but it's not my stomach. It's the music – it's awful. I don't want to disappoint you...'

'You won't,' I grinned. 'I hate it too. Let's finish our drinks and go home.'

I was draining my glass when I noticed the crowds parting to make way for a band of *gaiteros* coming along the road.

'This is more like it,' I beamed.

Shielding my eyes from the sun, I scanned the approaching troupe of musicians. They cut an impressive crew in their immaculate regional dress. The women wore puffed white blouses and long, full burgundy skirts trimmed with black. The men wore crisp white shirts, burgundy waistcoats, black knee-length trousers, and thick white gaiters. I sucked gratefully on my ice cube and wondered how they could bear to wear such heavy clothing in the heat.

'Look!' exclaimed Gary. 'There's Masi with his snare drum!'

'Never!' I gasped. 'Where?'

He chuckled, delighted to have fooled me and I cuffed him playfully on the arm. This was the old Gary, the one I'd married; as daft as a brush, but fun. I smiled at him fondly. 'Trust you. Come on, let's pay the *cuenta* and get out of here; at least we'll be home in plenty of time for Rose.'

At twenty past six Gary looked at his watch for the umpteenth time and frowned. 'What time did you tell Nina and Marcus?'

'Seven o'clock at Farelo's. It'll give us plenty of time to have a natter and a beer, then it's only a two-minute wander round the corner to the Casa de Cultura. If we're there for quarter past eight we'll get a good seat.'

'We won't get a seat at all if Rose doesn't get a move on. Did you tell her we were meeting up with the others first?'

''Course I did. Stop panicking. She'll be here.'

'I don't like standing about waiting with the van in the middle of the lane. What if the cows come past?'

'Gary, stop whittling. Look, why don't we drive up and wait by the church to save time?'

He gave an exasperated sigh and climbed into the van. I was opening the passenger door, when I heard hurried footsteps approaching from the corner of the annexe. Sure enough, it was Rose.

'Hiya,' she panted, with a grin. Her faced was flushed and her fringe was plastered to her forehead. She was clutching the strap of her handbag to her shoulder and holding a bulging carrier in the other hand. 'Sorry I'm late,' she said breathlessly. 'I stopped for coffee in Monterroso while I was waiting for the shops to open. I've got something really important to tell you…'

I shook my head vigorously and nodded towards the van.

'Sorry,' she grinned sheepishly. She was about to open the door but paused as if she'd remembered something. She held up the carrier bag. 'Have I got time to put this…'

I held up my palm and looked at her fixedly. 'Rose,' I mouthed. 'Get in.'

As we wound our way out of the *aldea* Rose was quiet and I wondered if she was sulking.

'I'm really sorry,' she said eventually. 'I hope I haven't made us late.'

'Don't worry,' I smiled. 'You haven't. Hey, now that the panic's over, why don't you tell us your news?'

'Not now. I'll save it for later. It's not just the usual news, you see – it's something special. In fact it's so mind-blowing, Gary would probably crash with the shock. Wait 'til we get back from the concert and then I'll have your undivided attention. I promise you it'll be worth the wait.'

Outside Cafe-Bar Farelo, the tables on the terrace were all taken. People, both seated and standing, spilled out onto the pavement and excited children were running around the small *plaza* outside the *concello* building, chasing a dog with a ball.

'Crikey,' I said. 'It looks as if the whole of Antas is out in force.'

'Do you think they're all going to the concert?' asked Rose.

'No,' grinned Gary. 'They're drowning their sorrows after an afternoon at Santa Mariña. They'll all be in desperate need of a beer.'

I was about to suggest that we look for a table inside when a voice boomed out, 'Gary!' Nina and Marcus had arrived already and had bagged a table and three extra chairs.

When we reached the table Nina and Marcus stood up to greet us. I hugged Nina warmly, while Rose leaned forward to kiss Marcus on both cheeks in the traditional Spanish way.

'One more,' Marcus insisted. 'In the Netherlands we give three kisses, not two.'

'That's madness,' said Gary. 'There are five of us. Do you realise how many kisses that is? By the time we've finished, we could have been to the bar and ordered the beers.'

'And drunk them as well,' laughed Marcus. 'It is a good point, Gary. No more kissing – we should drink.'

Once we were settled with beers, Gary gave a colourful account of our excursion to the Santa Mariña fiesta. He soon had the others in stitches and it was a joy to see him laughing and joking and back on form. It would have been easy to sit there soaking up the ambience for the rest of the evening but we had Rudi's concert to attend.

'Come on,' I said eventually. 'It's almost twenty past, we'd best make tracks.'

Gary strode ahead with Nina and Marcus. I waited while Rose gathered up her belongings and we fell in behind.

'Sorry about earlier,' I said, still wondering if she'd taken the hump. 'I could see how excited you were, but Gary was blowing a gasket. Come on, while nobody's listening – what's your news?'

'Later,' she whispered. 'I'm not being iffy. I want to tell you both together. I can't wait to see your faces – I promise you'll be really surprised.'

The Casa de Cultura was a single-storey concrete building, set behind metal railings. Flanked by patches of waste ground on either side, it took up the entire side of the tiny back street.

'Hardly a fitting venue for a soirée of chamber music,' giggled Rose.

'Wait until you are inside,' whispered Marcus. 'It has a ceiling like the Sistine Chapel and the seats are trimmed with gold.'

Rose gasped and her mouth fell open.

'Ignore him,' I grinned. 'He's having you on.'

The auditorium, though modest, was not without decorum. The walls and stage were panelled in pine and there were rows of proper theatre seats upholstered in red velour. The tasteful understatedness was refreshing after the kitsch of the fiesta we'd left only hours before.

At eight-thirty precisely the lights lowered and the group of a dozen musicians took their places on the stage. Rudi stood up to announce the Tchaikovsky. He asked the audience to refrain from clapping between movements and save their applause until the end. Rose and I turned to each other with a knowing grin.

Tchaikovsky had never been one of my favourite composers, and the serenade's opening sonatina did little to change my mind. The ensemble played expertly, yet the piece seemed unremarkable except for the repetition of a scale, and a section that sounded like a swarm of flies. It came as no surprise when, as the movement drew to a close, there was a smattering of applause amongst the audience. Heads turned and there were some embarrassed faces as the clapping quickly died down. The waltz which followed was a different kettle of fish entirely. My heart soared as the violins moved into a higher octave and took me racing through meadows and tumbling down hills. This time there wasn't a sound when the strings fell silent and I revelled in the brief moment of absolute stillness, until the elegy carried me off into a fantasy world once again. I imagined grey-tinged clouds moving above me as I stood at the bottom of the valley, drifting almost imperceptibly, then scudding and thinning to give intermittent glimpses of the sun. Suddenly, Tchaikovsky was the master of suspense and I was spellbound; would the clouds give way to brilliant sunshine or would they merge and darken and bring the onset of rain? The answer came with the finale. The clouds parted, the sun beamed down and I felt the urge to tilt my face towards the warmth of its rays. The radiance, however, was short-lived and a moment later, spiccato bowing signalled the first patter of raindrops, and it was time to run. As I moved across the meadow the mizzle fell lightly, but it soon gathered momentum and I quickened my pace towards the shelter of the trees. In the shade of the forest, the rain fell fitfully, and I shifted between the respite of leafy canopies and drizzle in the glades. When I emerged into the open the shower was subsiding. As the last scale ascended in crescendo, the sun shone down through the petering droplets of the cadenza, and a rainbow triumphed across the sky.

As the musicians lowered their bows, a tremendous round of applause filled the auditorium. When the clamour faded, Rudi came to the front of the stage. After thanking everyone for coming, he spoke about the work of Quercus Sonora, and how donations would help the group to fulfil its objectives over the coming year. He explained that some friends he'd met recently had told him about a large charitable organisation in England called the National Trust. I glanced at Gary and he nodded, smiling – Rudi was talking about us! He went on to explain that the trust did exactly the same kind of work as Quercus Sonora but had tens of thousands of members. He hoped that Quercus Sonora would continue to gain support and popularity, with the existing one hundred and fifty members swelling to thousands over the years to come.

When we left the auditorium, a cool breeze had tempered the earlier warmth of the evening. The street was cloaked in shadows as the sun made its western descent towards the hills, and the moon would soon be casting a soft translucent glow across the sky. As the van wound its way along the main road I gazed out at the woodlands and wondered what secrets they revealed after sunset that were never seen in the day. I thought of Maruja's sister's unfortunate hens and shuddered. I hoped I'd be home in time to shut my flock away before the fox was on the prowl. The fence *looked* secure but…

Suddenly, I was aware that Rose was saying my name.

'Liza?'

'Sorry, Rose. I was miles away.'

'I was just saying – Quercus Sonora. It's a great idea, isn't it? And such a worthwhile cause. That's why I gave twenty euros. I took a leaflet on the way out – I think I'll join.'

Rose had a heart like a Tardis, yet the news of her generous donation surprised me. She'd spent a fortune over the summer and had told us she needed to budget. The way she was going her funds would be quickly depleted. She was already struggling from week to week and I wondered how she was planning to get by. Friendship or no, it was none of my business; I erred on the side of diplomacy and focused on the performance instead.

'I liked the Tchaikovsky,' I said. 'I wasn't sure at first – the beginning was a bit dour, but I loved the waltz part, and the last movement was brilliant. It was great the way it revved up to the climax at the end. I tell you what though, I found it strange, the way he stuck scales in all over the place – that was a new one on me.'

'I noticed that,' Rose agreed. 'Weird, wasn't it? I wonder what made him do that?'

'I think I can guess,' said Gary.

I looked at him in surprise. 'Really?'

Up until now he'd said nothing. Unless he was cursing he wasn't usually given to talking while he was at the wheel. What's more, although he loved music and his taste was very eclectic, he knew next to nothing about rudiments and theory, so I was intrigued to hear what he was going to say. 'Go on.'

'Well, it's obvious, isn't it? He needed a riff.'

'A riff?' echoed Rose. 'What do you mean?'

'You know, something catchy that folks would recognise.'

'Ah,' I nodded. 'You mean a theme.'

'If you say so. Anyway, p'raps he couldn't come up with a *theme*, so he just thought, "sod it, everybody knows this one – it'll have to do."'

I imagined Tchaikovsky sitting at a piano with a quill poised over a note pad, frowning and tugging at his beard. From the backseat, Rose giggled and I guessed she was thinking likewise. Without warning, I was in bits. I clutched at my sides and laughed until the tears came.

'Can you drive a bit quicker?' I spluttered. 'I think I'm going to wee.'

Back at the house, Rose was beside herself with excitement and quick to take charge. 'Straight up to the living room,' she told us.

'Be patient,' I said. 'I've got to shut the chooks and rabbits away while Gary puts the van in the barn. After that I need to go to the toilet. *Then* I'll sit down.'

Once we were all settled upstairs, I was keen to hear Rose's news.

'Right then,' I said. 'What's this announcement you wanted to make? We're all ears.'

'Not so fast,' she giggled. 'Hold on.'

She reached into the carrier bag and took out a bundle of knitting. I recognised it instantly as the shawl she'd been making for Verna. For a second I was speechless. What a terrible anti-climax; all this fuss just to celebrate a finished gift. I feigned an expression of interest as, slowly and deliberately, she unwrapped the shawl. Only then did I see that it was still attached to the needles; it wasn't finished but was protecting the rather expensive extra brut cava that was hiding inside.

'Crikey, Rose,' I exclaimed. 'Aren't you meant to be on a budget? That stuff must be close to a tenner a throw.'

'And the rest,' she grinned. 'The budget's out of the window. Don't worry though – all will be revealed.'

'I'll fetch us some glasses, shall I?' asked Gary.

'No,' said Rose. 'Not glasses, flutes. I want to do this properly. You'll understand why when I tell you – it's something really big.'

I couldn't help smiling. The last two weekends had been filled with music. Flutes seemed a rather fitting way to end the night.

'So what are we celebrating?' asked Gary, when he reappeared with three flutes and set them down on the coffee table.

'Wait,' said Rose. 'Let me open the bottle first.'

I was growing impatient. Like the Tchaikovsky, Rose's performance was getting off to a slow start. I watched as she twisted the metal loop and gave it a jiggle to loosen the strands of wire.

'Ready?' she grinned.

I tensed instinctively, waiting for the cork to pop. When it didn't Rose gave it a nudge with her thumbs.

'Damn,' she cursed. 'Hold on.'

I sighed inwardly. It really *was* like the Tchaikovsky; there was even a repetitive theme. Rose wedged the bottle between her knees and gripped the cork firmly. She grunted as she tried to twist it and her hand slid round the top of the bottle when the cork refused to move.

'Talk about killing the moment,' she giggled. 'Here, Gary – you have a go.'

As Gary rose manfully to the challenge I wondered if the cadenza would be worth the wait. His jaw clenched as he gripped the cork and twisted for all he was worth. I was about to suggest we give up when there was an ominous hiss, followed by a pop and a bang as the cork hit the ceiling. Scholes leapt off the sofa as froth showered out onto my newly washed throw.

Gary poured what was left of the plonk into the flutes and passed them round.

'A toast!' declared Rose. 'To me!'

'To Rose!' we chorused, and clinked, still none the wiser.

'Well,' said Gary. 'Are you going to explain?'

'In three weeks' time I'm leaving Galicia.'

'You're moving back to England?' I gasped.

'No. Barcelona. I've found a job.'

Liza Grantham

Tchaikovsky's Riff

Tchaikovsky's got composer's block,
He's on a downward spiral;
He wants to emulate the greats
'Cos Mozart's work went viral.

He sits on his piano stool,
'What shall I write?' he wonders.
He wracks his brain but nothing comes,
He strokes his beard and ponders.

He wants to write a masterpiece,
A timeless composition,
A classic magnum opus that
Outshines all competition.

The theme itself need not be grand,
Nor complex, nor too clever;
Just something that the folks will love,
And memorise forever.

It has to be a catchy riff,
An earworm for the masses;
He casts his mind back to the stuff
He learned in music classes.

Arpeggios and sharps and flats,
The major keys and minor,
And then at last the penny drops;
A scale; what could be finer?

He'll make it rise, he'll make it fall
In sweet diminuendo,
He'll harmonise it into chords,
Exalt it in crescendo.

He'll call it 'Serenade for Strings',
A certain hit, he'll wager,
And all thanks to his catchy riff,
That simple scale; C major.

Chapter 10

Hold Your Horses

On Sunday morning it was still dark when I took my coffee out to the bench. I lit my cigarette and watched the smoke curl lazily up into the still air under the light of the streetlamp. An owl hooted from the oak wood and I shuddered involuntarily; there was something intrinsically hibernal about the sound, whatever the time of year. I wondered briefly where Rose would be spending Christmas. The news of her move surprised me, and I knew that when summer drew to a close it would bring with it the end of an era. Rose had enhanced our lives chaotically, but sweetly, and I was going to miss the effortless warts-and-all friendship that had grown over the last two years. I knew she wasn't an early riser, but this morning I was hoping she'd be up before Gary. I wanted us to spend some time together and I had a surprise of my own to unveil.

When I came in from letting out the chooks and rabbits, Rose was already in the kitchen drinking tea.

'Morning,' I smiled.

'Morning,' she beamed. 'Well, what a splendid evening – didn't we have fun?'

'We did,' I grinned, as I walked over to the sink to fill the kettle. 'But I'm glad we don't make a habit of it. You and your posh cava – it went straight to my head.'

'Good stuff, wasn't it? I slept like a baby. I'm looking forward to the horse fair, are you?'

'I s'pose so, as long as this headache wears off. I don't reckon it'll be much of an event though – just a few locals galloping round a field.'

She shook her head. 'I read an article about it in *la Voz de Galicia*. There's a proper racetrack – it's quite a big thing. People are coming with horses from as far as Portugal. There's a horse show first where they're judged to a standard, and then the racing. They have classes for Arabs and English and wild Galician horses as well. '

I put the kettle on the hob and perched myself on the edge of the marble surface. 'Wild horses? Here in Galicia? I didn't know there was such a thing. Fancy that.'

'You must have heard of the *Rapa das Bestas*?'

'No. *Rapa*? That means shaving doesn't it? If it's something barbaric I don't want to hear.'

'It isn't. It's classed as a national tourist event. They don't shave the horses anyway, they cut the manes and the tails.'

'Why?'

'It's a tradition. I suppose it was a sort of trophy back in the old days as well as a way of knowing which ones had been caught. Nowadays they're chipped and vaccinated and recorded in stud books before they're released back up to the mountains. The government's set up a protection programme because the numbers are so low.'

'Wow. First Rudi's project and now this. We're certainly doing our bit to support the environment. It's encouraging to know there's so much conservation work going on.'

'Not everybody would agree with you there.'

'What do you mean?'

'The *Rapa das Bestas*. The animal rights people have protested about it, saying it's cruel.'

'But why? Cutting the manes and tails doesn't hurt horses does it? They have their hair done for the show ring after all.'

'It's what happens when they get them down into the town and pen them that's the issue. In Galicia it's the custom for the men to wrestle the horses into submission by hand. The protestors say it causes the horses excessive stress and fear.'

I thought about the way of life out in the *aldeas*. Many of the customs and practices went way back in the mists of time. People couldn't fully understand how rural communities worked unless they were actually a part of one, and I'd have bet my bottom dollar that the protestors came from the cities and towns. Doing things the old way often had drawbacks but they weren't always without good reason. Hunting was a case in point. It was more than a blood sport; from a farmer's point of view it made sense to protect livestock by reducing the population of foxes and wild boars. The *matanzas* were another prime example. Pigs were led by a hook through their jaw and tied to a table, the carotid artery was severed and the animals would bleed to death. To an outsider the process might seem barbaric, but how much more so was the alternative? Pigs being transported for long distances in cramped trailers? Being stunned ineffectively so that they were still conscious when plunged into vats of boiling water to loosen their hair? What many people didn't know about the *matanzas* was that every effort was made to keep the pigs calm, because it was in people's interests not to have the meat spoiled by the taste of adrenalin. It was easy to protest about rural practices in ignorance, especially when it involved a ritual that appeared to glamourise the process, but meat bought from the supermarket had probably endured far more brutal, painful treatment before it reached the shelves. It was always going to be a swings and roundabouts situation and everyone was entitled to their own point of view.

'I can see why people might have a problem with it,' I mused, 'but the horses would have to be rounded up *somehow* to be treated and chipped and recorded, so they'd get scared anyway, wouldn't they? There'll always be a difference of opinion on these kinds of issues, but to me, on balance, it sounds as if the advantages to the horses far outweigh the bad.'

I lifted the kettle from the hob and took it over to the dresser. Fate was playing into my hands this morning; Gary was still snoring in the bedroom above.

'Let me make this coffee,' I said, 'and then I've got something to show you. It's *my* turn to give *you* a surprise.'

'Ooh, that's intriguing. I can't... Shh! Wait a minute – what's that noise?'

'What noise?'

'There – did you hear it? It's like a low growling – is it Lenda? Oh no, she's here.'

I followed her gaze as she looked up at the ceiling. At once the penny dropped. I chuckled. 'That's Gary snoring. He's still out for the count.'

'Never! It's awful. No wonder you get up early. I'm surprised you can sleep.'

'I can't always. Sometimes I have to kick him or prod him in the ribs. The longer he sleeps the better to be honest. He's not been right lately – a lie-in will do him good.'

'Has it been the heat?'

'We're not sure. The doctor's put him on tablets for his blood pressure and she's referred him to the hospital for his stomach – it's been acting up.'

'Oh, no. You should have said.'

'I didn't think, to be honest. It's all been a bit sudden – he's only been like it a couple of weeks. Anyway, you'd got enough on your plate, what with the neighbour and the builders, and now you've got a big move and a new job. Are you nervous?'

'Not really. I can always hand in my notice if I don't like it. Come on then, you said you'd got news as well.'

I smiled, pleased to move on from the subject of Gary's affliction. Deep down I was concerned about him being referred to a specialist and I'd been trying to push it to the back of my mind.

'Right,' I said. 'I'm going to show you my knitting. It hasn't half grown, and not just lengthways. It isn't a scarf anymore – it's a pair of britches or at least it will be when it's done.'

Rose frowned. 'Britches?'

'Yes, britches. You know – drawers; knickers; pants. Something's happened to it that wasn't meant to, but it looks fantastic. Wait 'til you see.'

When I unfolded what I considered to be my splendid achievement, Rose shrieked in delight.

'Oh my God!' she giggled. 'What on *earth* have you done? I didn't believe you, but you're right – it's half a pair of woolly pants. Actually, it's about your size.'

'I know,' I grinned. 'Perhaps I could plait some strands together and turn it into a thong. Seriously, though, I can't work out how it's happened. I've made all these stitches and I haven't a clue what I've done.'

'Let's have a look,' she said, as she took the knitting from me. She studied it for a moment. 'Ah, I see. You need to make sure that the yarn's at the back when you push the needle through the stitch. This is what you've been doing – watch. You've pulled the yarn over and under, see?'

I nodded.

'So, when that happens the bottom part of the stitch gets pulled across the needle and then you've got two loops where you should only have one.'

I nodded again. 'So I've been knitting into them both as though they were two separate stitches? It's so obvious now you've shown me. In future I'll be looking out for it and I won't make the same mistake again.'

Rose laid the work on the marble surface and smoothed it flat with her hand.

'You've made good progress. Look how your rows are neater, more even. By Christmas you'll be a confident knitter, you'll see.'

With Rose already in situ, there was no danger of us being late for the horse show. I'd suggested making sandwiches to take with us for a picnic, but Rose was insistent that she wanted to thank us by buying us lunch. It was becoming apparent that her first wage slip couldn't come soon enough.

'You don't have to,' I told her, while Gary was getting the van out. 'You're bound to have bits and bobs to buy when you get to Barcelona. Perhaps you should hang on to your cash.'

'I don't want to break the habit,' she giggled. 'I've been out for lunch every day this week.'

'Has all your veg finished then?' I asked, surprised. Even given the Galician microclimates I wouldn't have expected the harvest in the south of the province to be over for the year.

'Oh no,' she said. 'The beans have finished but the peppers and courgettes and squashes are still going bonkers. I've grown more lettuces and cabbages and caulis than I'd ever be able to eat.'

'So what have you done with them?' I frowned.

'I've given a lot to Verna and Ben, and I've used some in soups and salads. The rest can be left to rot down and that way the beds will be composted ready for next year.'

I was speechless. Rose had spent a small fortune on setting up the raised beds but had done little to reap the rewards. As for next year, she'd be hundreds of miles away in Barcelona. Her logic beggared belief.

Regretting the cava, I dozed on and off for most of the journey, but as we approached Palas de Rei, Gary nudged me awake. I was to keep my eyes peeled for signs for Vilar de Donas. According to the map book it would be roughly six kilometres when we'd turned right out of the town. If he'd been thinking we might miss the turn-off he needn't have worried. There were handmade placards for the *feira do cabalo* at even the smallest of junctions along the way. Less than ten minutes later I spotted a metal signpost pointing us right for Vilar de Donas. I felt a tingle of anticipation as we turned off the main road.

We drove down a wide country lane flanked on both sides by thickets and fields. People were milling about beside 4x4 vehicles with trailers and horseboxes, while their horses grazed in the shade of the trees. Up ahead was a hand painted sign saying '*Aparcamento*' and we pulled off onto a sparse, bumpy field to the right.

I climbed out of the van and took in our surroundings. Up ahead to the left I could make out a row of awnings and a big marquee. Across to the right was the racetrack, judging by the size of the assembled hordes. As we strolled up to the showground, we passed a van selling pizza, hotdogs and fries.

'There you go,' giggled Rose. 'If all else fails, we can have hotdogs for lunch.'

I looked at Gary and pulled a face. He grinned back at me knowingly. During our time in the Canaries we'd learned that the Spanish *perritos calientes* weren't *quite* the same as those we'd enjoyed in England. There was a boiled frankfurter in a soft bread roll, but the similarities ended there. As every Englishman knows, the key to a good hotdog is a liberal dollop of fried onions, with plenty of caramelised, unctuous juice soaking into the bread. Alas, there was no such luxury on the island; the flimsy frankfurters were topped with finely diced raw onion and, if that wasn't travesty enough, they were tarnished with watery ketchup and cheap mayonnaise.

'Come on,' said Gary. 'There's the racetrack. Let's go and have a look.'

The racecourse was a dusty earthen track surrounded by a waist-high crash barrier that was nothing more than a single metal pole.

'It's smaller than I'd expected,' said Rose.

I studied it for a moment. It looked roughly the same size as the running track I'd loathed in my early teens. 'It's about a thousand metres,' I said.

'Wow,' gasped Rose. 'How did you work that out?'

'It's like the one they tortured us with at school.'

'You're right,' said Gary. 'It's getting on for five furlongs and that's not unusual on the flat. It's not a bad size and it's a good hard surface, so the going will be fast.'

'Wow,' gasped Rose again. 'You're quite the expert, Gary. I'm impressed.'

'Don't be,' I grinned. 'It was one of his vices in England. He's watched more races than I've had hot dinners and I don't doubt he's lost a small fortune too.'

'Rubbish,' said Gary. 'I had more wins than losses.'

'Right,' I frowned. 'If you say so. Thank goodness there won't be a bookies here today.'

Beyond the track there was a van selling snacks and drinks, a bar, and a restaurant marquee. There was also a row of handicraft stalls and, most surprisingly, a dog-grooming tent.

'*Belleza Canina*,' said Gary. 'Is that what I think it is – a doggy beautician?'

''Fraid so,' grinned Rose. 'Let's go and see.'

A small papillon-type dog sat like a prima donna on a pristine table, having her nails clipped by a woman in a starched white coat.

I looked at Gary. 'I can't imagine Lenda putting up with that. It takes me all my time to get a comb through her hair.'

'What a pretty little dog,' said Rose to the groomer, in Spanish. 'She's exceptionally well-behaved.'

'She is,' smiled the woman. 'Her name's Lua. She's mine.'

'Hello, Lua,' said Rose, switching to English. 'Aren't you a little bimbo? I bet you're raking it in for your Mum.'

I giggled. Rose was incorrigible. I was going to miss her so much when she'd gone.

As we turned to walk away, Gary nudged me and pointed over to where Helen and Paul were making their way towards us. We waved and mimed our 'hellos' above the hubbub of the crowd.

'Did Fred come home okay?' asked Paul, as they reached us.

'No,' I said sadly. 'We've not seen him since that night.'

Paul and Helen glanced at each other, and I sensed their discomfort before Helen moved swiftly on.

'We've been watching the judging,' she told us. 'They've had quite a good turnout this year.'

'Were there many Galician horses?' I asked her.

'There were a dozen. It doesn't sound a lot, but I was talking to one of the organisers – he said that's a real success. Even though they've been a protected species since the nineties, the numbers are still dwindling. Apparently they've fallen by half in the last forty years.'

'So what's the cause?' asked Gary.

'They've lost a lot of their grazing land because of the forestry plantations in the mountain areas. On top of that, many get eaten by wolves.'

'I wouldn't mind having a look,' said Gary. 'Are they still judging now?'

'It finished about an hour ago,' said Helen. 'I wouldn't worry. You'll still see most of the horses in the races. It'll be starting anytime now.'

'We're going to have to miss it,' sighed Paul. 'We've got to get back for Pepe. It's a shame we'll miss the donkeys, but we can't really leave her all day.'

'The donkeys?' I frowned.

'Yes,' laughed Helen. 'According to the locals it's the highlight of the fair.'

Over at the racetrack there was an air of excitement as the Arabs lined up at the start. Every one of them looked keen and powerful; if Gary's theory on the going was right, I didn't want to be near to the track when the hooves came thundering by. I looked at the crash barriers and the happy smiling families behind them; a stampeding herd on a small track sounded like a recipe for disaster to me.

'Here'll do,' I mumbled, as we eased our way through the throng.

'Don't you want to stand at the front?' asked Gary.

I shook my head. 'We're taller than most folks, they won't see over our heads.'

'*I'm* not,' said Rose. 'Come on, let's go a bit further and get a good view.'

I followed reluctantly, hoping the riders would keep control of their horses as they came hurtling round. We were only a metre from the barrier when the tannoy crackled. '*Uno... dos... y TRES*!'

And they were off; not at a gallop as I'd been expecting, but at a brisk yet elegant trot.

'Amazing!' gasped Rose. 'I wasn't expecting this!'

'Neither was I,' I grinned. My fingers unclenched and my shoulders relaxed, and I watched in fascination as the hooves beat a staccato rhythm on the hard-baked dirt. As dust showered up from the track, masking the robotic, alternating movement of the legs, it seemed as if the horses were gliding gracefully through a cloud.

For the best part of an hour we watched the Arab and English horses trotting at speed around the track. I was beginning to think I'd seen enough when the voice on the tannoy announced that it was time for the Galician horses to come to the start. The horses were, like their owners, short and stocky in stature and it came as no great surprise that they were believed to have been brought over to Galicia by the Celts. With no money riding on it two more races was enough.

'I'm starving,' said Rose. 'Shall we grab some lunch?'

Gary and I nodded eagerly and we made our way over to the catering marquee. The restaurant was a vast area under canvas, set out with tables and benches with a kitchen area at one end. One of the longest sides was open with further tables and benches set out in the sun.

'Sun or shade?' asked Gary as we dithered on the side lines.

'That one,' I said pointing to the table closest to the kitchen. 'We can watch them cooking from there.'

The menu, though limited, was far from disappointing.

'*Pulpo a feira* or *churrasco*,' said Gary. 'That's your lot.'

'That's easy then,' giggled Rose. 'I'm buying. We'll have both.'

Thinking of Rose's bank balance I was about to protest when a plump woman in a calf-length apron bustled over and set down a basket of bread and three forks.

'Would you like *pulpo* or *churrasco*?' she smiled.

'Both,' grinned Rose, taking a hunk from the basket. 'We'll have the *pulpo* first and then the *churrasco*, please.'

From where I was sitting I had a clear view into the kitchen area. I watched as a second, equally plump woman took a pair of tongs and lifted an octopus arm, complete with suckers, from an enormous metal vat. With a huge pair of scissors she snipped the arm into bite-sized chunks onto a wooden plate, then drizzled it with olive oil and sprinkled it generously with what I guessed were the traditional condiments of paprika and salt.

The *pulpo* was cooked to perfection and it didn't take us long to devour the whole plateful, spearing the succulent chunks with our forks and mopping up the juices with the soft, spongey bread. No sooner had the first woman whisked our plates away than the second appeared with glistening pork and beef ribs heaped high on a plate. For the next ten minutes we hardly spoke as we did justice to the *churrasco*. Eventually, against all the odds, only a pile of bones remained.

'Gorgeous,' said Rose.

'I'll second that,' agreed Gary.

'I'm stuffed,' I sighed. 'And I could do with the loo.'

'Me too,' said Rose. 'I'll pay the *cuenta* and we'll go and find them. It'll be good to walk off the lunch.'

Crammed full of octopus and ribs we walked around the outside of the racetrack. A sign for the *aseos* pointed us in the direction of the main road.

'Oh, heck,' frowned Rose. 'I hope it's not far.'

'It won't be,' said Gary. 'I reckon it's just the other side of the racetrack. There look…' he pointed. 'Where that cluster of trees is. I can see a tent.'

We strode the hundred metres or so across the grass to where, sure enough, a row of green portaloos were located beneath the canopies of the trees. The 'tent' was a small marquee which stood within a cordoned off enclosure. A sign across the entrance said 'Protectora de Lugo' and a couple of girls in fluorescent tabards were exercising dogs for adoption on leads. The volunteers were friendly and were happy to chat to us about their wards. The first was an oatmeal coloured, rough-coated dog with floppy ears and soulful brown eyes.

'Aw,' said Rose. 'Isn't he lovely? I wonder what breed he is?'

'I think he's a griffon,' I said, 'but I thought they were bigger. I can't be sure.'

'He is a griffon,' said the girl, in English. 'They come in different sizes. His name's Dante.'

Dante wagged his tail and looked up at the girl. It was then we could see that the bottom third of his ear was missing. I swallowed hard.

'What happened to his ear?' asked Gary.

'It was cut,' said the girl sadly, 'to remove the tattoo. Hunters often abandon their dogs at the end of the season. This way they can't be traced.'

I looked at the griffon. He was so small, so vulnerable. I reached down to fuss him and he wagged his tail. It was hard to believe that he could be so trusting after the cruelty he'd been subjected to. He was a gem of a dog and I was in no doubt that he'd soon have a loving home.

'And what about this one?' I asked, nodding towards the larger dog that the second girl was walking. Everything about him was typically German shepherd, except for the fact that he didn't have upright ears.

'This is Xoani,' smiled his walker, ruffling his head fondly. 'He's very timid. He's been with us for six months and it's taken all that time to get him to this stage. He was living in complete isolation under a woodpile for months.'

I wanted to ask more about Xoani: how had he survived? Had someone been feeding him? Why had it taken so long for the Protectora to be called in? Knowing only too well that the answers might upset me I kept schtum and gave my attention to Xoani instead. I held out my hand and he sniffed it cautiously, but when I smoothed my fingers over the top of his head he started to wag his tail. There was something about him that reminded me of Anxo, and I thought for a second I might cry. His walker began to speak and I turned to her, grateful for the distraction.

'He'd take up a lot of time and patience,' the girl explained. 'He needs a home where someone's there all day, but where he can be outside for as long as he wants to. Most importantly, it would have to be a quiet household with no young kids.'

I looked at Xoani and pondered on what the girl had told us. 'Xoani' was the affectionate form of 'Xoán', and it hadn't escaped my notice that the name was an anagram of Anxo. There was something about Xoani that made me want to love him. I looked at Gary, wondering if he felt the same.

'We'd be the perfect home,' I ventured. 'He'd make a lovely playmate for Lenda and he doesn't look very old.'

Gary sighed and turned to Xoani's girl. 'Do you know what he's like with cats?'

'I don't,' she replied.

'He's still young though,' said Dante's girl, 'so he should be easy enough to train.'

I smiled keenly, but Gary frowned.

'It might take ages,' he said sensibly. 'And in the meantime, where would that leave Scholes?'

I nodded sadly.

'And what about Lenda? It's alright saying she needs a playmate but sharing you and her house with another dog's a different thing altogether.'

He was right and I knew it. I nodded sadly again.

'Right,' said Gary, sensing that the danger, at least for now, had passed. 'Come on, you needed the toilet didn't you? And then we ought to be heading home.'

'Aren't you staying for the donkey race?' asked Dante's girl.

Rose looked at Gary.

'You should,' added Xoani's girl. 'It's the highlight of the day.'

I had reservations, but Rose looked at Gary imploringly. '*Please*,' she crooned.

He sighed and shrugged his shoulders. 'Alright.'

As Rose and Gary began to walk towards the portaloos, I turned to give one last ruffle to Xoani's head.

We were heading back towards the racetrack when the air rang with a loud crackle and an unwelcome screech. A voice boomed out from a tannoy that the donkey riders should make their way over to the track. I trudged reluctantly behind Rose and Gary. I wasn't sure about the donkey racing at all.

Packed like sardines around the racetrack, the crowd seemed twice the size it had been for the trotting; the donkey race really was a popular event.

'I'm not sure about it,' I mumbled. 'I hope it's not making fun of the donkeys. I don't want to be part of anything cruel.'

'I'm sure it won't be,' said Rose, reassuringly. 'Let's have a look. If there's anything you're not happy with, we can walk away.'

We eased our way through the crowds towards a space near the barrier. With a clear view of the track I could see that only five donkeys were lined up at the start. The tannoy crackled and the announcer called for the sixth rider to join the other contestants at the line. When all six donkeys were finally in position, the announcer began the countdown.

'*Uno… dos… y…*'

The donkey that had turned up last shot forward and a cheer went up from the crowd. Only a short distance along the track the donkey stopped dead. His rider turned him round and rode him back to the start line and the announcer gave the starter's order again.

'*Uno… dos… y…*'

Once more the same donkey bolted forwards and stopped in the same spot as before. This time when his rider tried to turn him, he refused to budge. The crowd laughed as the donkey looked first to one side, then to the other, looking for all the world as if he was having fun. The rider dismounted and managed to tug his maverick mule back to the start line. Leaving nothing to chance, two men came over to steady the beast until it was time to go. Satisfied that there would be no further hiccups, the announcer began again.

'*Uno… dos… y… TRES!*'

This time, they were off.

Shouts went up from the crowd as five of the donkeys took off at a surprisingly brisk pace but, as if in an act of rebellion, the erstwhile livewire refused to budge. His rider flicked at the reins and kicked with his heels, but the beast was not for shifting. Shaking his head, the rider climbed down and a groan went up from the crowd. Right on cue, the donkey took off in pursuit of his rivals as if in a bid to appease the throng. Seconds later, the first of the competitors crossed the finish line, to shouts and applause.

A Donkey Speaks Out

I will not obey you,
Or do as I'm bidden,
Asserting my rights
I refuse to be ridden.

I will not conform
As you dangle the carrot,
I will not perform like
A dog or a parrot.

Don't say that I'm stubborn,
Contrary and mulish;
Your actions are thoughtless,
Uncaring and foolish.

My ancestors carried
Sweet Mary and Jesu,
So show me respect;
I'm not here just to please you.

Don't treat me unkindly,
Don't be so demanding,
And then we might reach
A combined understanding.

Chapter 11

Ye of Little Faith

When I woke on Monday morning I'd have been happy to lie in bed for another hour; a fiesta, a concert *and* an equine extravaganza had more than taken their toll. It was little more than a month since I'd committed myself to an action-packed social calendar, and if the truth be told, I was ready to revert to my comfortable stay-at-home ways. Gary, on the other hand, had seemed completely unaffected by our forays out into civilisation; he'd eaten, drunk and made merry, and had taken it all in his stride. It was hard to believe that only a week ago he'd picked at his meals and had been laid low with exhaustion. I wondered if it might have caught up with him this morning, but he looked as fresh as a daisy when he came through the kitchen door.

'Morning,' I smiled as I passed him his cuppa.

'Morning,' he yawned. 'I can't believe it's Monday already. I have to say, it was a thoroughly good weekend.'

I giggled. 'You *are* a strange one. You hated the fiesta as much as I did.'

'I didn't hate the fiesta. It was the pop group I couldn't stand.'

'*And* you had a strop on at night when Rose was nearly late.'

'Ah, well. That was understandable, but I loved the concert. You can't beat a bit of Tchaikovsky and his catchy riffs.'

'You did well. It's me that's shattered. I couldn't do it all the time.'

'Well, you can have a break now 'til the virgin goes on the rampage again.'

'You what?'

'The Virgin Mary – your favourite icon. Don't tell me you'd forgotten? It's the village fiesta in just over a week.'

I grimaced. I hadn't forgotten. I'd attended the village fiesta every August for the last three summers and my feelings towards the effigy had been different every time. During our first summer I'd been excited about the procession, but when the icon had made her appearance I'd been spooked by her sinister eyes. The second year, armed with prior knowledge, I'd attended the mass but fled the scene before the avatar had left the church. The third year, Maruja had given me a photograph that had helped me to think of Nuestra Señora in a different light.

'She can rampage all she likes, but *I* won't be there to watch her.'

'Why not? I thought you'd made your peace with her. Last year you were pleased 'cos she'd answered your prayer and made it rain.'

'That was a coincidence, you said so yourself. It was only drizzle anyway – it had stopped by the end of the afternoon.'

'So what's made you change your mind?'

'It was when I lost Anxo. I had faith in Nuestra Señora, but where was she when I needed her? I got down on my knees in the churchyard and I begged her to save him. That proves it's all a load of old codswallop if you ask me.'

'Hmm.'

'Hmm, what?'

'Is that what you *really* believe, or are you just being arsey?'

'What d'you mean?'

'Well, that's what usually happens when you can't have your own way.'

I pouted and reached for my tobacco.

He chuckled. 'See?'

I grinned in spite of myself. 'Let's change the subject, shall we? Have you forgotten it's Monday? You're usually quibbling about the shopping list by now.'

'Where is it?'

'It's here.' I passed it over and waited while it fell under his critical, tightarsed gaze.

'Green yarn. D'you mean twine?'

'No, I mean yarn. You know, to knit with.'

'Ah, wool. What sort of green, though? It doesn't say.'

'That's because I'm going to show you. Hold on.' I crossed the kitchen and took a bottle of olive oil from the top of the dresser. 'Here,' I said, as I handed it over. 'See the label? Not the picture, the bit at the top?'

'Yes.'

'That's the colour I'm after – olive green.'

'Khaki.'

'If you say so. It doesn't have to be exact, something similar will do.'

'I'll do my best. Have you used all the wool that Rose gave you?'

'Nearly. There's a bit left, but that was for the practice piece. I'm going to do some *real* knitting. I'm going to make a jumper – I've made up my mind.'

'A *jumper*? Are you sure? You started a scarf and it turned into a triangle. Still, it's up to you.'

'Trust me, I can do it. I'll have it finished by October and I'll wear it for the End of the World.'

When Gary came home with the shopping, I was dying to see what he'd bought me. For once he'd paid attention and I was overjoyed with my yarn. Not only was it a tasteful olive green, but he'd chosen a lovely chunky thickness as well.

'It's perfect,' I beamed. 'Thanks.'

'I thought the thick stuff would be better for winter,' he said, as I squidged it approvingly. 'And I've invested in some craft materials of my own.'

'Really?' I thought of his oil paints and charcoals and sketch books gathering dust upstairs in the cupboard. Six balls of yarn didn't come cheap, but at least they'd be put to good purpose. God forbid that he'd squandered a small fortune on one of his fads.

'Can I see?'

''Course you can. Hold on.'

He went out to the barn and reappeared with a broomstick.

'A *broom*stick?'

He nodded. 'And these as well.' He plonked a plastic bag of inch-long nails onto the marble surface. 'Go on then – guess.'

It didn't take a genius to work out that he was going to knock the nails into the broomstick, but the million euro question was *why*? The result would be something akin to an oversized loo brush with the nylon bristles replaced by spikes. Would it be a gadget for collecting the leaves up in autumn? A *matanza* comb for dehairing a pig? Surely he wasn't planning on using it to kill the cockerels?

'Go on then, put me out of my misery – I honestly don't know.'

'You're hopeless. I'm going to make the *charrasco*, of course.'

'Oh, of *course*. How on earth was I supposed to guess when you've missed out the vital components? What are you going to use for the discs?'

'Aha, that's where my genius comes in.'

'Oh, yes?'

'You know how Paul's such a hoarder?'

I nodded.

'Well, I remembered he had a boxful of beer bottle tops in the courtyard. I noticed it ages ago, when I went round to put buckets under the leaks. Anyway, I mentioned it to him the day after the percussion workshop. He's still got them and he told me to help myself.'

'Amazing. So all you'll have to do is bash them flat with a hammer, then nail them on?'

'Not quite. I'll need to drill holes in them so that they'll jiggle. And I'll have to knock the end of each nail over so the discs don't slide off the end.'

'I'm impressed. You're really creative when you put your mind to it. It sounds like a fiddly job.'

'It will be, but if I start it today it'll be ready in time for the fiesta. Remember last year, when Masi was playing his trumpet? This year I'll be able to join in.'

Straight after lunch I took my extra virgin olive yarn and size five needles out to the bench. I'd only been knitting for a fortnight, and hadn't a clue how to follow a pattern, but what could be difficult about knitting a jumper? I'd make rectangles for the front, back, sleeves and neck, then stitch them all together; it seemed like a fool-proof plan. To get the right size I'd measure the stitches on the needle against one of my winter woollies; all I had to do now was cast on. I tried to remember how Rose had done it, but she'd worked so quickly I hadn't a clue. I looped the yarn around the needle and tied a knot in it, then wound it round and round. Something told me this wasn't quite the way to do it and when I poked the needle into the first loop it quickly became apparent that it wasn't going to work. I wound and looped and knotted and fiddled until I could bear it no longer. In exasperation I dashed up to the church to ring Rose.

Half an hour later the van screeched out of the *aldea*. Gary was not a happy man.

'I can't believe I'm driving all the way into Antas so you can watch a YouTube video. Rose'll switch her phone on eventually. You're too impatient, that's your trouble. I don't see why it can't wait.'

As luck would have it, my casting-on crisis couldn't have come at a better time. As I was logging on to the computer I heard a high-pitched trilling from inside my bag. To my surprise, Matt from the Ghost House was calling. Adey had finished the ceilings but he wouldn't have time to paint them. Matt wondered if Gary would like to do it instead. By the time we left Cafe-Bar Olga, my impatience had all but been forgotten. I'd cast on a hundred and twenty stitches and Gary had accepted the job.

'Are you looking forward to doing Matt's painting?' I asked, when we settled down with our beers that evening.

'I am. I enjoy painting, but it won't be straightforward. It'll mean poking into the contours where the plasterboard meets the beams.'

'I don't envy you. The living room ceiling was a nightmare. I had a heck of a job wiping the emulsion off the wood.'

'And half of it's still there now. I'm not like you – you dive straight in and you're clumsy. I've got a steady hand and I'm happy to take my time.'

'It'll probably be a full week's job then, will it?'

'At least. It's a big area. And when I've finished the painting he wants me to oil the beams.'

'Crikey. That's brilliant. The extra money'll really come in handy. When are you going to start?'

'I'll go tomorrow if you don't mind. I'll kill the two cockerels while you're out walking Lenda. You can spend the day plucking – it'll give you something to do.'

I was out on the bench with my knitting when Gary came home on Tuesday. When he climbed out of the van he looked like the cat that got the cream.

'Hello,' I smiled. 'You look happy. I take it the painting went well?'

'Not bad. It's going to be trickier than I thought, but I'll get there. Anyway, forget the painting, wait 'til you see what I've got in the van.'

I could tell by the tone of his voice that it was something really exciting. I put down my knitting and stood up.

'No, stay there. You can have a ringside seat while I unload them one at a time.'

I clasped my hands in my lap and looked on eagerly. I couldn't for the life of me think what the treasure might be.

'Ready?' he grinned, as he reached into the van. 'Exhibit number one,' he announced as he brought out a bulbous green bottle. 'What do you think?'

'Wow! It's an old demijohn! It's gorgeous! Wait, don't put it down there, the shingle's sharp and the glass might be fragile. Put it down gently, here look, on the bench.'

As Gary reached back into the van I began to smooth the dust off the bottle. It had a narrow neck and was in perfect condition apart from an unpleasant coating of mildew on the inside. I was still admiring my prize when Gary set a second bottle down beside it. Its companion was smaller, but otherwise identical in colour and shape.

'Another one?' I gasped. 'That's fantastic! They'll look great on the floor in the terrace once they're cleaned.'

'I thought you'd like them. I'm surprised Matt was getting rid of them really, but he did say everything had to go. Right, are you ready for the next exhibit?'

'There's more?'

He nodded. 'This time it's a set of eight.'

I was enjoying myself. On a limited budget, presents were few and far between. Working at Matt's was turning out to be a good thing in more ways than one.

This time when Gary leaned into the van there was a lot of huffing and puffing. Eventually he heaved out a sack of mortar and plonked it against the wall of the barn.

'Crikey!' I exclaimed. '*Mortero*! Now that *will* come in handy. And you said there're eight?'

'Yes. I couldn't believe my luck when I found them. Come on, you can give me a hand to get the others out of the van.'

I waited patiently while Gary dragged the next sack forward. 'Here,' he said. 'Stand it next to the other one against the wall.'

'I've got a better idea,' I grinned. 'I'm smaller than you are. I'll get into the van and shunt them forwards. You can carry them over to the wall.'

I stepped up into the boot space and began to shove the next sack forwards. Only then did I realise that the mortar was rock hard.

'Gary,' I frowned. 'This one's set solid. If you've still got some trips to the tip to make you might as well leave it in the van.'

He shook his head. 'They're all like that. That's why Matt didn't want them. Surely you didn't think he was chucking out sacks of perfectly good *mortero*?'

'I thought it was strange, but I think it's even stranger that you've brought them home with you. What on earth do you want them for?'

'I'll use them to make another raised bed. If I lay them sideways they'll be about the same height as breeze blocks. They'll do the job just as well and they won't cost a cent.'

I looked at him admiringly. For the last three years he'd bodged and cobbled and made use of things that nobody else would have given barn space. It wasn't the first time I'd thought how well he was suited to peasant life.

'There were some rolls of fibreglass insulation as well,' he continued. 'They'd have been perfect for our roof space but I didn't dare take them. He's probably forgotten they're there, but I'm sure he wouldn't have wanted me to chuck them out.'

'You could always ask him.'

'I could do, I s'pose. I might ring him when I get there tomorrow, see what he says.'

'Oh, you're still going are you? I wondered if you might have a day off, seeing as you're going for your blood test results.'

'The appointment's at nine so I thought I'd go straight from the doctor's. Do you mind?'

'Not really, it's just that…'

'You'll be worrying. I know. I tell you what, if the results are okay I'll go on to Matt's place, but if it's bad news I'll come home.'

'Fair enough. I'll have a relaxing day's knitting. The world's my lobster now I can cast on.'

'Let's have a look then. I might as well see the fruits of my driving.'

'Here,' I said, picking it up off the bench to show him. 'It's a good start isn't it? Look, I've nearly done four rows.'

He chuckled. 'And there was me thinking you meant *this* October. I'd like to think I'll still be here to see you wear it, but I don't hold out much hope.'

'Gary!' I gasped. 'Don't say that! You know how I'm worried about you seeing the specialist. I don't know what I'd do if I lost you. I'd...'

'Liza. The doctor as good as said it's just a precaution. You need to get those ridiculous thoughts out of your head.'

'I'm sorry. It's only because I care about you.'

'Rubbish. It's because we're in the middle of nowhere and you can't drive.'

When Gary wasn't home by breaktime on Wednesday I guessed that all was well with his blood test results and he'd gone straight to Matt's. Sure enough, when he came home that evening he was smiling from ear to ear.

'The blood test results were fine. My iron's slightly high, but the doctor reckons that's not a problem. Apart from that everything's normal. *And*....'

I looked at him expectantly.

'I've got you another present in the van.'

'From Matt's?'

He nodded. 'Shut your eyes.'

'But...'

'Shut your eyes, and don't open them 'til I tell you. I want you to see them all together and they'll take me a minute to unload.'

I screwed my eyes up and waited. I heard a scraping, then a clanking, like metal hitting metal. The sounds came again and again. Eventually Gary said, 'Right. Now open your eyes.'

In the middle of the lane were a pile of rusting poles, not much thicker than a finger. A couple were bent into V shapes, while the rest were straight and of varying lengths.

I leaned forward to peer at them. 'They look like tent poles,' I frowned.

'That's 'cos they are.'

'And they're a present for *me*? What am I supposed to do with them?'

'You're not going to do anything. I'm going to build you a new maternity wing for Mrs Brown.'

A smile spread across my face. I was about to stand up to hug him when he turned and pulled a shrink-wrapped roll of chicken wire out of the van. 'There's this as well.'

I gasped in amazement. 'I can't believe he was chucking *that* away.'

'He wasn't. I bought it from the *ferretería* on the way home.'

I gaped in astonishment. Up until now the very mention of chicken wire would have caused a domestic; I wondered what had caused such a drastic change.

He smiled at me. 'Don't look so surprised, I'm not such an ogre. Mrs Brown's chicks are due in a fortnight, and sooner or later we're bound to have rain. I'll build her a run that's rainproof and windproof. I know how upset you were over losing Waynetta's. You won't have to worry about it happening again.'

A wave of emotion swept over me. As I looked at him now, it was hard to believe how nasty he'd turned only recently. Had his brush with ill-health pulled him up by the bootstraps? Or was he putting on a brave face because he was scared that something was wrong?

For the next two days, Gary went off to work at the Ghost House, while I set about the laborious task of weeding the lane. The regular passage of tractors and cows had left cracks and chasms all over the surface and the weeds that took root there grew with far more determination than any veg.

'I think you should leave it,' said Gary at breakfast on Friday. 'Paul won't be weeding his bit. Nor Carmen. It'll take you ages. Personally, I think you're mad.'

Despite his misgivings, I'd carried on with my mission in earnest. I wasn't going to neglect my role as a citizen; Cutián was a community, and it was only right that I played my part. In less than a week, people would be coming from all over Spain to visit their family parish and attend the mass. They were sure to wander down the lanes when the service had finished and I was determined to do what I could to make the village look its best.

By late afternoon the lane, though not perfect, looked far more presentable. My back was aching and my knuckles were bleeding; it made sense to call it a day. As I eased myself up off my knees, I noticed something white sticking out of the mailbox. It must have arrived in the morning while I'd been out walking Lenda. I shook my head in disbelief, wondering how I could have missed it when it had been there all day.

When Gary came home, I was sitting with a coffee in the kitchen.

'You're as white as a sheet,' he exclaimed. 'What's wrong?'

'You've had a letter. It's got the health service logo on the envelope. I think your appointment's come.'

He relaxed visibly. 'That's good then, isn't it? There's no need to look so scared.'

'Gary, it's not even a fortnight since she referred you. She said it'd take at least a month.'

'Let's see what it says first, shall we? It might not be 'til Christmas for all we know.'

As he opened the envelope I reached for my tobacco. I willed him to hurry as he started to read.

'Well?' I asked impatiently.

'You've got yourself into a state for nothing. It's for September the fourteenth.'

When we settled down with our beers that evening Gary seemed slightly distracted. He didn't look red or flustered or grumpy, but something was definitely not quite right. I wondered if the prospect of the hospital appointment was bothering him after all.

'Penny for 'em?' I ventured, once I'd plucked up the courage to ask him.

'Eh?'

'You seem a bit... I don't know... anxious.'

'No, I'm alright.'

I watched as he drew hard on his ciggie. 'Are you sure?'

'I said so, didn't I? I'm fine.' He paused for a moment then looked at me intently, as if he was weighing up whether he should tell me what was on his mind. 'Look, there *is* something... you'll think it's daft.'

'You won't know unless you tell me.'

He cleared his throat. 'I think I've met the ghost.'

My eyes widened in astonishment. 'You're having a laugh.'

'I'm not. It was this afternoon. I'd been painting non-stop for about an hour when all of a sudden with no warning I heard an almighty bang upstairs.'

'A bang?'

'Yes. Like something heavy had fallen over or somebody had lifted something up and dropped it on the floor.'

Hadn't Adey told him that the ghost threw things? Perhaps there was some truth in the story after all.

'So what did you do?'

'Don't laugh. I chucked my brush down and legged it outside.'

'Really? It was enough to put the wind up you then?'

'Oh, yes. I mean, you expect weird noises in old houses, don't you? The wind blowing, doors banging, mice charging about – we get all that here. But this was something entirely different. I don't mind admitting it, I was scared.'

'So then what? You must have gone back in?'

'Eventually. I smoked a couple of fags and tried to think logically. There's no such thing as ghosts so something must have fallen over upstairs.'

'And had it?'

'No. That's what's really creepy. I looked in every room, but nothing was on its side or on the floor, and all the windows were fastened. I don't s'pose I'll ever know what it was, but I only hope it doesn't happen again.'

When Gary came in at breaktime on Saturday morning he had news.

'I've had a message off Matt. They're driving up to Taboada tomorrow and they'll be staying 'til next Saturday. He's tiling the floor in the kitchen and living room, so I've got next week off.'

Whilst it would be nice to have him at home for the fiesta I was surprised that he seemed so elated. He was enjoying the painting, but he'd only been at it since Tuesday. I wondered why he was keen to have time off so soon.

'Is it because of the ghost?' I asked him.

'I don't understand what you mean.'

'You seem really chuffed about getting a week off. Has it put you off going, the business with the ghost?'

'Don't be daft. It was probably just a bird or something. I wouldn't have thought anything of it if it wasn't for Adey and all his guff. I'm pleased 'cos I'll have time to catch up on the jobs that want doing. The rabbits need killing and I can build the new maternity wing so it'll be ready in plenty of time for the chicks.'

When I went up to the wheelie bin after lunch, I had a surprise when I reached the farmhouse. The poster for the village fiesta had appeared on the telegraph pole at the top of the lane. Maruja was standing in front of it, leaning over and peering. Flea-pelt was running excitedly in circles around her feet.

'*Hola*, Maruja,' I called, as I approached with my binbag.

'*Hola*, Elisa,' she smiled. 'The poster's up.'

I leaned forward and peered alongside her. On the fifteenth of August, three masses followed by a procession would take place at the parish church of San Xoán de Cutián.

It was exactly as I'd expected. The poster was the same every year.

'Young Javi's here already,' said Maruja. 'He came down last night with Másimo, Solina and Begoña. José Antonio and his family will be here this afternoon. Ivon and Marcos are coming tomorrow morning, and the family from number twelve should arrive tonight.'

I looked at Maruja. She was excited, and who could blame her? Our sleepy hamlet was about to change beyond all recognition. I supposed it was like the poster; it was the same every year.

Over the weekend the *aldea* came alive with the sound of vehicles and voices. Cars were parked up on

every spare patch of wasteland and by Sunday evening
the village community had tripled in size.

Whilst the upsurge in people had been fully expected, on
Tuesday morning the news of a further population
increase took me completely by surprise.

'The kittens were under the fig tree,' said Gary, when
he came in for coffee at breaktime. 'There weren't two,
there were three.'

'Never. Are they still there?'

'No, they scarpered down onto the track when they
saw me. They're half wild.'

'Are you *sure* you saw three?'

''Course I'm sure. There was the ginger one, like
Fred, but hairy...'

I nodded. 'I've seen that one.'

'And the splodgy one...'

'Splodgy?'

'Yes. White with splodges of ginger and black.'

'Ah, I'm with you. I've seen that one too.'

'So it's the motley one you haven't seen yet.'

'Motley?'

'Why d'you keep repeating me? It was mainly black,
mottled with ginger. I don't see what's so hard about
that.'

I smiled. 'Sorry. It's called a tortoiseshell. It's a
female, more's the pity. That's Sophie, Splodgy and now
Motley – the village'll be overrun with kittens this time
next year.'

When I came down from the shower that evening, Gary
was out on the bench drinking wine.

'Crikey,' I said. 'Has the fiesta started already?'

'No,' he grinned. 'But it's about to. Go and fetch
yourself a beer.'

I knew he was planning something but I had no idea what he might be up to. Saying nothing, I nipped through to the kitchen and took a can from the fridge. As I came back through the passage I heard a peculiar jingling. When I opened the backdoor Gary was standing, holding a *charrasco*, in the middle of the lane.

'There you go,' he said proudly. 'Well, what d'you think?'

'I think it's brilliant,' I laughed. 'You didn't tell me it was finished. Come on then, let's hear you play.'

'Wait,' he smiled. 'There's more.' He slipped his hand into his pocket and pulled out two small pieces of wood. 'Here y'are – *tejoletas*. I thought we could have a bit of a practice. I want to be on top form tomorrow night.'

Haiku for the Masses

Look at the poster!
An invite to the masses;
The same as last year.

Chapter 12

The Big Bang

On the fifteenth of August I was up before sunrise. Although I'd quarrelled with Nuestra Señora, I was excited about the fiesta; the festivities would continue down in the village long after the masses and the procession were all done and dusted up at the church. People would stroll past the house, pointing, nodding, laughing and perhaps even shedding a tear as they reminisced about loved ones and times gone by. Some would smile warmly and bid us '*Buenos días*', while others would stop to share memories of happy hours they'd spent in the *aldea* years ago. Meanwhile, the family would party with gusto, their celebrations shifting between the farmhouse and number fifteen throughout the afternoon. Not to be outdone, I was keen to make the most of the atmosphere and was planning a barbecue party of our own.

By the time Gary surfaced, a selection of freshly picked veg was piled up on the marble surface and there were rabbit portions soaking in a tandoori marinade in the fridge.

'Morning,' I smiled, as I passed him his cuppa.

'Morning,' he yawned. 'Has Masi been out with his trumpet?'

'Not yet. But I've heard him singing and whistling. Don't worry, I'm sure you'll get chance to bash your *charrasco* before the day's out.'

'I hope so. I'm looking forward to it. I'm looking forward to having a barbecue as well.'

'I was thinking about that. I wondered if we should've asked Paul. I s'pose it's too late now, I've only defrosted one rabbit. I didn't think earlier, I feel a bit mean.'

'Well don't. If it wasn't for the extra people milling about, Paul wouldn't even know that today was a fiesta. Would he have done anything special if he'd been in England? Of course he wouldn't. To him it's just August the fifteenth.'

'I s'pose you're right. He seems happy doing his own thing anyhow. He can always ask Carmen for a game of pétanque and a dip in the pool.'

It was a little before eleven when I stood on the doorstep to call Gary in for his coffee. Unlike me, he had no intention of changing his routine this morning; he was loping up from the *río* with his eyes fixed on the bumpy track, and a bucket of water in each hand.

'Coffee, Gary!' I called.

'Whooh,' he panted, as he drew closer. 'I'm sweating like a glass…'

'Pig.'

'A glass pig? Hmm, it's not got the same ring to it somehow. Why's coffee early anyway? Are you going to the service after all?'

'Don't be daft. I want to be out in the garden when the first mass finishes. I like to watch all the folks walking past.'

'Be honest. You want to hear them ooh-ing and aah-ing and saying, "Doesn't José Val's house look nice?" You've spent hours weeding and sweeping and scrubbing the paintwork. They'll think your standards are slipping – last year you painted the door.'

'I painted everything, actually. I'd have done it this year if we could afford it, but I'm trying to be careful. In case you'd forgotten, at the end of the month Lenda needs to be spayed.'

'I hadn't forgotten. I'm trying not to think about it. I bet we'll be looking at a hundred and fifty quid.'

'Probably double. Still, it's worth the investment. I don't think I could cope with another canine siege.'

After coffee, I popped Lenda into the garden, then settled with my knitting out on the bench. In ten minutes or so, the eleven o'clock mass would be ending and the first round of visitors would begin to drift by. I was knitting my second row when I heard the clanging of the church bell. Lenda shot up from the threshing floor whining and ran to the gate. Suddenly, there was a mighty 'whoosh' and seconds later a loud explosion. I glanced up at the sky, expecting to see the rocket shooting up overhead. There was a second 'whoosh-bang', then another *and* another. When I looked back to the threshing floor, Lenda had disappeared.

Laying my knitting carefully to one side, I crossed the lane and opened the gate. There was no sign of her on the lawn or under the fig tree. I set off down the garden, thinking she might have sought safety under the shade of the trees. She wasn't there, or in the veg plot or in the chooks' pen. I wondered if she'd managed to climb over into Carmen's or Paul's. I was coming back through the gate when I spotted Gary making another shuttle back from the *río* with his buckets.

'Is Lenda with you?' I called.

'What?' he shouted.

I cursed and tapped my foot impatiently as he plodded the last few metres up to the gate.

'What's the matter?' he panted, as he set down his buckets.

'Lenda's escaped.'

'Rubbish. She can't have. Was the gate shut?'

I nodded.

'Well then. The garden's completely escape proof. She'll be hiding somewhere. Have you looked under the trees?'

'Yes. And in the chooks' pen and the *huerta*. There's no sign of her anywhere. I'm telling you, Gary, she's escaped.'

He pushed past me. 'Let *me* go and look.'

'Please yourself, but she's not there. I'm going to see if she's round Carmen's or Paul's.'

As I stepped into the lane, Lenda came skulking sheepishly from round the corner of the barn.

'Gary!' I shouted. 'Don't bother, I've found her! I'll take her inside. See if you can work out where she got out, will you? She came from down the side path.'

Inside the kitchen, Lenda lay down by the dresser.

'Oh, Lenda,' I sighed. 'You did have me worried. Look at you, you're shaking. Nothing can hurt you in here.'

She looked at me anxiously, and the wisps of hair on her ears fluttered as she trembled. I wanted to hug her, but I knew that to do so would only affirm her fear. I looked at the clock. There were two more masses ahead of us, and that meant a *lot* more rockets. I couldn't take Lenda back to the garden, but there was no reason why *I* couldn't be out there; she wouldn't fly into a panic now she was safely indoors.

Ten minutes later, Lenda had stopped shaking and, leaving her in the kitchen, I resumed my place outside on the bench. It wasn't long before I heard voices; an elderly couple had paused at the top of the lane. They were talking to Paul, who was standing in his boxers and flip-flops and clutching a wine box. '*Vino*?' I heard him ask them. I wasn't really surprised when they declined.

As they came past they nodded a polite '*Buenos días*,' but showed no signs of wanting to linger. I could only assume that after meeting one Englishman they'd seen enough.

I relaxed into my knitting, the needles clicking softly in contrast to the abrasive clackety-clacking and jingly-jingling coming from inside the barn. After a while I paused to stretch out my work and admire my progress. The front (or back, depending on how many stitches I dropped) had grown to almost three inches. It was beginning to look as if I wouldn't be wearing it when the world ended after all. I gave a sigh of resignation and was contemplating nipping indoors for a ciggie, when the church bell clanged again. At the first whoosh-bang of a rocket there was a terrible crash from the kitchen. I tossed my knitting down and dashed indoors. The saucepan that I'd left on the drainer was lying on the floor and Lenda was trying her damnedest to scramble up into the sink.

'No, Lenda, no,' I shouted, wrapping my arms round her middle and pulling her back against my legs. As the ensuing volley resounded she shook herself free from my grasp and hurled herself up at the cooker. Wrapping my arms around her a second time, I leaned over and spoke to her gently, rubbing my chin on the top of her head. Eventually, I was able to lead her into the passage, where she lay hunched on the tiles, quaking with fear.

I plonked myself down on the step in the doorway, holding my head in my hands in despair. The third mass was still to come, and the final barrage was sure to be more protracted. If I kept my eye on the clock I'd be able to pre-empt a disaster by keeping her under control on her lead. With almost an hour to wait, it made sense to use the time wisely. I'd make Gary a sandwich for his lunch, and there were dressings for the salads to prepare. I went back into the kitchen and took mayonnaise and oil from the cupboard beneath the dresser. As I slammed the door closed, Lenda shot through from the passage and cowered at my feet.

'That wasn't a rocket,' I told her. 'It was me.' To show her what had made the noise, I opened the door a second time. Before I had chance to close it, Lenda jumped in. As she pushed her way further into the cupboard, I heard bashing and clanking and rustling. I prayed that nothing had broken as tins and packets bounced out onto the floor.

'Lenda,' I called, in a voice that I hoped belied my frustration. 'Lenda, there's nothing to be scared of. Come on, be a good girl.'

I coaxed and cajoled, but Lenda was determined to stay in her hidey-hole. Resigned to defeat, I knelt on the floor and pulled as much of the contents of the cupboard as I could salvage from underneath her. When I called Gary in for his sandwich there were dented boxes and packets heaped up on the marble surface, and a scattering of chickpeas and lentils all over the tiles.

'What's happened?' he asked, as he cast his eyes over the kitchen.

'The rockets,' I frowned. 'They sent Lenda into a frenzy and she dived into the cupboard for cover. I've tried coaxing her out with rabbit and ham and all sorts. There's no way I can shift her, she's flatly refusing to budge.'

'Poor Lenda,' he sighed. 'I've found out where she escaped.'

'Oh, where?'

'It was the bit where the sandy dog and the shepherd got in when she was in season. I put a plank of wood across the top and that's how she managed to get purchase. I'm going to have to take it down again and run twine through the wire to hold it taut.'

After lunch, Gary worked on making the fence escape-proof, while I sat with Lenda in the kitchen for the rest of the afternoon. I was beginning to think we'd have to cancel our barbecue, but around five-thirty Lenda finally decided that the coast was clear.

'Right, madam,' I told her. 'I'm going to put everything back in the cupboard and we'll have no more of your nonsense. When I've finished we'll go for a nice walk over the fields and then you'll come with me into the garden. You'll be safe now, because everything's back to normal. I promise there won't be any more fireworks until next year.'

Out in the garden we chatted and sipped on our beers while the rabbit sizzled on the barbecue and the marinade hissed as it dripped onto the embers beneath. For a while, Scholes had watched eagerly, but soon turned his attention to a blackbird that was pecking about on the lawn. He crouched down on his haunches and stalked it almost to the end of the garden, until it took flight over the wall into Paul's. In what appeared to be an exaggerated display of indifference he charged all the way back down the garden sideways then shot up into the fig tree with his tail bushed out, looking for all the world like a demented squirrel. Throughout his performance, Lenda had remained oblivious. Exhausted from her earlier escapade, she slept on soundly under the shade of the broom.

As the evening wore on I kept an ear out for the sound of a trumpet or a snare drum; Gary had worked hard on his instruments and I knew he'd been dying to use them, but apart from the shouts and the laughter, the only music to be heard from Másimo's garden were the pop songs blasting out from the radio inside his van.

By eight o'clock, the party at number fifteen had gone quiet. The music had stopped and so had the shouting and laughter. Now and again there was a clank or a bang, as though people were clearing up rubbish and moving tables and chairs. Poor Gary. The festivities were over and there would be no percussion tonight.

By now, the sun had sunk behind the house, casting a shadow over the threshing floor.

'I'm going in to fetch a cardi,' I shivered. 'It's starting to get chilly out here.'

'Why don't we go upstairs?' he suggested. 'We can play Scrabble, if you want to. I reckon I can beat you now I'm back on good form.'

'D'you know what?' I yawned. 'You probably will do. This afternoon's really taken it out of me. So much for the party – I'll give you one game and then I could do with an early night.'

Once satisfied that Lenda was settled in the passage, I joined Gary upstairs in the living room.

'I'm glad that's over for a year,' I sighed, as I reached for my tobacco. 'I can honestly say I was as stressed as Lenda by the end of the afternoon.'

'It's a shame I didn't get to play my instruments,' he said, as I opened out the Scrabble board. 'It's turned out to be a bit of a damp squib really. Still, there's always next year, I s'pose.'

'Not if I can help it,' I grimaced. 'You can build me a bunker out in the *campo*. I never want to go through such a nightmare again.'

We were halfway through the game when I looked up from the board and listened. If I wasn't mistaken I could hear drumming outside in the lane.

'Listen,' I said. 'That's Másimo's snare drum, can you hear it? It sounds as if he's standing outside.'

'You're right,' he nodded. 'I'm going to have a look.'

He got up from the sofa and walked over to the open window. He stuck his head out and I watched as he waved and smiled, then turned and gave me a thumbs-up from across the room.

'It *is* Masi. He's going up to the farmhouse and I think he wants me to join him. I'll take the bodhran, the *tejoletas* and the *charrasco*. Do you want to come?'

I shook my head. 'You don't mind do you? I wouldn't be much fun – I really am tired. I'll have half an hour on my knitting and then I'm going to bed.'

As I was clearing away the Scrabble, Scholes came in through his cat-hole.

'*You* were no trouble, were you?' I smiled, as he padded over to greet me. 'Rockets, tractors, cows, dogs – I don't think there's *anything* that you're scared of. Perhaps you could have a word with Lenda, she's such a wimp of a girl.'

Scholes leapt onto my lap and lay down as I started to stroke him. Soothed by the softness of his fur and the gentle rhythm of his purring, I leaned back on the sofa and was soon drifting off to sleep.

More than an hour had elapsed when I woke to the sound of barking. Lenda, though a coward when it came to rockets, made a *very* reliable guard. Down in the passage she was doing her best to sound ferocious, intent on seeing off the intruder who was hammering on the back door.

'Elisa!' came a voice, amidst the banging and the barking. 'Elisa!'

'Damn,' I muttered, as I eased myself forward and lifted Scholes gently onto the floor. I rose from the sofa and shuffled over to the window. Masi's son, José Antonio, was staring up at me from the lane.

'Elisa,' he grinned. 'I've come down from the farm to fetch you. You can't sit here on your own while your husband's enjoying the fiesta. Come on, I'll wait for you and we'll walk up together. Maruja's got plenty of food and beer.'

'I'm fine,' I protested. 'It's been a long day and I'm going to bed in a minute. You go back and enjoy the party. I'm quite happy here.'

It was odds on that José Antonio had been drinking since lunchtime, and I knew from experience that he wouldn't take no for an answer when he was under the influence of booze.

'Elisa,' he persisted. 'You *have* to come. It's the festival of Nuestra Señora. You're part of the community and you're missing the fiesta of Cutián.'

I sighed in exasperation. I'd had a hell of a day and the last thing I needed was a drunken knees-up. I wracked my brain for an excuse that I could fob him off with, but whatever I came up with was going to sound lame.

'Okay,' I nodded. 'I'll drop in for a beer, but I won't be stopping long because I'm tired. You go on, and I'll catch up with you. Give me ten minutes and I'll be there.'

'No, Elisa,' he persisted. 'If I go, you won't come, I know it. Do what you have to, but I'm going to wait here.'

'Listen,' I said calmly. 'For as long as you're there, Lenda will keep barking. I'll go to the bathroom then I swear I'll be right behind you. I give you my solemn promise I'll be there.'

When he smiled and nodded I knew that I'd managed to convince him. 'Ten minutes,' he reminded me, as he strode back up the lane.

Despite my misgivings, I couldn't help smiling. When we'd first moved into the village, I'd hoped that we'd be made welcome. Over the years I'd seen how our neighbours worked together as a close community and wondered if we'd ever truly belong. Tonight, José Antonio had been sent on a mission to drag me along to the party. It was testament to how far we'd come on that journey of acceptance and all of a sudden I was glad to have been roped in.

At the top of the village, an unlikely band of musicians was making a terrible racket outside the farmhouse. Gary on the bodhran and Masi on the snare drum were a half-decent duo together, but the addition of young Javi on the *tejoletas*, Maruja on the *charrasco* and José Antonio clapping and stamping had turned the percussion recital into one heck of a row.

When Másimo saw me approaching he stopped drumming, gave me a wink then frowned.

'Oh, Elisa,' he groaned. 'Can you hear them? What a disaster! I've raised two sons and neither has any idea of rhythm. I've told them over and over they must listen to what they're playing. They're too drunk to concentrate and they can't keep the beat.'

I glanced across at Maruja, who gave me an embarrassed smile from the doorstep. I thought of the pipe band in Santa Mariña; in her pinny, thick tights and work boots, Maruja didn't quite look the part.

My arrival had caused a break in the performance and José Antonio called out for more beer.

'Yes!' cheered young Javi. 'More beer and then we'll sing!'

Maruja bustled off into the kitchen and reappeared with four bottles of lager, which she handed to her nephews, Gary and me.

I sipped from my bottle and smiled at Gary, pleased that he was finally having fun.

'I'm sorry,' he whispered. 'I told him you were tired.'

'It doesn't matter,' I assured him. 'I'm glad I came.'

'Okay!' announced young Javi, as he drained the last of his lager. 'It's time for Manolo!'

'Manolo?' I echoed, looking round expectantly.

'It's a song,' chuckled Másimo.

'It's not just any song,' grinned José Antonio. 'It's the special song of Cutián!'

Másimo picked up his drumsticks and his sons began to sing.

As their voices boomed out in slurred *galego*, I could only make out the gist of the story. Manolo was a simple chap with a pretty young cow and twenty bulls. The tale turned rather saucy when he acquired a pretty young wife as well.

When the song ended, young Javi turned to Maruja. 'What time are we having the meat?'

'When Javier and José Manuel have finished milking,' she told him. 'I suppose I could go and see to it now.' She turned to me. 'Come on Elisa, you look frozen. It'll be warmer inside.'

I smiled gratefully and trailed in after her. The percussion was fun, but there was only so much bashing and pounding I could bear.

Inside the kitchen, Ivon was standing at the sink making cheese.

'*Buenos tardes*,' I smiled. 'I thought you'd gone home.'

'No,' she laughed. 'We're staying at Solina's until tomorrow. The children haven't gone to bed yet. I came here to get some peace.'

'Really?' I chuckled.

'I know,' she grinned. 'It was poor judgement on my part, but it isn't so bad in the kitchen. We're frying the meat soon, but you should help yourself to the buffet while you wait.'

I was about to protest but it was hours since I'd eaten rabbit and salad. I looked at the spread before me and was sure I'd manage to eat something after all.

'Sit yourself down,' said Maruja. 'I'll get you a plate.'

The spread, laid out on a plastic tablecloth, covered the whole of the marble surface and the top of the range. There were homemade cheeses, cured meats and chorizos, *ensaladilla* and a green salad that glistened with oil. As I settled on the bench, Ivon brought over a bowl of crisps and a basket heaped high with fresh bread.

'It's left over from earlier,' added Maruja as she passed me a plate and a fork.

I thought, not for the first time, how much I loved sitting in Maruja's kitchen, with the buckets of curds and whey and another full of potato peelings, the mud that had fallen from work boots and wellies, and the *jámon* that hung above Javier's place on the bench. There was something so warm and wholesome about the set-up, it was like returning to the safety of the womb.

'Here,' said Ivon, passing me some wine in one of the tumblers that they also used for coffee.

'Oh,' I said, embarrassed. 'I don't usually…'

'Drink it,' she said, with a chuckle. 'It's only once a year.'

While Ivon scooped the curds into sieves and Maruja fried hunks of *ternera*, I munched on the buffet and told them of the trouble I'd had with Lenda that afternoon.

'Is that why you didn't go to the mass?' asked Maruja.

I shook my head, thwarted momentarily by a mouthful of cheese. 'No,' I said eventually. 'I hadn't planned on being there anyway. I made up my mind last year.'

'Because of Nuestra Señora?'

'Yes.'

'But I thought you felt better after I gave you the photo?'

'I did. I wasn't scared, I was angry with her. And I suppose I was angry with God.'

Maruja looked at me intently. I sensed she was willing me to carry on.

'When Anxo was dying, I went up to the church and I prayed. I prayed to God and Nuestra Señora. I cried and begged them to save him. I lost my faith when they let me down.'

'You still miss Anxo, don't you Elisa?'

'Yes,' I smiled sadly. 'I do.'

I was aware that the drumming had stopped, and suddenly there were footsteps and laughter in the passage.

'Come on,' said Maruja, 'let's get the meat onto the plates – the men are hungry.'

Ivon crossed the kitchen and took two metal salvers from the dresser. As she walked back to the cooker she leaned over and touched my arm.

'Are you still angry with God, Elisa?'

I nodded.

'Then you haven't lost your faith.'

Next morning, while I waited for the kettle to boil I took the photograph of Nuestra Señora out of the back of my diary. I studied it for a while and felt sure she was smiling. 'I'm sorry I didn't make it,' I told her. 'I'll try and be there next year.'

It was approaching eleven o'clock when Gary finally surfaced. I could hardly blame him; he'd done well to stay up into the wee small hours and had expended a fair amount of energy, pounding away on his trusty bodhran. I'd half expected him to spend the day taking it easy, but he was keen to start building the luxury nursery unit for Mrs Brown. For the next three days he became an almost permanent fixture down in the chooks' pen, turning the air blue and swotting at flies. On Saturday evening the maternity house, along with Mrs Brown and her precious cargo, sat proudly inside a giant trapeziform enclosure, complete with a roof, an awning and roll-down plastic sides.

Gary returned to the Ghost House the week after the fiesta. He assured me he'd made a fabulous job of the ceilings and the overall effect was rather impressive now that the beams were oiled. There were no more unexplained disturbances, and he took that as a sign that the ghost thought so too.

Manolo and his Heifer

Manolo was a kindly man
(Though sadly not too clever)
Who had a fine and handsome bull,
And one delightful heifer.

The people said, 'One mate won't do –
A beast like that needs plenty.
To keep it happy and fulfilled
It needs a herd of twenty.'

And so on market day, he went
To town with loads of lolly,
And came back home with nineteen bulls
To keep his heifer jolly.

As time went by he met a girl
Called Lola, and they married.
Each day he went out to the fields,
At home fair Lola tarried.

She wasn't on her own for long;
Young men came by to visit.
Manolo heard of this and wept:
'It isn't true, dear is it?'

Fair Lola smiled, 'Manolo, dear,
Don't ever doubt I love you;
My feelings run deep as the sea
And all the sky above you.

But just one mate is not enough;
A girl like me needs plenty
To keep me happy and fulfilled
I need a herd of twenty.

Liza Grantham

I promise I'll stay by your side
Until the Twelfth of Never,
Provided I remain fulfilled
Just like that sweet young heifer.'

Chapter 13

Home and Dry

Life in the *aldea* seemed to fall rather flat after the busyness of the fiesta. Másimo and Solina's relatives went back to their homes in A Coruña, and the family at number twelve returned to Bilbao. Children could no longer be heard squealing as they pricked themselves on brambles or shrieking with delight as they free-wheeled on their bicycles downhill from the farmhouse to the end of the lane. Visitors who had ventured to the region from the cities had returned to work, and people from neighbouring *aldeas* no longer wandered through the lanes in the evenings; the air was growing cooler and the nights would soon be drawing in.

As August drew to a close, the climate became more temperate and so did the pace of village life. The *fincas* were sparser now; the last of the maize and tomatoes had been harvested, and the bean plants stood decked in scrunched foliage and the swollen pods which held the promise of new life for the coming year. Row upon row of drooping yellow leaves signalled that it would soon be time to gather in the year's potatoes, and sow turnip seeds when the earth was furrowed anew. In our own small *huerta* there were still peppers, squashes and courgettes to pick. The pumpkin, approaching the size of a beachball, would be ready well before Halloween.

Down in the chicken run, Mrs Brown fussed and fretted over her recent arrivals. There were only two chicks this time and one was much tinier than the other. Mrs Brown didn't seem to notice, but there was no mistaking the fact that Waynetta was really its mum.

In previous years I'd welcomed the lull after the summer. I'd spend the afternoons pacing over the garden, filling bucket after bucket with windfall apples and, in the mornings, the kitchen would be filled with the spiced fragrance of chutneys and the sweet cinnamon scent of crumbles and pies. The routine would follow the same pattern this September, but with one small difference; I'd be counting down the days to Gary's consultation and, although his appetite was almost back to normal, I was scared. If that wasn't enough to worry about, there was another appointment to be organised; it was time for Lenda to be spayed.

When I heard Gary stirring on Saturday morning, I drew slowly on my cigarette. I wasn't looking forward to reminding him of the big expense we'd be faced with in the coming week. There was no point in treading softly; it was better to wade straight in.

'White rabbits,' I smiled as I passed him his cuppa. 'I'm going to ring the vets this morning, see if I can get Lenda booked in for next week.'

'Good idea,' he yawned. 'I thought we were taking her in August to be honest. I wondered if you'd forgotten.'

His lack of resistance surprised me, but I was about to discover the cause.

'I've been thinking about appointments actually.'

'Oh, yes? Why?'

'Well, I'm supposed to be going to the hospital this month, aren't I?'

I nodded.

'The thing is, I've been feeling fine for weeks now. I'm beginning to think that stomach thing's sorted itself out. I'm wondering if it's worth me going to the hospital after all.'

I frowned at him. 'It doesn't matter whether it's better or not, you'll go regardless. *You* might not be worried, but it's *me* that's had to put up with your mood swings. For both our sakes you should get it checked out.'

He rolled his eyes skywards and gave a protracted sigh.

'Don't look like that. We're lucky to have full medical cover and it makes sense to use it. Not all ex-pats have that privilege – never look a gift horse in the mouth.'

He chuckled. 'I never understood that. What's it mean?'

'It means if somebody's offering you something don't quibble, snatch their hand off.'

'I know that. What I meant to say was, where does it come from? It sounds daft.'

'It's from the olden days when folks used to decide if a horse was any good by looking at its teeth.'

He chuckled again. 'I wonder what they'd say nowadays? "Don't look under the bonnet", I s'pose. That's what you'd do if you were buying a car.'

I couldn't help but giggle as I thought of our liability of a van. I had no idea whether Gary had looked under the bonnet when he'd bought it, but he'd certainly managed to turn a deaf ear to its screeching brakes.

'You see what I'm saying though, don't you?' I persisted. 'Free health care's not to be sniffed at – you'd be mad not to go.'

'Alright then,' he sighed. 'I'll go if it makes you happy. I'll even let you come with me if you like.'

Before break I went up to the church to ring the veterinary clinic. When Gary came in for coffee I gave him the news.

'I've made Lenda's appointment. It's on Tuesday at ten o'clock.'

'That's good then. Did you ask the vet how much it'll cost?'

''Course I did. Two hundred and eighty euros. I don't think that's bad.'

'Not bad? If she has one of those every day she'll be booking a cruise for Christmas. I reckon *I* should have been a vet.'

'Make your mind up. According to you, you should have played for Man United. Honestly, Gary, you're such a dreamer. You're as bad as him up the road.'

He smiled wryly. 'Not quite. At least *my* dreams are normal. *I'm* not planning a party for the end of the world.'

I giggled. 'True.'

'Anyway, you're as bad – you were going to have the jumper finished by then.'

I grinned sheepishly. 'I'll have you know it's coming on lovely. I'll be starting the front this afternoon.'

'I thought that was the front that you've been knitting?'

'It was. I've dropped a few stitches so I'll have to darn where the holes are. I've got better as I've gone on so the next piece will be perfect. Just wait 'til it's finished – you'll be wanting one too.'

When I went out to Warren Place on Tuesday morning, the floor of Doe's hutch was covered in fur. Unlike her springtime litter, none of the babies had been tossed out of the nest to perish, so it was safe to assume she'd had her usual kindle of nine.

Wayne and his wives had been quick to lose interest in the luxury unit that had sprung up inside their enclosure. This morning when I opened the hen house, Wayne threw back his head and crowed before strutting over to the hens as they jostled and bickered around the feeder. Inside the five-star maternity wing, Mrs Brown fussed over her two little chicks as they hopped out into their run.

As I made my way back up the garden I was briefly saddened by the thought that Lenda would never have puppies. While Mrs Brown and Doe were absorbed in the joys of motherhood, this morning Lenda would forgo all hopes of ever becoming a mum.

At nine-thirty I hovered uncomfortably in the passage, while Gary fetched the van out of the barn. Driving with him could be challenging at the best of times, but this morning I was expecting it to be an ordeal. Despite our conviction to accustom Lenda to travelling, four months had passed since we'd visited Nina and Marcus. I crossed my fingers and hoped she'd stay calm.

Inside the van, Lenda's breathing quickened. As soon as Gary released the handbrake, I knew we were in for another rough ride. She whinged and fidgeted as we wound along the main road towards Antas, but once we turned onto the straight run into Monterroso she settled down. I was relaxing into the journey but when the van turned right past the medical centre the brakes gave a protracted, agonised screech as it crawled to the brow of the hill. Lenda threw herself against the window and buffeted her head against the driver's seat. It was all I could do to control her until the van began its descent towards the main road.

By the time we arrived at the clinic, Lenda was panting heavily.

'She's very stressed,' I explained to the vet. 'She hates travelling in the van.'

'Don't worry,' she smiled kindly. 'We'll weigh her and then I'll give her a sedative to keep her calm. You can stay with her until she falls asleep if you want to.' She looked down at Lenda. 'Hello, Lenda. I'm María. Are you going to be a good girl?'

Lenda wagged her tail and I smiled gratefully. 'Can you fit her with an identichip while she's here?'

Gary raised his eyebrows. 'You didn't mention that before.'

I shrugged dismissively. 'I'd forgotten about it 'til now.'

Up until then I hadn't known that María spoke English. She was quick to tell Gary that dogs *had* to be chipped by law.

Once Lenda was sedated and comfortable, we left the clinic. As we drove out of Taboada I battled silently with an irrational inner fear. The last time I'd left a dog in the vets he'd died there. I rolled a cigarette as I fought back the tears.

Back in the *aldea* I laundered Lenda's bedding and replaced it with a fresh blanket; there would be less chance of her wound becoming infected if her bed was spotlessly clean.

After lunch, I took my builder's bucket out to the lawn to carry on collecting the windfalls. As I stooped beneath the trees a terrible thought struck me and I froze in horror. I was doing exactly what I'd been doing almost a year ago when our old vet, Eli, had brought Anxo's body home. I tossed the bucket aside and fled back to the kitchen. I sat on the bench and slumped over the marble surface, my shoulders shaking as my sobs came in waves.

Back in the garden I spent the next two hours cutting back the sweet Williams and calendula, and shaking the seeds into margarine tubs, ready to be sown in the spring. It was the simplest of tasks, yet it brought with it a welcome catharsis. Just as the lifeless heads brought forth the seeds of new beginnings, so Anxo was at peace, and Lenda would blossom in the years to come.

When Lenda came home from the clinic that evening she was drowsy and inappetent, but when morning came round she was fine. Nevertheless, she'd had surgery and would need a period of convalescence. There would be no running, jumping or climbing until the wound had properly healed. For at least a week, her exercise would be limited to shorter lead walks. Instead of our usual route through the eucalyptus woods and out into the five fields, I'd take her along the track, past Másimo's *huerta* and the *río*, and up into the oak woods for a leisurely stroll.

On Saturday morning Solina was pegging out her washing when I came back along the track with Lenda.

'*Hola*, Solina,' I called. '*Buenos días.*'

'*Buenos días*, Elisa,' she smiled. 'We're going to pick the potatoes this morning. In the afternoon, Maruja will be picking hers.'

I thought of the field where Maruja and Javier grew their potatoes. It was a little way out of the village, along the main road to Facha. It was a massive area and the yield lasted Maruja all year.

'That sounds like a lot of work,' I frowned. 'I'm surprised they manage to do it in an afternoon.'

'They don't do it on their own,' laughed Solina. 'Alfonso and his wife help, and a couple of others come down from Facha. Maruja cooks them a meal and they take some potatoes home.'

That was typical of life in rural Galicia. People kept themselves to themselves and minded their own business, but when help was needed, everybody mucked in.

'And then it will be time for the *nabos*,' I smiled.

For the last three years I'd paid careful attention to what went on in our neighbours' *fincas* and I knew that the turnips were planted after the potato harvest each year. The root channels stopped the soil from compacting as the ground hardened over winter, and the dense foliage helped to suppress the weeds.

'That's right,' nodded Solina. 'José Manuel will bring the tractor over to plough the *finca* on Saturday morning. Másimo will be sowing the *nabos* in the afternoon.'

I chuckled as I thought back to the previous year's calamitous caper. José Manuel had caused such a commotion with the tractor, bashing the plough attachment repeatedly into the sides of the lane. The whooping and cheering that had ensued had been better than any pantomime. I made a mental note to be around the following Saturday. If there was going to be a repeat performance I wasn't going to miss it for the world.

For the whole of the next week the sun continued to shine. It wasn't the intense, burning sun of the summer months, nor was it the watery, pallid sun of autumn. It was the sun that caressed bare arms and kissed faces but issued a rebuke like a spurned lover if you lingered too long in the shade. Under normal circumstances, this was the kind of weather that cheered me, yet I was feeling increasingly subdued as the week wore on. Since Gary had been taking his blood pressure tablets his behaviour had returned to normal. He was as daft as a brush and his hearty appetite had recently returned with a vengeance. His stomach, however, gurgled loudly from morning through until bedtime, and in my heart of hearts I was still convinced that something was wrong.

When I called Gary in at breaktime on Thursday morning, he looked at me and sighed as I passed him his brew.

'Liza, look at your hands, they're shaking. I wish you'd stop worrying. It'll all be over and done with by this time tomorrow. Anyway, this'll cheer you up, I've got news.'

I looked at him eagerly; village news, however small, was always guaranteed to be fun. Today, the distraction would be more than welcome. 'Okay,' I smiled. 'Go on.'

'Paul's in his plunge pool.'

'Never! He can't be! It's September. It might be pleasant, but it's not warm enough to take your clothes off. In fact it's quite chilly when you move into the shade.'

'Well, that's what he's doing. I went down to chuck some apples in the composter and I heard all this splashing. I knew it wasn't Carmen, so I pretended I'd run out of screws and nipped round.'

'Oh dear. Did he have any clothes on?'

'I doubt it. I couldn't tell, to be honest, he was submerged up to his neck. He said he's making the most of the weather. The forecast says rain for tomorrow.'

'Really? I'm not surprised.'

'He's worried that it might set in and ruin his bash.'

'He's serious about it then? The End of the World party?'

'Oh, yes. He reckons he's bought enough pasta to feed… a hundred? …a thousand? I forget how many. Oh, and he's having the stuff delivered to lay the concrete for the pétanque court next week.'

On Friday morning I woke Gary at half past seven. I was keen for everything to run smoothly before the journey to Lugo so that he'd remain calm. I'd take Lenda for her walk as the sun was rising and I'd let out the chooks and rabbits just before we set out. Gary would have plenty of time for breakfast and a second cuppa, and he'd be bright-eyed and bushy tailed by the time we took to the road.

We left the village a little after eight-thirty. Galician farmers, unlike the English, didn't lead their herd out at sunrise and it was a safe bet that we weren't going to get stuck behind cows. State-of-the-art robots hadn't found their way into the heart of the Galician countryside and, like Javier and Maruja, most families still milked by hand. For many, it was a long process; milking would begin around eight and the cows would go out to the fields any time after ten.

It was almost nine-thirty when we drove into the centre of Lugo. We'd missed the worst of the morning rush hour, and a steady flow of traffic moved through the dreary city as the rainclouds gathered above us in the ever-darkening sky. The traffic lights worked in our favour and I hoped that this was a good omen. We arrived at the hospital with plenty of time to spare.

Inside the main foyer we hovered, overwhelmed by the size of the four-storey building and baffled about where we were supposed to go.

Opposite the revolving doors were a couple of women in white coats sitting at a table labelled '*Información*'. It seemed as good a place as any to start.

'I'll go and ask at that table,' I told Gary. 'Here, give me the letter. You wait there.'

Two minutes later I was all genned up on our destination, but Gary was missing. I glanced round and spotted him hovering by the cafeteria door.

'Right,' I said. 'We need to go to that machine over there – by the stairs, look. When you stick your card in, it'll give you a ticket. You have to take one even though you've got a *cita previa* and a piece of paper. Don't ask me why.'

As it turned out, the ticket was neither use nor ornament. It merely repeated what was written in the letter; the appointment was at twenty past ten.

Gary looked at his watch. 'It's only five to ten. Let's go and get a coffee.'

'I don't think we ought to. You've stuck your card in the machine now and it'll register on the computer. If anyone's cancelled they might call you in early because they know you're here.'

'You should have said so,' he tutted. 'We could've gone to the café first.'

'Why not take one up with you? Look, there's a vending machine.'

My suggestion seemed to appease him and ten minutes later we were walking along a corridor on the fourth floor. To the right were the different departments, labelled A to K.

'This is it,' said Gary. 'Gastro-wotsit – B.'

We turned into the waiting area and plonked ourselves down at the end of a row of plastic seats. Opposite were half a dozen doors and three screens spaced evenly along the wall.

'What number are you?' I asked.

He looked at his ticket. 'Oh-three-five. And it's room four-oh-four.'

'That one,' I said, nodding towards a door down on the left.

Gary stood up. 'We ought to move along a bit, really. Come on.'

I sighed impatiently. 'I've sat down now. I'm damned if I'm moving. They don't come out and call you anyway, you have to watch that screen on the wall.'

Satisfied that I was right, Gary stayed put and sipped on his coffee. I was reading a poster about the early warning signs for colon cancer when he spoke.

'I s'pose they'll just ask me what my symptoms are and give my stomach a bit of a prod.'

'I should think so,' I nodded. 'They'll probably want to have a look at your bum as well.'

'Don't be horrible. I'm surprised at you. This is hardly the time to joke.'

'I wasn't joking. It's a digestive problem. They'll want to know about what comes out at the end, not just what's happening in the middle.'

'My shit's normal.'

'No it isn't. It floats.'

'Rubbish. It's perfectly normal. And don't you go saying otherwise when we're in there. I don't want folks poking things up my arse.'

'Gary. Now that you're here you need to tell them everything. There's no point…'

There was a loud 'Bong!' from the screen on the wall, and the number zero thirty was replaced by zero thirty five.

'That's me,' said Gary. 'Come on.'

Inside the consulting room the doctor, who looked no older than thirty, was sitting behind a desk looking at a computer screen. A nurse sat at the end with a pen and pad.

'*Buenos días*, Harry,' smiled the doctor. He looked at me. 'Are you his wife?'

'Yes,' I nodded. '*Buenos días*.'

The doctor scrolled through the notes on the screen nodding occasionally. This was a good sign. Perhaps he recognised the symptoms and would be able to tell us what was wrong. Eventually he turned to Gary. 'You've been having trouble with your stomach. Have you been having pain?'

'No,' said Gary. 'It didn't hurt. There was a... I don't know how to explain it. It was, erm... a sensation. I didn't know if I was empty or full. The thing is, it's gone back to normal. Whatever it was has gone.'

Gary was making a sterling effort but it would be quicker and easier if I took over. 'Do you want me to explain?' I asked him.

He nodded. 'Yes, please.'

I looked at the doctor. 'He was fine in the mornings. He'd have two or three eggs for his breakfast as usual. The problem started around mid-day. At lunchtime he'd say he was starving but then he'd pick at his meal. He was sleeping through the afternoons, but in the evenings he'd eat on and off until he went to bed.'

'And the symptoms have gone now?'

'Most of them. His appetite's back and he feels full when he's eaten, but his stomach's still making a gurgling noise.'

The doctor nodded and looked back at Gary. 'And what about your stools?'

'They're normal,' said Gary.

'They're not,' I frowned. 'They float.'

Gary glared at me. 'They don't.'

'Gary, I'm telling you they do. When I go up for my shower...' I stopped in mid-sentence. Was I *really* sitting in front of a complete stranger, arguing with my husband about the appearance of his poo?

'Thank you,' said the doctor diplomatically. He looked at Gary again. 'If you'd like to go behind the screen for a moment I'll give you a quick examination. Would you like your wife to come through as well?'

'That won't be necessary,' I said quickly. 'He'll be fine.'

The doctor led Gary into the inner sanctum and the nurse followed on behind. For a few seconds all went quiet then the nurse told Gary to take off his lower garments and lie on the bed. I recognised the clank of Gary's belt buckle, then a soft thwack followed by another. I shuddered as I imagined the doctor donning his rubber gloves.

I sat like an unwitting fly on the wall until, after what seemed an age, the doctor said, '*Listo*. All done.'

There was a lot of shuffling and fumbling and eventually the trio reappeared from behind the screen.

Once everyone was seated, the doctor began to type on the keyboard. Gary leaned forward and cleared his throat.

'I did wonder if the wife's been trying to poison me,' he said quite earnestly.

The doctor eyed me suspiciously and I wanted to crawl under the table and hide. Instead, I glared at Gary before turning to the doctor with an apologetic smile. 'I'm ever so sorry. It's his English sense of humour. He's joking because he's scared.'

The doctor's expression softened and he looked at Gary. 'There's no need to worry,' he said gently. 'I'm going to make you an appointment for an *endoscopia*. We'll put a tiny camera down your throat and have a look at what's going on inside you. It won't hurt but it will be uncomfortable, so you have the option of being sedated. If you do, you won't be able to drive straight afterwards, but you don't have to notify us until the day.'

I looked at Gary. 'Did you understand all that?'

He nodded. 'More or less.'

The doctor continued. 'You won't be able to eat or drink after midnight before the procedure, but I'll give you an information sheet that tells you exactly what you need to do.'

He began to tap away on his keyboard and eventually there was a high-pitched buzz as two sheets of paper slid out of the printer. He passed them across the desk to Gary. 'This tells you everything you need to know; this one's your appointment. I'll see you on the eleventh of October at half past eleven.'

I swallowed hard but said nothing. The eleventh of October was already etched on my memory. It was the day that Anxo had died.

When we left the consulting room I glared at Gary a second time. 'What*ever* possessed you to say that?'

'I was only having a joke. It made him smile.'

'Believe me, it didn't. He must have thought you were a nutcase. That's the last time I'm coming with you. From now on you're on your own.'

When we drove out of Lugo the rain was torrential. The van's wipers swept manically across the windscreen and I was thankful that, unlike the brakes, they didn't squeal. Our experience with the consultant had done little to quell my fears about Gary's condition but, as we drove along the N-540 homewards, a more pressing worry was growing in my mind. Waynetta's chicks had been three days old when they'd been lost in the rainstorm. Mrs Brown's brood weren't that much older and she was out with them now in the new pen. I drew hard on my cigarette and willed Gary to put his foot down. Try as I might, I couldn't shake off the terrible sense of déjà vu.

Back in the *aldea*, I leapt out of the van even before Gary had turned off the engine. Down in the chooks' pen the dust bath hollows had morphed into poultry-sized plunge pools, but the hens clamoured beneath the canopy of the chestnut tree, unwilling to take a dip. I squelched through the quagmire, slowing as I reached the maternity wing. I inhaled deeply, steeling myself for the horrors I was convinced I'd find. I ducked under the lip of the awning and peered through the wire. There wasn't so much as a puddle in the enclosure and Mrs Brown and her chicks were as dry as a bone. Gary's construction was every bit as windproof and rainproof as he'd promised; the state-of-the-art nursery was a huge success.

As I strode back up the garden I felt a whole lot brighter. All was well with Mrs Brown and her babies; I only hoped that the same would be true for Gary too.

White Coat Syndrome

You've heard of White Coat Syndrome?
It's a form of hypertension;
It affects a lot of people
Seeking medical attention.

It's brought on by the doctors
In their antiseptic get-up,
And the sights and sounds and smells
Of such a super-sterile set-up.

The heart beats harder in the chest
(You almost hear it thumping),
It sends the pulse rate through the roof
And sets the blood a-bumping.

It causes temperatures to soar,
Leaves palms and brows perspiring,
But some folks get it really bad –
It messes up their wiring.

Some say the most offensive things,
Some lie and turn abusive;
A character so calm can change
To one that's quite obtrusive.

To loved ones who support them
They might well turn heavy-handed
But don't stand for any nonsense –
Speak your mind, be bold and candid.

It's only White Coat Syndrome,
And you know it can't be thwarted;
Next time there's an appointment
Let them go there unescorted.

243

Chapter 14

Invalid Food

On Saturday morning the sky was blue and completely cloudless. All that remained of yesterday's downpour were the tell-tale puddles in the lane. As soon as I came back from walking Lenda I brought the laundry basket into the kitchen. At this time of year every dry day was a wash day; once the autumn torrents set in the opportunities for pegging out would be few and far between. Over the last few months I'd begun to question my commitment to going back to the old ways. Wringing out had begun to cause pain in my finger joints; three years without a washing machine or a tumble dryer were taking their toll.

It was approaching breaktime when I finally finished the pegging. Up until now there had been no sign of José Manuel and the tractor and I was beginning to wonder if he was leaving the ploughing until the following weekend. I wiped my hands down my pinny and was about to return to the kitchen when I heard a medley of shouting and screeching. It seemed that my patience was finally being rewarded; the disturbance was coming from number fifteen.

I dashed through the gate, down past the barn and along the track past Másimo's garden. The commotion was coming from the *huerta*, not above the thrumming of a tractor, but amidst a cacophonous squawking and flapping of wings. As I stared through the chain-link fence, a full-blown slapstick was unfolding before my eyes. Masi was shouting at the top of his voice as he stumbled through the kale in pursuit of a fat brown chicken, while Solina was pacing along the row cursing as she jabbed with a mop in between the closely planted stems. From the perimeter, Begoña was laughing and squealing and as Másimo lunged forward to make a grab for his quarry he stumbled and landed on his knees in the soil.

It was just after lunchtime when I finally heard the tractor approaching. From the doorstep, I watched as José Manuel slowed it almost to a halt at the corner of the annexe, before turning it expertly onto the track. I set off at a safe distance behind it as it chugged the short stretch down to Másimo's *huerta*, where a section of the fence had been swung back far enough to allow for a vehicle to pass through. A couple of metres from the entrance, José Manuel turned the steering wheel just a fraction, easing the nose of the tractor through the opening and guiding it effortlessly in. I didn't mind for a moment that there had been no dramatics; the village pantomime had already surpassed itself this year.

At teatime I considered taking Lenda on a longer walk across the *campo*. Her wound was healing nicely but she was growing increasingly restless and I could tell that, like me, she was ready to get back to our regular routine. Erring on the side of caution, I decided to stick to the shorter walks until the weekend was over and on Monday morning we'd resume our treks over the five fields. As we set off along the track, Lenda's ears pricked up and she began to pull forwards. Thinking she needed to do her business, I let her off the lead. Instead of snuffling in the weeds until she found a spot to suit her, she charged off ahead and stopped dead at the chain-link fence. When I caught up, I cast my eyes over the *huerta* and saw in an instant the cause of her fascination. The errant brown chicken was back, pecking and scratching about in the newly furrowed soil. Although the fence had been closed back up I began to panic when I noticed that the board across the bottom hadn't been replaced. I unravelled the lead from around my wrist as Lenda sank onto her belly and began to scrape at the earth beneath the fence. I leaned forward and grabbed her around the waist, but as she scrabbled harder I lost my grip and my feet gave way beneath me. Lenda took off across the *huerta* and I fell sideways onto my elbow in the mud.

Cursing under my breath, I stood up and yelled with as much authority as I could muster, 'No, Lenda! *No!*'

The hen squawked and Lenda, heedless of my commands, took off across the furrows, the thick, damp clods kicking up behind her as she gained on her terrified prey. The poor bird flapped its way over the ridges and past the kale, before taking off over the dense thicket of bramble and into the pasture below. I breathed a sigh of relief, but Lenda, consumed by primal instincts, hurtled onwards and bulldozed her way through the undergrowth like a beast possessed. For the next few seconds, time seemed to stand still, and I whispered a desperate prayer as I listened to the rustling, cracking, flapping and squawking which ensued. Suddenly all fell silent and I was beginning to think the hen had eluded her hairy predator when Lenda emerged a little way along the track, wet, muddy, and with her trophy clenched firmly between her jaws. Not to be thwarted in my efforts to save her hapless victim I lunged sideways as Lenda hurtled past me, back towards the lane. I took off in pursuit, but my efforts were futile. As I neared the barn, I watched helplessly as she sped off onto the path that led into Paul's and Carmen's gardens. Whichever route she chose, it would be a nightmare trying to find her; each was an overgrown wilderness and I hoped that both of the gates were closed.

When I reached the path there was no sign of Lenda or the chicken. Carmen's gate was shut, but Paul's was wide open. I shook my head in frustration. The chances of finding her were as good as zero if she was hiding out in Paul's. I charged through the gate but stopped in my tracks when I came to the threshing floor. I wouldn't need to go searching; Lenda was lying beneath the apple tree, surrounded by feathers and licking her paws.

I stared in horror as the dreadful reality dawned on me. My dog was a killer of livestock. In a Galician *aldea* this was a grave situation. Once our neighbours found out it was *not* going to go down well.

'Lenda!' I gasped. 'What have you *done*?' I marched over to where she was lying. There wasn't so much as the head or a claw remaining; I couldn't believe she'd devoured the whole chicken in such a short space of time. 'Come here *now*,' I said firmly. 'You're a bad girl. A very *bad* girl.'

Once she was back on her lead I kept her close to my side as I stomped back down the lane. Gary must have heard the commotion. He was waiting outside the barn.

'What's happened?' he asked. 'I could hear you shouting. Why have you come that way? I thought you'd been walking her past the *rio* and up to the woods.'

'I have,' I grimaced. 'It's a long story.' I looked behind me. 'Come on, let's go inside.'

Back in the kitchen I made straight for my tobacco.

'Oh dear,' frowned Gary. 'Bad news?'

I nodded. However much I was dreading telling Gary, it was going to be even harder to own up to Solina. I might as well come straight out with it; whatever I said wouldn't sugar the pill.

'We were *going* to go the woods way, but we didn't make it. Solina's chicken was loose again and Lenda spotted it and the fence hadn't been put back properly and…'

'Don't say she got into Másimo's *huerta*?'

I nodded. 'I tried to grab her but… Anyway, the thing is, she went charging after the chicken and…'

'Shit! She didn't disturb the seeds, did she?'

'The seeds? If only. It's worse than that, Gary – she killed the hen.'

'You're joking? So much for neighbourly relations. Are you sure it was dead and not just stunned?'

'Of course I'm sure. Trust you.'

'There's no need to be stroppy, it's not *me* that let her run riot. I'd have kept her on the lead 'til we were out of the village. Still, she's your dog.'

I glared at him. 'Spare me the lectures, will you? I've still got to go round and face Solina. What the hell am I going to say?'

'Doesn't she know yet?'

I shook my head.

'That's good then. Perhaps it's better you don't tell her. Where's the hen?'

'Lenda ate it. I was going to tell you if you'd have let me finish. She ran off up the lane and there was nothing left but a pile of feathers by the time I got to Paul's.'

'That's a pity. It's only a matter of time before Carmen spots them. She was probably watching anyway, you know what she's like. You'll have to come clean then. Rather you than me.'

I sighed as I stubbed out my cigarette. 'I think I'll go now and get it over with. The longer I leave it, the worse it'll be.'

I walked over to the fridge and took Gary's wallet down from the telly shelf.

He looked at me in astonishment. 'What are you doing? You can't just…'

'I only want a fiver. It's a gesture. It won't cover the cost of the chicken, but it'll go some way to making amends.'

Before he had chance to argue I dashed into the passage and out through the back door.

Outside Solina's gate I dithered for a moment before grasping the hand-shaped knocker and rapping it twice. I fidgeted nervously, wondering if Solina would hear above the telly. I needn't have worried; within seconds she opened the gate.

'Solina,' I stammered. 'One of your hens was loose in the *huerta* and…'

'I know, Elisa. That was this morning. Másimo caught it. It's back in the chicken run now.'

'No,' I protested. 'This was half an hour ago when I was walking Lenda. She was off her lead and she got under the fence and caught it. She ran off up the lane and she ate it round Paul's.' I held out the five euro note.

'What's that for?' she frowned.

'It's to pay for the chicken. I'm ever so sorry. I didn't realise that the fence…'

Solina laughed and shook her head. 'Elisa. Keep your money. The hens are two years old so they won't be laying much longer. They've slowed down already. We'll be killing them and buying some new ones in the new year.'

Her words took me by surprise and for a moment I fell silent, wondering if I'd misunderstood. The hens were only two, but they were already destined for the table? It didn't make sense. Solina was Javier's sister and had been born into farming. She'd probably been feeding chickens and collecting eggs since she'd first been able to walk. Surely she'd know that fertility varied according to the seasons? Hens stopped laying when they moulted in the summer and slowed down when the daylight hours declined throughout the winter months. All she had to do was be patient and her hens would be laying again in spring. I was about to proffer my theory but thought better of it. Lenda was off the hook and no more would be said about it; it made sense to quit while I was ahead.

When we settled down with our beers that evening I was still feeling shaken about the business with the chicken. I considered myself lucky that we had such reasonable neighbours and was grateful that Solina had been so kind. Gary, however, was nowhere near as understanding. He was decidedly lacking in sympathy and quick to remind me what a narrow escape I'd had.

'I should think you've learned your lesson,' he admonished. 'You'll be keeping her on the lead until she's over the fields from now on.'

Too jaded to argue, I said nothing. Despite what I'd told her earlier, Lenda was a good dog. It wasn't *her* fault she'd killed the chicken; she'd been the victim of instinct and circumstance. The chicken was loose and the fence hadn't been replaced properly and that was Másimo's responsibility, not ours. By the time they left for A Coruña tomorrow, the *huerta* would be secure and there would be no likelihood of a repeat performance. I was damned if I was going to let Gary dictate to me. And I was damned if I was going to keep Lenda on her lead.

On Monday morning I stepped out of the shower and shivered as I reached for my towel. There had been a sharp chill in the air at daybreak and it was a sure sign that autumn had truly arrived. A long, brisk walk over the five fields had been welcome after a fortnight of ambling, and now, after ten minutes under the hot water I was refreshed, enlivened and ready for the day ahead.

I was tying my laces when I heard the sound of an engine at the top of the village. It was too loud for a car, yet too smooth and steady to be a tractor. Whatever it was, it was getting closer; it couldn't be Bread Van or Shop Van because they always stopped outside the farm. I pulled on my fleece and hurried downstairs to discover the source of the invasion. Leaving Lenda safely in the passage, I slipped out of the back door and listened from the step. The noise was louder now and it seemed to be coming from behind the house. I set off round the corner of the annexe and stopped when I reached Solina's gate. A monster of a lorry was edging its way towards me and I tucked myself in against the wall. I needn't have worried. The lorry came to a halt by the waste ground under Paul's dining room window, where Paul was now standing, waving his arms. The engine stopped and the driver climbed out of the cab. He shouted and pointed, then clambered up onto the back of the lorry, out of view. Seconds later, he returned to the cab and started the engine. I watched as a winch hoisted a huge cubic sack up from the lorry and onto the ground. When two further sacks had been deposited my curiosity was sated. As I turned to go back to the house, Solina's gate clanged open and Maruja came out with Luna and Flea-pelt in tow.

'*Hola*, Elisa,' she smiled. 'It looks like Paul's having a delivery. Is he going to do some work on the house?'

She looked surprised and it was no wonder. Paul had bought his house eight years ago and had yet to earn a reputation for forays into DIY.

'No,' I grinned. 'He's building a *pista de petanca*.'

Maruja pulled a face. I couldn't quite work out whether her expression was one of bafflement or disapproval. Either way, it was unlikely she'd make sense of Paul's foibles. It was easier to change the subject than to try to explain.

'Has Másimo mended the fence around the chicken run?' I asked her.

'Yes,' she nodded, 'He did it on Sunday morning. The hens had been flying up into the plum tree. He's sawn the lower branches off and made the wire higher. They won't be escaping again.'

'That's good then,' I smiled, pleased that there would be no more embarrassing mishaps. 'Did Solina tell you about Lenda and the hen?'

'Yes,' nodded Maruja. 'It wasn't a problem – she's used to it. Pastor was always chasing them when he was a puppy. He grew out of it eventually. So will Lenda, given time.'

It wasn't so much that Lenda had *chased* the hen that bothered me, but the fact that she'd *killed* it. I had a sneaking suspicion that Solina had omitted that part of the story to spare my blushes, so I decided to keep schtum.

'He wouldn't catch one now,' Maruja continued. 'He's half blind and as deaf as a wall.'

I smiled at the idiom. It seemed strange that walls were deaf in Spanish, yet in English they had ears.

'Where is he?' I asked. I couldn't ever remember seeing Luna out and about without him, except when she was having her season and she'd been shut away.

'He isn't well, Elisa. He's not been eating much and he's lost a lot of weight. He's in the cowshed where it's warm. He has good days and bad.'

I felt saddened as I pictured dear old Pastor, with his motheaten ears and his bobbly eyes. 'He's old though, isn't he?' I said gently.

She nodded. 'We had him when José Manuel was seven, so that makes him…' she paused and thought about it. '…nearly thirteen.

'That *is* old,' I agreed. 'So José Manuel's twenty now?'

'Nearly. His birthday's next month, the eleventh of October. It's the day before *Día de la Hispanidad.* When he was little he used to say it was a lucky birthday. It was like an extra present, having the next day off school.'

'I hope it's lucky for Gary. That's when he's at the hospital. He had some problems with his stomach over the summer. It's better now, but I said he should keep the appointments just in case.'

'That's sensible. You'll be going with him, I suppose?'

I faltered. I didn't want to say that Gary had been a pain in the backside and I'd vowed not to go with him again. I'd never heard Maruja say a bad word about Javier and I was keen not to sully my reputation as a devoted village wife.

I shook my head. 'He says I fuss too much and he's right, if I'm honest. He'll stay calmer if he goes without me and I can do my worrying at home.'

'You're like me, Elisa. I worry about everything. You'd feel better knowing he could call you if there was a problem. Come up and see me before his appointment. I'll give you the number of our landline to put in his phone.'

I smiled gratefully. 'That's ever so kind of you. Thanks.'

'*De nada.* Well, I should be getting back, Elisa. I still have the calves to see to and then it will be time to make lunch.'

I was about to thank her again but was distracted by movement behind her. I gasped in delight as Hairy Fred and Splodgy poked their heads out from under the gate. It was over a month since Gary claimed to have seen three kittens under the fig tree, but I still hadn't seen Motley. I stared hopefully at the gate, wondering if I'd finally meet her today. Following my gaze, Maruja turned to look behind her. The kittens, startled by the movement, shot back under the gate.

'It was the kittens,' I laughed. 'They're lovely, aren't they?'

Maruja frowned. 'They're a nuisance. Solina says they've been shitting in the woodstore. They don't really bother her, but I'm not very keen.'

'Gary said there are three altogether, but I've only seen two.'

'There are only two left now. Ivon took one home after the fiesta. She's like you – she likes cats. It's going to live in the house.'

I smiled my approval, but it was clear that Maruja didn't like the sound of it at all.

'Solina said we could have one. I'm tempted, I must admit.'

'You wouldn't be able to get near them now, Elisa. They've grown up nervous. I've just given them some milk but they wouldn't drink it while I was standing there. They're not used to people because there's nobody here in the week.'

As I walked back to the house I thought about the kittens. Motley would have a good home with Ivon, but what would become of the others? Scholes would be five in the spring and was still an overgrown kitten. He'd enjoyed having Fred as a playmate; I wondered how Gary would feel about adopting Splodgy and Hairy Fred.

I couldn't wait for Gary to come home with the shopping. I had so much to tell him and was determined to grab his undivided attention before he disappeared with the football paper into the barn. As soon as I heard the van at the top of the village I put the kettle on for a brew. When he'd dumped the last of the carrier bags in the passage I dived in.

'Don't dash off, I'm making you a coffee.'

'I'm alright, thanks. I had one in town.'

'Honestly, Gary. *Marca* won't turn into a pumpkin before lunchtime. All I want is ten minutes, now come and sit down.'

As soon as I mentioned Paul's delivery, Gary was all ears.

'Three tonnes? You're having a laugh.'

'I kid you not. I'm surprised you didn't notice – you drove past.'

'I can't see round corners. I'll have to nip and have a look before lunch.'

'I'll look forward to hearing your verdict. Three tonnes seems excessive to me.'

'He's obviously intending to do a thorough job. Good luck to him. Hopefully I'll bump into him and get an update straight from the horse's mouth.'

'You be careful. Don't go getting us roped into his bloody party.'

'When is it?'

'October sometime. I don't think he told me the exact date.'

'Perhaps there isn't one.'

'What d'you mean?'

'Perhaps we're all going to shrivel slowly, rather than go out in one big bang.'

I shuddered. I didn't believe for one moment in all the End of the World gobbledygook, yet I still found it creepy. I was ready to change the subject. Now he'd forgotten about *Marca* it was safe to mention Splodgy and Hairy Fred.

'The kittens came out of Solina's while I was watching the delivery. They haven't half grown.'

'You've seen the motley one then?'

'No. Ivon's adopted her. She'll be a proper pet cat. I bet she'll have all her treatments. I bet she'll be spayed as well.'

'That only leaves Splodgy and Hairy Fred then. It's a shame she didn't take all three.'

'That's what I thought. There's always us though.'

'Us? But I thought you weren't interested. What's made you change your mind?'

'When Solina mentioned it back in the summer I'd just lost Fred and I was heartbroken. I was too upset to even consider another one and I hadn't given up hope that Fred would come home.'

'Is that what you want to do then – adopt Splodgy and Hairy Fred?'

'It is. It won't happen overnight though. Maruja said they've grown wild because they're not used to people. I don't know about "wild" but they're ever so skittish. It'll take a lot of time and patience to get them to trust us. I thought we could start to encourage them by feeding them every day in the barn.'

When Gary came in at lunchtime he was looking pleased with himself. It didn't take a genius to work out that he'd been round to see Paul.

'I'd have made a great detective,' he boasted. 'Not only do I have the lowdown on Paul's delivery, but I can give you an update on the pétanque court as well.'

I sighed impatiently. 'Go on.'

He cleared his throat. 'Two tonnes of coarse white sand and a tonne of fine grey gravel. *And* six sacks of cement in the courtyard as well.'

'Crikey!'

'Oh, and two new builder's buckets.'

I giggled.

'It's surprised me really. It must have cost him a bob or too. I shouldn't think he'll have had much change out of three hundred quid.'

From what we'd seen up until now, Paul definitely wasn't the last of the big spenders. Apart from his economy roof job he'd barely spent a penny on the house or garden in the last four years. Paul had been talking about his intention to build a pétanque court since we'd first had the pleasure of meeting him. Knowing that he was given to dreaming, I hadn't thought for a moment that the project would really go ahead. 'He's taking this pétanque lark pretty seriously then?'

Gary nodded. 'And it looks like it won't be a bodge job either. He's filled the hole up to six inches below the surface and now he's making it level. After that he's going to cover it with smashed up roof tiles for the hardcore. I have to say I'm impressed.'

For the next two weeks, Paul worked like a Trojan on the pétanque court. From mid-morning through to early evening the creaking and scraping of the sun lounger was replaced by a medley of rasping, sloshing, clattering and clanking as Paul mixed his concrete and trundled backwards and forwards with his barrow between the garden and the lane. Carmen spent an unusual amount of time hovering about on her doorstep, and her shortcut through Paul's land to her tiny oakwood was by far the most well-trodden it had ever been.

Sophie soon discovered the food in the barn and it wasn't long before the kittens were tucking in with her. They were hovering in the garden most mornings, scrambling up the trunk of the fig tree or running and pouncing over the lawn. Whenever I passed them I called them by their names in the hope that they'd eventually get used to me. For the time being I didn't stand a chance of handling them but I was sure that, in time, I'd win them round.

On the last Saturday in September, Gary went back to the Ghost House to see to the garden. While he was out of the way, I wore my jumper as I worked in the kitchen. It wasn't *quite* finished, but even with one sleeve and no collar it looked terrific; I was looking forward to wearing it for the End of the World.

The End of the World

The world's going to end in October,
The hour of our Judgement is near;
It'll be a momentous occasion,
So let's have some fun while we're here.

It's true, 'cos it said in the paper
(The tabloids are full of bad news),
So let's live it up while we're able;
It's better than singing the blues.

I've bought lots of cheddar from Lidl,
And stocked up with pasta and booze,
So let's get together and party;
From now on there's no time to lose.

I've built us a lovely pétanque court,
And on it we'll have so much fun;
We'll play to the death, maybe longer,
Or at least 'til the tournament's won.

You can have a rosette or a trophy,
Crack open a wine box or beer,
But please make the most of your vict'ry;
There won't be a rematch next year.

Above us the clouds are amassing,
It looks like that could be a sign,
But if they've predicted in error
Make sure that you leave me some wine.

Chapter 15

The End is Nigh

October was always such a magical month in rural Galicia. Mists hung heavy over the valley in the mornings and the sun cast its gauzy light over the village throughout the afternoons. Out in the *campo*, the pasture had been restored to its former emerald glory, and up in the oak woods the trees were a profusion of oranges, russets and golds. The forest floor was jewelled with toadstools in all manner of shapes and colours, and the pungent smell of lichens and leaf mould mingled with the fresh scents of eucalyptus and pine.

It was a fortnight since Maruja had mentioned José Manuel's birthday, and since then I'd had it in mind that I'd like to buy him a gift. Life on the farm meant there were few opportunities to socialise and little time for pursuing the kind of interests that were typical for someone of his age. Each day followed a similar pattern and I felt sure that receiving a present would add a touch of sparkle to his special day.

When we'd first moved to the *aldea*, José Manuel was a teenager. He'd been shy at first, but little by little he'd come out of his shell and we'd come to know him as the polite, cheerful and warm-hearted lad that he was. He was helpful to Carmen, gentle and patient with the animals and worked tirelessly alongside Javier around the farm. In the last four years he'd grown from a teenager into an adult. He wasn't worldly-wise or highly educated, but he was diligent, well-mannered and selfless. He'd become a young man whom Javier and Maruja could be truly proud of. Not only that, he was a competent farmer to boot.

Deciding on a suitable gift hadn't been easy. It couldn't be much; Maruja knew that we weren't well off and she'd be embarrassed if she thought I'd dipped deep into our limited funds. Books weren't too expensive, but he didn't read for pleasure. He wasn't interested in football, so I couldn't buy a mug with the logo of his favourite team. Eventually I decided I'd opt for something practical, yet personal; with winter approaching a pair of thermal socks would be just the job. As luck would have it, the first of October was a Monday. Not only was it shopping day, but it was also market day in Monterroso. The timing was perfect and I decided I'd tag along.

'White rabbits,' I smiled, when Gary came into the kitchen.

'Crikey,' he yawned. 'October already? That's soon come round.'

'Hasn't it just? Do you realise, in a fortnight we'll have had Lenda a year?'

'It doesn't seem that long, does it? It doesn't seem five minutes since Anxo...' He faltered and looked at me sadly. 'I'm sorry. I didn't think.'

I shrugged my shoulders. 'It's okay. There's not a day goes by when I don't miss him. Avoiding the subject won't make it less painful. Grief's a lot tougher than people think.' I drew hard on my cigarette. Anxo's death had affected me more deeply than I could ever have imagined. I had Lenda now, and I loved her dearly, but the bond I'd shared with Anxo would always remain.

I smiled at Gary. 'I'll cheer you up, shall I? I'm coming with you today.'

'Eh?'

'To Monterroso.'

There was no mistaking his disappointment, but I pretended not to notice when his face dropped a mile. 'There you are – I knew you'd be pleased.'

'I'm not. I mean I *am*. It's just that…'

I could see that he was struggling. Whatever he said now would only dig him deeper into the hole. I looked at him expectantly. 'Well?'

'It came as a surprise, that's all. You usually hate shopping. What's so different today?'

'It's José Manuel's birthday next week. I want to buy him a present. I thought I'd have a look round the market and get him some socks.'

His brow furrowed. 'You don't usually get him a present.'

'That's because I didn't know when his birthday was. I do now.'

'We're s'posed to be on a budget, remember?'

I glared at him. 'I could hardly forget. Listen, Gary. Maruja and Javier are good to us. They give us wood and cheese and milk and… damn it, it's not even about that. Maruja's more than a neighbour, she's my friend. She teaches me about history and customs, she finds time to answer my questions, she corrects my Castilian, she understands when…'

'Alright, alright, I get it. Just don't go spending a small fortune, okay?'

'God forbid.' I stood up to make another coffee and noticed that Gary was still frowning. I didn't have to wait long to find out why.

'I s'pose you'll be wanting to go to the Hotel Río Ulla as well?'

So that was the *real* reason for his misery-guts expression. Monterroso would be heaving with traffic; if we went to the ex-pats' get-together it would be a nightmare finding somewhere to park. I felt a twinge of guilt for misjudging him. He wasn't being a cheapskate; it all came down to his IDS.

'The ex-pats' thingy? Not likely. I feel as if I've spent the whole summer socialising. I just want to get round the market and come home.'

The change in his mood was instant and he smiled. 'It's a nice idea to buy José Manuel a present. How old will he be, nineteen?'

'Twenty. Unbelievable, isn't it? He's old enough to marry, yet how is he ever going to find a wife?'

'I hadn't thought of that. It won't be easy. He only ever goes as far as Monterroso to sell his honey and do the shopping. Actually, he's a bit like you.'

I nodded meekly. 'You're right. The thing is, Gary, I'm at my happiest here in the village. I only promised to make the effort to get out more for your sake. I felt guilty that you were missing out.'

'You should have said so. I was worried it might become a regular thing, all that visiting people and having them over. It's alright once in a blue moon but I prefer it when it's just us and the animals. I'm quite content digging the garden and chopping wood.'

When we settled down with our beers that evening I took the birthday socks out of my rucksack to wrap them up.

'Ah, the socks,' said Gary. 'Can I have a look?'

I handed the three-pack over. They were a chunky wool and acrylic blend with Fair Isle patterns in greys, blues and browns. They'd be perfect with work boots or wellies and I was sure José Manuel would be thrilled to bits. Gary gave them a good squeeze.

'They'll be great,' he nodded. 'It was good thinking on your part to get a three-pack. It'll save me a job.'

I looked at him puzzled. 'A job? What do you mean?'

'Darning. I'm ready for some new socks – all mine are in holes. A pair for José Manuel and two for me. Which colours can I have?'

I couldn't believe what I was hearing. There was me thinking I'd done him an injustice earlier. Three pairs of socks had cost me a fiver; Gary was being a miserly devil after all.

'None, sorry. I'm wrapping the pack as it is. If you wanted socks you should have said so. You can get some at the market next month.'

I was up long before dawn on the eleventh of October. My heart was adrift on a sea of emotions; my thoughts writhed and twisted somewhere above me, like snakes on a Gorgon's head. I needed coffee; I needed a cigarette; but above all I needed silent contemplation. It was Anxo's anniversary and Gary's endoscopy appointment. I was consumed with grief, love, fear and anxiety, and I knew I'd have to dig deep to do battle with the day ahead.

As the sun began to cast its pale rays over the valley I went out into the garden. When I'd let out the rabbits and the chickens I knelt down beside Anxo's grave. He'd been a fun-loving dog and I was always convinced he had a sense of humour. He wouldn't want to see me moping, so I chuckled as I told him about Lenda and Solina's hen.

Back in the kitchen I rolled another cigarette and considered my next hurdle. I'd felt so embarrassed during Gary's first appointment and I'd meant it when I'd told him I had no intention of accompanying him again. A month had passed since then and my stance had mellowed, though only slightly. Was I being unreasonable by not going with him today?

At a quarter to nine I heard Gary stirring. I wondered how he'd manage to kill time without a cuppa; his appointment was at eleven thirty and he wouldn't have to leave until ten.

After half an hour he was becoming twitchy. It was almost nine-thirty when he said, 'I think I'll go. I'll be early but at least I'll be able to buy a paper. It's no fun sitting here watching you drink coffee. It'll be easier if I've got something to do.'

'Alright,' I nodded. 'You've got your medical card, haven't you?'

'Yes.'

'And the phone?'

'Yes.'

'And you know I've put Maruja's number in it?'

'*Yes*. Look, Liza, I'll be okay – it's *you* I'm worried about. You'll be sitting here getting yourself all worked up about nothing. I think you might feel better if you came.'

His words were transparent and I bristled. He wanted me with him but was too stubborn to ask. Well, two could play at that game; if he couldn't ask me outright I wasn't prepared to give in.

'I'm fine,' I said airily. 'I haven't got time to go gadding off to Lugo. I want to take José Manuel's present and then there's the apples to see to. Once I get started I won't have time to fret.'

As the van screeched out of the village, I felt guilty. Secretly, I'd have liked to have gone with Gary to support him and I was certain that he would have liked me to be there to translate. We'd reached an impasse and regardless of what we were really feeling, neither one of us was prepared to back down. Since Gary's appetite had come back and his behaviour had returned to normal it had been easy to forget how unwell he'd been in the summer. I wasn't expecting the endoscopy to show up any problems, but if it did… I could only imagine how bad it would be for him if he was stuck in Lugo having to shoulder the bad news on his own. He was right, I *did* worry, but I'd been far too proud to give in.

At half past ten, I set off up to the farmhouse. Luna was lying by the doorstep but there was no sign of Pastor. She looked up from her dozing and thumped her tail when I reached over to ring the bell. Javier would still be milking, but José Manuel kept the tradition of stopping for his *merienda* of coffee and biscuits. It might be his twentieth birthday, but Maruja adored him and indulged him like an overgrown kid.

When Maruja opened the door her face lit up when she spotted the present.

'*Hola*, Elisa,' she beamed. 'Is that for José Manuel?'

I nodded and smiled as I handed it over. 'It's not much, but I think he'll like it. Men are hard to buy for at the best of times, and twenty's such an awkward age.'

Maruja smiled. 'I know what you mean. He isn't a child anymore but he's not quite a man either. We've given him money and he can spend it how he likes. He'll be back for *merienda* any minute, you can join him for coffee. Come on inside.'

I shook my head. 'I'd like to, but I've got so much to do while Gary's at the hospital. I want to get the cleaning done and cook something nice for his lunch.'

'I saw him go off this morning. I haven't been out to collect the eggs yet in case he rings.'

'Thanks,' I said gratefully. 'I'm struggling for eggs at the moment. I'm lucky if I get three a day. The hens slowed down in summer when they were moulting and they've not picked up again since.'

'They won't do, Elisa. They're too old. They're the same ones you had when you moved here, aren't they?'

'Yes. We bought them that first February. They're only about three.'

Maruja sighed. 'There you are then. They're old. We kill ours when they're two. Solina does the same with hers. You're better to kill them now and buy some more before winter. By the new year you'll have plenty of eggs again.'

As I walked back down the lane I pondered on what Maruja had told me. I still wasn't convinced that my hens had given up laying. With the shorter daylight hours it wasn't surprising that the egg count was feeble. I resolved to let them rest through autumn and winter and see how they fared in the spring.

It was getting on for half past two when Gary arrived home from the hospital.

'I could eat the back out of a sofa,' he announced as he came through the door.

'You'll be having nothing until I've heard how you got on with your appointment. Sit down and tell me what happened. I've made you rabbit stew with dumplings. By the time you've given me all the details it'll be warmed through.'

'Well, I arrived early, so I went for a coffee before I put my card in the machine. It's a nice cafeteria. The *menú del día* looked good value for money. There was...'

'Gary. I couldn't give a shit about the menu. I want to hear about you.'

'It wasn't as bad as I was expecting, put it that way. I had to lie on the bed and the nurse sprayed the back of my throat with some stuff. The doctor poked a tube down my throat and at first I thought I was going to vomit. The doctor said not to worry, that was just a reflex, and once the tube was in my stomach I was fine.'

'So then what?'

'It lasted about fifteen or twenty minutes, I reckon. I was glad it wasn't much longer – I was dying for a fag. Anyway, he said that from what he could see on the screen, everything seems normal. Later he'll look at it more closely with another doctor. If there's a problem I'll know within the fortnight, and the same for the biopsy results.'

'They did a biopsy? Shit, Gary, he doesn't think…' My voice trailed off as I summoned up the courage to say the word.

'He doesn't think what? Spit it out.'

'That it might be cancer?'

To my surprise, Gary laughed. 'Don't be stupid. It's just routine.'

'And he said that did he? You understood?'

He nodded. 'It was a different nurse this time, a young one. She spoke really good English and the doctor asked her to translate. She said it's usual to take a biopsy because while they're down there they might as well.'

I raised my eyebrows. 'They might as well' didn't sound much like medical speak to me. I reached for my tobacco. 'So when will you have the results?'

'It'll take a while. It'll go to the lab to be analysed, and unless there's something urgent they'll give me the results on the same day as the results of the scan.'

'The *scan*?'

'Yes. You know, where you lie on a conveyor belt that goes into a tunnel and…'

'I know what a bloody scan is, Gary. It's starting to sound a bit drastic. Why does he want you to have one, did he say?'

'It's to make sure there's nothing wrong with the surrounding organs. He said it's just to be on the safe side. There're things that can affect your stomach that are somewhere else in your digestive system, or something like that. So, if they don't find anything serious I'll get the results of the endoscopy and the scan together. It could be as late as December. I'm beginning to wish I hadn't kept the appointment. At this rate it'll be dragging on for months.'

My heart went out to him. 'Poor you. At least they're being thorough. So far it all sounds very positive. I've got a feeling they won't find anything. I still think it was down to the heat.'

'I'm sure they won't. I've been eating apples every day since they've been falling. I should have been a doctor. I think I've cured it myself.'

Over the next week, Gary continued to eat his apples and seemed unperturbed by the prospect of his ongoing investigations. There were jobs to be done in the garden and he set about them as though there was nothing wrong at all. He pulled up the squash and courgette plants and gave the lawn its final strim before winter. He dug cow muck into the raised beds and raked the dried leaves beneath the chestnut trees, ready for the first prickly cases to fall.

On Thursday morning, Gary was waiting on the doorstep when I came back from the fields with Lenda. He was holding an envelope and wearing a troubled expression. It was only a week since the endoscopy, but word from the hospital had arrived.

'I waited for you,' he mumbled. 'I thought you'd want to be here when I opened it.'

'Okay,' I nodded. 'Let's go inside.'

Back in the kitchen I looked on anxiously as Gary tore open the envelope. He unfolded the letter and peered at it for ages. Eventually he started to grin.

'I'm invited to a Bonfire Party. How does the rhyme go? Remember, remember, the fifth of November?'

I looked at him blankly.

'Ten-thirty, Monday the fifth of November – it's the appointment for the scan.'

I began to walk over to hug him when he suddenly leapt up from the bench. 'Hold on, you've had some cards and a massive parcel. I forgot because of the letter. I've left them in the barn.'

When Gary came in at breaktime I was squeezing my parcel. I looked up and saw that he was wearing a grin.

'Hey up,' I laughed. 'What's tickled you?'

'The Apocalypse must be imminent. Paul's already out playing pétanque.'

We hadn't seen much of Paul since he'd finished the pétanque court, but the repetitive thud of the balls hitting the gravel could be heard for hour upon hour in the afternoons. We were over halfway through October and there had been no further mention of the party. The clock was ticking and Paul would have to get his skates on if he was going to make his announcement in time for the End of the World.

'You're probably right,' I nodded. 'He doesn't usually surface this early. What shall we do if we're invited? We'll need to come up with an excuse.'

'Perhaps we should go if he asks us? It'd look rude if we didn't, we're neighbours after all.'

I grimaced. 'You can if you want to, but I'm digging my heels in on this one. I have to be honest, Gary – I think the whole thing's really twisted. If you ask me there's something downright sinister about celebrating the End of the World.'

'I don't know about sinister. Downright miserable's how I would've described it. I can't see any pleasure in drinking beer in that dark, damp courtyard or standing freezing outside in October playing pétanque.'

I shuddered. Gary was right. It *would* be freezing outside and it would probably be even colder in Paul's courtyard. Although our reasons differed it was clear we were of the same opinion. We'd be giving the Doomsday knees-up a wide berth.

I started to smile. 'He can't *really* believe the world's going to end though. For a start, he wouldn't have put so much time into building the pétanque court if the first tournament was going to be the last.'

'True. And if he's invested in enough pasta to feed the five thousand...'

'P'raps he's hoping everybody'll be starving on the night.'

When Gary came in at lunchtime he was grinning again.

'Crikey,' I said. 'Are you going for a hat-trick?'

'You what?'

'You look like you're bringing more news.'

'I am, as it happens. I know when the End of the World is. You'll never guess?'

I shrugged my shoulders. 'Halloween?'

'No. Guess again.'

'Gary. Just *tell* me. And stop hovering, will you, you look like an overexcited kid.'

'You can talk. You've been feeling that present all morning. Actually that's a clue.'

'What is? Oh no, not my birthday? This Sunday? I don't know whether that's a good sign or an omen. The world's going to end on my birthday – imagine that.'

'It's worked in our favour really. We'll just tell him it's your birthday and we've already made plans.'

'Perfect. That's sorted then. What do you think's in this parcel? Here, do you want a squeeze?'

On the eve of my birthday it was nearly dusk when I grabbed my coat off the peg in the passage. Once I'd shut the chickens and rabbits away and showered, I'd be ready for my birthday countdown to begin. I was about to open the door, when Lenda started barking. I paused and listened; sure enough, there were footsteps coming down the lane. I wasn't expecting visitors and, as far as I was aware, none of the ex-pats knew that it was my birthday. Who on earth could it be at this time of night? I wondered if it was Paul, coming to persuade us to go to the party, but then I heard Flea-pelt yapping and Maruja's voice calling, 'Elisa!' I shut Lenda in the kitchen and opened the back door.

Out in the lane, Maruja was standing beside a wheelbarrow. Inside was a feed sack, half full and tied up halfway with twine.

'*Hola*, Elisa,' she smiled. '*Feliz cumpleaños*. It's tomorrow isn't it? I've brought you some potatoes.' She glanced round nervously, before leaning towards me. 'Don't say anything to Javier or José Manuel.'

'Thank you,' I murmured. I fumbled for a better phrase to convey my gratitude. The gift was so generous, so thoughtful, yet beyond my feeble 'thank you' I was lost for words.

She hoisted the sack from the barrow and plonked it down in the lane. 'Keep them somewhere dark,' she told me, 'and if they start chitting, cut the eyes out. They'll last longer that way.'

'It's so kind of you,' I said. 'It's a big sackful. Are you sure you can spare them all?'

'I'm sure. They've done well this year. They haven't had mildew. We'll have more than enough to last us the year.'

I was about to thank her again, but she leaned over and touched my arm. 'Take them in now, Elisa. If

Carmen comes by she'll see them. She'd be bound to tell Javier – you know what she's like.'

I nodded. I'd be the first to admit that I was nosy, but Carmen's snooping went far beyond curiosity. With little to occupy her beyond the ducks and chickens and the *finca*, she was always on the lookout for a bit of gossip and couldn't be trusted to keep schtum. I grabbed hold of the neck of the sack and heaved it inside the passage. With a firm shove from my work boot it was secreted safely behind the back door.

When I returned to the doorstep, Maruja had already grabbed hold of the barrow. 'I'll have to go now, Elisa. Javier and José Manuel are over the fields and I'm expecting the slaughterman. We lost a cow in the night.'

'Oh no,' I said sadly. 'How?'

'She went into labour and the calf was stuck. It was a big one and we couldn't turn it. We called the vet out, but by the time he arrived the cow and the calf were both dead. Maybe she haemorrhaged, maybe she was just exhausted – we'll never know.'

'I'm so sorry,' I said, and meant it.

'That's farming, Elisa. It could have been worse – it could have been one of the younger cows. At least this one was old.'

I wasn't sure what constituted old as far as cows went. I wondered if it was roughly the same as cats and dogs. 'As old as Pastor?'

'Almost. Ten, maybe eleven.'

'Oh.'

'They usually make fifteen,' she continued, 'but after eight or nine their seasons slow down. She didn't have many more breeding years left in her. It would probably have been her last calf.'

I couldn't help but feel a pang of sadness. It didn't do to get sentimental about livestock, but it wasn't only the loss of life that made me sorry. From Javier and

Maruja's point of view, losing a cow meant losing money, and I doubted that anyone would want to buy ten-year-old meat.

'What will happen to her now?' I asked. 'Will you eat her yourselves?'

Maruja chuckled. 'No Elisa. She's far too old to be eaten. She'll go for *polvo* instead.'

'Powder?' I echoed, wondering if I'd misheard.

'Listen,' said Maruja. 'The meat's no good for people but it's fine for pet food. They dry the meat and process it into a powder. That's how *piensos* are made.'

I nodded my understanding. I'd often wondered where the 'meat' in Scholes' and Lenda's kibble came from; now I knew.

'Have a good day tomorrow,' she smiled, as she started off up the lane. She'd only gone a few paces when she turned back and looked at me. 'And don't forget, Elisa, you really should kill those hens.'

When we settled down with our beers that evening I told Gary what Maruja had said about the hens.

'So what are you going to do?' he asked me. 'If she's right and they're past it, killing them would make sense.'

'I know,' I nodded. 'But the thing is, Gary, I'm not sure she *is* right. The chickens I kept in England carried on laying on and off until they died.'

'There you go then. It'll be the same with these.'

'It might not though. Mine were bantams.'

'Surely a hen's a hen?'

I shook my head. 'All breeds are different. The Galician sort don't go broody, remember? Perhaps there are other differences too.'

'What're you going to do then?'

'I'm not sure yet. I need time to think.'

When we went to bed that night I lay awake for a while, pondering my dilemma. It wasn't that I had a problem with killing the livestock; the whole point of keeping them was to produce meat. I'd skinned, gutted and butchered goodness knows how many rabbits and I hadn't batted an eyelid when I'd asked Gary to kill the cockerels, even though I'd reared them from chicks. The hens were a different matter entirely. They'd served us well and up until now I hadn't given any thought to eating them; their job was simply to lay eggs.

Since our disastrous first year with the *huerta* we'd made it our rule of thumb to copy whatever the neighbours did. There had been times when their practices hadn't made sense to us but their knowledge had been passed down through countless generations; they were the experts and it made sense to follow their lead. If they knew what was best for the vegetables then the same must hold true for the livestock. I was beginning to think Maruja was right about the chickens, and as I drifted off to Dreamland I came up with a way to make absolutely sure.

When I came down to the kitchen on Sunday morning, I had seven cards and a very big parcel to open. I stuck the kettle on the hob and reached for my tobacco. My birthday wouldn't be starting for at least an hour. I needed coffee and a cigarette *and* I had a hungry menagerie to feed.

A month had passed since I'd started feeding the kittens. Sophie had been spending less and less time with them and now they were waiting every morning on the log stack in the barn. For the past three days, Splodgy had stood nearby, watching as I'd put the food down, but she'd wait until I was standing well back before she'd let down her guard and eat. This morning, as she bent over the food bowl, I edged forward and watched her closely. It was the first time I'd had chance to study her carefully; she had the prettiest calico markings I'd ever seen. There was a zig zag dividing the ginger and black along the length of her spine line and she had the colouring of a Bengal tiger, but with patterning reminiscent of an exotic snake. When she looked up momentarily from her breakfast, I noticed that her face had almost perfect negative symmetry; half black and half ginger extending from her white jaw, over both ears and the top of her head. If that wasn't special enough, her most unusual and endearing feature was a pronounced kink resulting in a question mark tail.

'Look at you,' I told her fondly. 'You're as pretty as a princess.'

She looked at me and miaowed the strangest, sweetest, 'eek-eek', before sloping shyly away.

Over in Warren Place, Doe's babies were eating like billy-o and growing accordingly. It was hard to believe they were already six weeks old. At the end of the month, four of the nine would need to be moved into the Death Row pens to avoid overcrowding in Doe's run.

Down in the chooks' pen, Waynetta and Humbug had continued to lay daily, but I was still collecting only one or two eggs from the older hens. If I took Maruja's advice I'd have less eggs than ever, but would that really be a problem? This was the time of year for stews, hotpots, broths and curries. If I bought some young hens from the market, omelettes and tortillas would be back on the menu when normal service was resumed in the spring.

It was almost an hour later when Gary came into the kitchen.

'Morning,' I smiled as I passed him his cuppa.

'Morning,' he yawned. 'Oh, and happy birthday as well. Sorry I haven't got you anything, but…'

'No problem. I wasn't expecting anything. This'll surprise you though – you're taking me out instead.'

'For a beer?'

'No, a coffee. I want to go to Cafe-Bar Olga after lunch. I'll check if I've had any birthday messages and I can find out about Galician hens.'

'That's a good idea. I hadn't thought of the internet. So if Maruja's right, what will you do?'

'Kill them. Or rather *you* will. Then we'll get some more from the market next month.'

'Fair enough. What was in the parcel from your mum?'

'A knitting pattern, some yarn and a big bag of stuffing to make hedgehogs. They look really good on the picture, here, have a look.' I passed the pattern over and waited while he fumbled for his glasses.

'Ooh,' he said eventually. 'That's clever, they're all glittery. It makes them look spiky. Let's have a look at the wool.'

I passed him a ball.

'Crikey. It's not like wool, is it? It's like tinsel. Won't it be hard to knit with?'

I grinned. 'Probably. I'm sure I'll crack it though. There's a couple of things on the pattern I'm not sure about but I'll look it up on YouTube later on.'

'You'll get there. You've done a great job with your jumper. It's a shame we're not going to the party – you could have worn it then.'

'I thought I might wear it when Ron and Miranda come. Miranda doesn't know I've been knitting and... Shit! I've not told you, have I? Hold on, where's the card?' I rifled through the pile and pulled out a card with sheep on. 'Listen to this. "We're going to visit my niece in Santiago for *Todos Santos*. It falls on a Thursday so there's a *puente* to make it a long weekend. We wondered if it would be okay to drop in on you on the way back. We'd arrive on Sunday but we'd only be able to stay two nights. Send me a text message and let me know." Are you pleased?'

''Course I am, but I haven't got a clue when they're coming. When's *Todos Santos*? Is it Halloween?'

'The day after. Halloween means All Saints' Eve, so All Saints Day is November the first.'

'I've got you. It's the big one where they put loads of flowers in the churchyard. And don't they do something weird with chestnuts up in the woods?'

I giggled. 'Well remembered. They do that the day after, on the second. That's *Día de los Difuntos* – it's Anxo's birthday as well. There's nothing weird about it, they leave chestnuts out to feed the dead.'

'And you don't think there's anything weird about that? You're turning Galician. Come to think about it, you're nearly as bad as Paul.'

'Bugger off. I'm not bonkers. Anyway, back to Ron and Miranda. If they're coming on Sunday that'll be the fourth and… damn! They'll only be here one full day and that's when you go for your scan!'

'You're joking. That's a nuisance. Still, the appointment's at half past ten. I won't be gone more than three hours. I should be back by one.'

When I went to shut the livestock away that evening, there was shouting and laughter coming from the garden of number ten. The master of ceremonies was whooping and cheering and doing a great job in motivating the competitors. The End of the World didn't matter; the pétanque court was a roaring success.

Wayne and his wives were already roosting when I closed the door to the henhouse. The six Galician hens had no idea that their day of judgement was coming; after tonight they'd never be roosting again.

When A Cow Dies

Estela the cow was expecting;
She went into labour at dawn,
The herd waited now for Dolores,
To hear if the calf had been born.

'Estela collapsed,' said Dolores,
'The calf was stuck edgeways inside,
The vet came and tried hard to save her,
But she and her baby both died.'

The rest of the herd started weeping
'She was everyone's friend,' said Belén.
'I just can't believe that we've lost her
And won't ever see her again.'

Inés said, 'I miss her already,
She's only been gone a few hours.'
Said Luz, 'she'll be happily grazing
On grass so much sweeter than ours.'

'It's true,' said Dolores. 'Don't worry.
It doesn't all end when you die;
Your spirit goes up into Heaven
To graze in a field in the sky.

At first there's a bridge to walk over,
A rainbow shines brightly above,
And when you've crossed over it safely
You'll find only kindness and love.'

'My word,' said Belén, 'it sounds lovely.
In fact I can picture it now;
Green pasture forever in sunshine,
A beautiful place for a cow.'

Chapter 16

A Prickly Subject

When I awoke on Monday morning, I wiggled my toes and fingers, then blinked to be doubly certain. There was no doubt about it; I was still alive. Not only that, but I was a year older and there was much to be thankful for. We'd be having chicken dinners throughout the autumn, while Paul would be living on pasta for months to come.

'Morning,' I smiled, when Gary came into the kitchen.

'Morning,' he yawned. 'So much for Doomsday. Do you still want me to kill the chickens today?'

'Yes please. I've only opened the hutches and the maternity wing this morning. I thought you could see to the hen house while I'm over the fields with Lenda. If you pull the door ajar, you'll be able to stick your arm in and grab a hen at a time. Just make sure you don't kill Waynetta, Humbug or Wayne.'

'Hold on a minute. You want me to do *all* of them today?'

'Yes. Hens aren't like rabbits, they're much more sensitive. If you do a couple at a time the rest will be traumatised. They'll be pacing round the enclosure wondering when it's their turn.'

'Don't be ridiculous. It's because you're fond of them. You're scared that if we don't get it over with...' he stopped and grinned at me.

'What?'

'You'll chicken out.'

'Trust you. You're not funny. I'll start the plucking while you're out shopping. You can take over when you get back, while I cook the lunch.'

'Will it be chicken?'

'Obviously. Unless you want to go and eat pasta round Paul's.'

'That's mean. Poor devil went to all that trouble getting ready to hide folks in his bunker...'

'What bunker?'

'The one underneath the pétanque court. You saw how deep he was digging. It was all a cover-up – there's a fallout shelter underneath.'

'And you called *me* ridiculous. Hey, there's a thought. Now the tournament's over he'll be looking for another contest – you know how competitive he is, and it just so happens it's that time of year.'

'I'm not with you. *What* time of year?'

I grinned at him. 'Autumn? October?'

He frowned for a moment, then groaned. 'Chestnuts. Oh *no*. Not again.'

The previous year, Paul had returned to Galicia especially to collect his chestnuts so he could take them back to England to be sold. The trouble was, he'd made it his business to collect everyone else's as well. Gary had explained to him that every chestnut tree belonged to someone, but Paul had ignored the warning. For over a fortnight he'd skulked about the woodlands performing a weird stooping and stamping ritual before stuffing his booty into his bag. In the meantime, Gary had been on a similar mission; for a handsome euro a kilo he'd be selling his chestnuts closer to home. Once Paul had caught wind of this he'd insisted on turning the activity into a foraging face-off. He'd thrown down the gauntlet to Gary and, come hell or high water, he was determined to win. Gary, however, had wanted no part in the contest; his sole objective had been to boost our rapidly dwindling funds.

It occurred to me that we still didn't know whether Paul had managed to sell his chestnuts. I was about to say so when Gary groaned again.

'Now what?' I frowned.

'Paul. If he collects them again this year he won't be taking them back to England, will he?'

'No. 'Course not. He'll want to sell them here.'

'Exactly. And he won't know where to take them because he hasn't bothered to learn any Spanish. He needn't think he's tagging along with me.'

'He won't do. He's too stubborn. He'll probably ask you where to take them and drive over himself.'

'I'm hoping it's the same place as last year – it was easy for parking. We won't know 'til the sign goes up at the garage. I'll check on the way home today.'

'It won't be up yet. The chestnuts are late this year. The ones that have fallen are tiny. They won't be worth collecting for at least a week.'

'That won't stop Paul. He'll be like a man possessed once he gets started, you mark my words.'

By the afternoon, the first of the hens was no more than a carcass and her sisters had been laid to rest in the freezer. The chooks' pen seemed bare with only Wayne, Waynetta and Humbug in the main enclosure and I was already looking forward to market day when I'd be able to replenish the flock. The sun's rays offered little in the way of warmth as they filtered through the spindly branches of the damson trees. The mists of early morning had left the air damp and clingy, but in the maternity wing, the chicks were tucked snugly beneath trusty Mrs Brown.

Back in the house, I took my knitting parcel up to the living room. While the sun radiated through the two large windows it would be a pleasanter workspace than the kitchen or the bench out in the lane. As I began to cast on the stitches, I was intrigued by the texture of my latest yarn. The ply was rough and twine-like, yet the wisps of spangly fibre gave it a soft and fluffy effect. It was surprisingly easy to work with and, after only half an hour, I was already into my stride. As I clicked away, I thought about Gary. As from tomorrow he'd be starting to collect the chestnuts. Progress would be slow at first; he'd spend hours out in the autumn chill, painstakingly working through the prickly cases for the few that had made a decent size. Then, over the next fortnight, the yield would improve and he'd be out with his bucket whatever the weather, with only a day's respite next week when he'd drive over to the Ghost House to strim the lawn. He wasn't the only one who worked hard, but he was the one that brought in the money. Over the past two years, it had been Gary who had been out earning a crust to keep the wolf from the door. I was grateful of course, but I also felt guilty. Not only that, but my lack of contribution left a dent in my pride. As the body of the hedgehog began to take shape, so did a marvellous idea. If the hedgehogs looked as good as the one on the pattern, I could knit dozens and eventually perhaps I could sell them on a market stall. I wouldn't mention it to Gary just yet; he'd be sure to tell me I was deluded. I'd keep the idea to myself for the time being, but it had all the makings of a splendid plan.

When I called Gary in at breaktime on Tuesday morning he looked frozen to the marrow. The way he curled his fingers gratefully around his Man United mug told me I'd have to be lighting the range sometime soon.

'How'd you get on?' I asked him.

'Not bad,' he nodded. 'A couple of kilos. I reckon we'll do alright this year, once the big ones start to fall.'

I giggled.

'What?'

'I was thinking about last year when you went to sell them. Remember the woman who left with her tail between her legs because she'd hidden a load of tiddlers in her sack?'

He grinned. 'How could I forget? It was priceless. She won't dare come back this year. The way folks were looking at her you'd have thought she'd sprouted horns. Paul's as bad though. I've been watching him from inside the chooks' pen. He's been picking up every chestnut that's fallen. And he's been doing that bloody dance again.'

'Did he see you?'

'Oh yes. I made a point of waving to him and shouting "Good morning". He'll be panicking like mad now he knows I'm collecting mine.'

'You rotter. I'd lay money on it he'll be round before the week's out. He'll be dying to know how you're getting on.'

As it happened it was only a matter of hours before Paul paid us a visit. At teatime he turned up on the doorstep. I was feeling mischievous and greeted him with a smile.

'Is Gary about?' he asked me.

I shook my head. 'He's weighing his chestnuts in the barn.'

Paul's face dropped a mile. 'Is he selling them today?'

'Don't be daft. They're nowhere near big enough. I was pulling your leg.'

His relief was visible, but then he frowned. 'Not big enough? What do you mean?'

'I mean they're only tiddlers. You'll find the odd one that's a decent size but that's about all.'

'I'd have to disagree with you there. I've found plenty. That's what I've come to see you about actually. I need to ask you about the trees.'

He'd lost me. 'The trees?'

'Yes. The chestnut trees around the village. Which ones can't I pick from? Now I'm living here permanently I don't want to cause offence.'

A wave of shame came over me. It seemed he wasn't here to play duelling chestnuts after all.

'Well,' I began, 'the best thing I can do is tell you about the trees surrounding the village. If you avoid those that the neighbours will be picking from you should be alright.' I stepped out into the lane. 'See down the track?'

Paul nodded.

'All the trees along there, right up to the glade at the top of the hill, belong to people in the village. You need to avoid them at all costs.'

Paul nodded again.

'The trees in this corner field...' I pointed past the barn, 'and the field behind the *río* – they're out of bounds as well. Oh, and the one at the top of the village near the wheelie bin – that's Hilda's, so Antonio picks them. Beyond that, you should be sound.'

'Right-o. And what about the ones along the roadside? Last year Gary said I had to be careful with those.'

'You do, but it's quite straightforward. If the trees border somebody's field or *finca*, then obviously you don't go over the boundary. It's better to avoid verges and grassy areas as well, to be on the safe side. All the *carreteras* are public, so you can pick up any that have fallen on the pavement or the road.'

'Thank you,' he smiled. 'That should be easy enough to remember. What about the trees up in the woods?'

'Crikey,' I frowned. 'Now *that's* a difficult question. There are grey areas, you see – even the Galicians themselves have trouble sorting it out.' I thought about it for a moment. All the trees belonged to someone, but that didn't necessarily mean that the owners were still around. There were families in Bilbao, Madrid, Barcelona… Some even lived as far away as Argentina and others, of course, were dead.

'Let's see,' I said eventually. 'You should be okay in the woods beyond the track – I've never seen anyone up there. Keep your eyes and ears open and if you *are* unlucky enough to get caught, look remorseful and say you didn't mean to molest anybody and…'

'*Par*don?'

'Just tell them you're sorry and sling your hook.'

Paul thanked me again and I was about to go back into the house when a thought occurred to me. 'Paul?'

'Yes?'

'We never did ask you, what happened with the chestnuts you took back last year? Did you get a good price for them?'

Paul shook his head. 'You wouldn't believe the attitude of people. They all want something for nothing these days. The man on the fruit and veg stall wasn't interested and I've spent a fortune with him over the years.'

'Miserable git. Did he say why?'

'Oh yes. He had an excuse ready. He said he used to do well with chestnuts years ago, but people stopped buying them once those portable roasting carts appeared.'

I nodded. I could remember the hot chestnut wagons he was talking about. They used to do rather well on the market in my hometown. They would appear at the beginning of December and vanish without a trace after Christmas Eve. I also remembered that they'd been rather pricey and I'd never forked out for their wares.

'Aren't they expensive?' I asked.

'Extortionate. Two pound fifty for half a dozen.'

'No way! That's more than forty pence a chestnut! You're having a laugh.'

'It's the truth. And people were *buying* them. If I'd have set up a table I'm sure I could have sold mine for two pounds a kilo. But you can't do that though, you have to have a permit.'

'So what did you do?'

'I told him he could have the lot for fifty pounds. He'd have been getting a bargain, of course, but he was determined to stick to his guns. I didn't want to take them all the way home with me – I'd already taken the best ones out for myself – so I said, "Look, I'll leave them with you and you can give me what you think's fair if you manage to sell them." You know, like sale or return.'

I nodded. 'So what happened?'

'I went back the next week. There wasn't a sign of a chestnut on the stall, but he was adamant he hadn't sold them. He told me he'd had to throw them away because they'd gone soft.'

'So you didn't get anything for them at all?'

'Not a bean.'

I giggled.

Paul frowned. 'It wasn't funny.'

'Sorry. I wasn't laughing about the money. You said "bean" and it was the veg stall, you see? So what did you do?'

'Nothing. There was nothing I *could* do really. You live and learn.'

I tutted and shook my head. 'We *told* you to sell them here, but you wouldn't have it. They were paying a euro a kilo. More fool you.'

'I know that now. I suppose I was being greedy. It won't happen this year, I'll take them to the place that Gary goes to. I saw him collecting his down in your chicken run this morning. Ask him to give me a nod when he goes to sell them won't you?'

'Okay,' I nodded. The visit wasn't solely about being a good citizen after all.

On the following Monday, Gary was smiling when he came home with the shopping. He tossed my copy of *El Progreso* onto the marble surface and said, 'I have news.'

'Don't tell me,' I grinned. 'The poster's up.'

'It is. It starts this Friday. Same time and place as last year.'

'Splendid. Will you be ready by then?'

'That depends on what you call "ready". If you mean will I have an amount worth selling, then yes, I should think so. I reckon I've got about forty kilos so far, but they're not all big ones. If I take the smallest out for the freezer I reckon I might have about thirty kilos at a push.'

'Brilliant. It'll cover the cost of the treats for when Ron and Miranda come.'

'Treats?'

'Yes. I thought we could choose some goodies from the market next Thursday. Chorizo, cheeses, perhaps a bit of wild boar pâté…'

'They won't have that at the market. I've only ever seen it at the *artesano* fair.'

'Yes, but it won't be the normal market, will it? It'll be the big November one, with the stalls going all the way down the back streets behind Plaza Antonio Rojo. There'll be coaches coming from all over because it's the big cattle sale as well.'

'Forget it.'

'Pardon?'

'I said you can forget it. I'm not even going to attempt to...'

'You won't have to.'

'What d'you mean, I won't have to? You don't even know what I was going to say.'

'Oh, but I do. "I'm not even going to attempt to park in Monterroso on market day. It'll be a nightmare." Am I right?'

He grimaced. 'More or less.'

'Well the fact is, Gary, you won't need to park in the town centre. You can do what you always do – drive straight through Monterroso and park round the back of the hotel.'

'You want to go to the hotel as well?'

'No. I didn't *say* that. We can park there because it's easy, then walk the five minutes back into town.'

'For the sake of a piece of cheese and a tub of pâté? That's ridiculous. In fact it's as stupid as Paul biking all the way to Lidl for his cheddar. I don't know which one of you is worse.'

'I take it that's a no then? Please yourself. It's no skin off my nose, I was thinking of our visitors. I'm sure they'll be just as happy with luncheon meat and processed cheese.'

I set my face in a pout and reached for my tobacco, while Gary stomped out to the barn to sulk over *Marca* until lunch. Once his chicken and mushroom pie was warming through in the oven, I sat down at the marble surface and began to thumb through the local rag. The ambulance-chasing reporters usually had no shortage of tragedies to write about in the autumn; chestnut feuds and hunting accidents made it a newsworthy time of the year. As I turned the pages, keeping my eyes peeled for seasonal disasters, a piece on the November market in Monterroso caught my eye. According to the feature, *A Feira dos Santos* dates all the way back to the Middle Ages, when fish traders, brandy merchants, and muleteers passed through the area on their arduous trek from the coast all the way to Castile. The feature explained that the market had since been heralded by the Galician tourist board as the best *feira* of the region, boasting seasonal products, cheeses, chestnuts, honey, meat products and sweets, as well as fifty octopus stalls distributed throughout the town. The best examples of Galicia's *rubia galega* cattle could be found on the showground, along with traditional musical performances and further gastronomic delights. The article left me more determined than ever that we should drive over to Monterroso on Thursday. I knew that I was in for an uphill battle; for the third year running Gary was being a party pooper and he wasn't going to give in without a fight.

On the thirty-first of October I brought the humdinger of a pumpkin in from the garden. I was going to work my magic better than any Fairy Godmother. I wasn't about to wave a wand and transform it into a stagecoach; I was planning on turning it into soup, curry and pumpkin pie by mid-day. In the afternoon I'd carve a ghastly face into the shell and at night I'd place a lighted candle inside it to ward away evil spirits for Halloween. While I was busying myself with the pumpkin, Gary would be paying his monthly visit to the Ghost House to do the garden. He'd also promised to give further consideration to a trip to the All Saints' market, but I wasn't going to hold my breath.

When he came back at tea-time he unloaded six rolls of fibreglass insulation from the back of the van.

'Crikey,' I said. 'Matt said you could have it then? You've not mentioned it since summer. I thought he must be keeping it after all.'

He shook his head. 'I kept forgetting to ask him, what with the blood tests and the hospital and everything. I remembered it when I was thinking about Ron and Miranda's visit. They've never stayed in the autumn before and it'll seem freezing compared to Granada. Not only that, we should feel the benefit ourselves when winter sets in.'

While Gary was changing out of his work clothes I warmed up some of the soup for his tea.

'Excellent,' he beamed, when he'd polished off a second bowlful. 'Good old me.'

I stared at him. 'Come again?'

'Not the soup – that was very nice by the way. I meant it's my very first homegrown pumpkin. I feel quite proud.'

'*Your* pumpkin?'

'Yes. I grew it.'

'You cheeky devil. You did not.'

''Course I did. *I'm* the gardener, remember? You look after the animals and the house.'

I knew he was teasing, but I couldn't help rising to the bait. 'I'll have you know *I* grew that pumpkin. I planted it in its bucket and when it was strong enough I transferred it – lovingly, I might add – to the garden.'

'The garden that I dug and fertilised. I haven't seen *you* on your hands and knees scraping cow shit off the lane.'

I chuckled. 'You do exaggerate. I've watched you scoop it up with a shovel. Anyway, I'm the one that watered it all through the summer *and* I put scrunched up bracken underneath it to keep it raised up off the earth.'

'I don't know why.'

'To give it a chance to grow bigger and to stop the shell going manky as well.'

'It wouldn't have made any difference. Even without the bracken it would have been fine.'

'That's not what it says in the gardening book. A proper gardener should know his onions. You need to read up.'

'Matt doesn't think so.'

'What d'you mean?'

'He must have faith in my gardening ability. He's asked me if I'll prune his vines.'

'Really? You didn't say.'

'I haven't had chance to, have I? I had a shower, ate my soup and then listened to you trying to take all the credit for growing the pumpkin.'

I giggled. 'And rightly so. Come on, be serious for a minute. What did Matt say?'

'When I sent the message about the insulation he rang straight back. He asked if I could prune the vines in December or January, but there's no real urgency, as long as it's done before spring.'

'Is it a big job?'

'Not really. It'll probably take a few hours, but he said he'll pay me for the full day. Do you realise, with the work I've done for Verna, Rose and Matt, I've earned over three thousand euros in the last two years?'

I swallowed hard. I'd had no idea that Gary had earned so much money, but I knew for a fact that we wouldn't have managed without it. Looking after the animals and the household chores was no mean feat, yet my role seemed so trivial compared to Gary's input. I made up my mind to work harder than ever on my hedgehogs so that I could have my market stall in the spring.

As the sun sank below the horizon I carried my pumpkin lantern out to the garden. I set it down on the larger of the two stone tables that stood beyond the threshing floor. The position was perfect; I'd be able to see it from the kitchen and living room windows, and it would be sure to ward off any ghoulies and ghosties if they happened to come creeping along the lane. For the rest of the evening I kept a frequent watch on the bloodcurdling beacon and was delighted to see that the candle was still burning when I went up to bed. Whether or not it would deter evil spirits, it had certainly exorcised mean ones; Gary had finally agreed to go to the market after all.

Liza Grantham

Honesty Pays

There's a man in Güimil who buys chestnuts;
He's there the same time ev'ry year,
It's a great way to earn a few euros
To pay for your bacca and beer.

You might have to queue for an hour,
And wait for your turn in the cold,
But then there's the lovely warm feeling
You get when your chestnuts are sold.

The man doesn't want to buy tiddlers,
He'll have a good look in your sack;
So make sure you take only big ones,
And then you'll be safe to go back.

But if he should find that you've cheated
He'll soon have you out on your ear,
And folks far and wide will all shun you,
And brand you the Cheat of the Year.

Chapter 17

Never-ending Story

On the first of November, for the first time ever, we were off to *A Feira dos Santos*. When I went out to see to the livestock I gave my menacing pumpkin the thumbs up. It seemed to be grinning back at me, its candle still burning away. Down in the chooks' pen I told Wayne the bad news and hoped that he'd understand me. It was nothing short of a miracle that Gary had agreed to go to the market. I didn't dare push my luck any further; we wouldn't be bringing any new hens home today.

It was approaching mid-day when we parked up behind the Hotel Río Ulla. The walk back along the main street was pleasant in the sun. Crowds were moving shoulder to shoulder in both directions, some towards the town centre and others happy to make the kilometre trek down to the showground to absorb the full atmosphere of the momentous event.

There was no chance of walking side by side when we reached the market. I shuffled forward at a snail's pace, edging round stalls and dodging past pushchairs and looking for gaps in the crowd. Ten minutes later I hovered outside the market hall. Smells of hot fat, boiled octopus and diesel were just on the nauseating side of intriguing. When Gary finally caught up I tugged at his arm impatiently, eager to be indoors.

Inside the hall, the usual local produce was laid out on trestles in the centre, whilst products of distinction were making their guest appearances on more elaborate stalls around the side. We eased through the crowds, pausing to sample cured meats, cheeses, breads, *artesano* sweetmeats and preserves.

Eventually we came to a stall selling top notch chorizos which were, according to a sign on the table, eighty per cent meat.

'Crikey,' I said. 'That's unusual, they only have to be sixty percent to get the quality seal. These must be extra special and they're only three quid a throw.'

'And you were right about the pâté,' grinned Gary. 'There's *jabalí*, look, and oh, what's *venado*?'

'Venison. I bet that's scrumptious.'

We settled for a tub of each and a couple of wild boar chorizos as well.

The next stall specialised in locally made *melindres*; glazed aniseed-flavoured donuts that tasted divine. At two euros a pack they were a bargain.

'What d'you reckon?' Gary asked me as he sucked the sugar off his fingers.

I grinned at him. 'Let's have two.'

By the time we emerged back out into the sunshine we'd added date and walnut bread and a couple of quality mark cheeses to our treats.

Satisfied that our visitors wouldn't go hungry we began the slow shuffle back towards Plaza Antonio Rojo. The crowds seemed more densely packed than ever and I resigned myself to being carried along with the flow.

'Look at it,' frowned Gary, pointing beyond the *plaza* to the street that ran parallel to the main drag. 'If we go that way it'll be half an hour before we get back to the van. We're not planning on buying anything else, are we? Why don't we just cut our losses and walk back down the main road?'

I looked at the stalls and crowds stretching out into the distance. We'd had a good time sampling and we had plenty of treats for our visitors. In principle, Gary was right, but this would probably be our first and only visit to *A Feira dos Santos*. 'Come on,' I grinned. 'It's a one-off – in for a penny, in for a pound.'

As we strolled down towards the Hotel Río Ulla I was stuffed full to bursting. The crumbly *artesano* chocolate, the clotted cream biscuits and the chestnuts in syrup had made it worth the effort after all.

Out on the hotel terrace the ex-pats were already heading for home.

'Look,' said Gary. 'There's Nina and Marcus.'

Nina spotted us and waved.

As we neared the terrace, Marcus was frowning. I knew that he was being mischievous when his manner was stern. 'You did not come to the meet-up,' he said accusingly.

'Sorry,' I grinned. 'Gary felt a burning compulsion to go to the market. Blame him.'

'Ignore her,' said Gary. 'I never want to go round the market at the best of times but I've always avoided the November one like the plague.'

'We went early,' said Nina, 'but it was already crowded. There must have been thousands here today.'

'It said in the paper they were expecting over twenty thousand,' I nodded.

'Enough to fill the Anxo Carro stadium three times over,' said Gary.

I looked at him. 'Eh?'

'Lugo's football stadium. You need to read *Marca*.'

I rolled my eyes and looked at Nina. 'Trust him.'

Nina giggled. 'Marcus is the same. We should send them off to a match together and spend the day drinking coffee and eating cake.'

'It's a great idea,' grinned Marcus. He turned to Gary. 'Have you ever been?'

Gary shook his head. 'I'd like to but we're always on a budget. I've not been to a game since we lived in Las Palmas. It must be over five years.'

'We could afford it *now*,' I said. 'What would it be? Twenty, thirty euros? With the money from Matt's and the chestnuts we could stretch to that.'

'She is a good wife,' nodded Marcus approvingly. 'Gary, we will go.'

Gary looked at me. 'Do you mind?'

Not only did I not mind, I was delighted. Gary had worked hard for the money he'd earned. A treat like this would go some way to assuaging my guilt.

'Not at all,' I smiled. 'It'd be nice to spend some time with Nina. In fact, I insist that you go.'

'Right,' he nodded. 'We'll go before Christmas. I'll look at the fixtures and we'll sort something out.'

On the second of November, I went down to Anxo's grave before I let out the livestock. I sang 'Happy Birthday' and told him he'd soon be having a visit from his Aunt Miranda and Uncle Ron. They'd both loved Anxo and the feeling, I was sure, had been mutual. He'd particularly adored Miranda; unlike Mum, she was a great stick thrower and had shoulder length hair he could chew.

Down in the chicken run, I let Mrs Brown and her babies out into the main enclosure. At ten weeks old they were ready to mingle with the big chooks. Both were hens and I'd named them Nutmeg and Juanita. I had a strong suspicion that Nutmeg was a *raza galega* daughter, but there was no doubt whatsoever that Waynetta was Juanita's mum.

Over in Warren Place, I bundled four of Doe's youngsters into Scholes' carrier, then deposited them equally unceremoniously into the Death Row pens in the barn. Unluckily for Buck, Doe wouldn't be paying him a visit for a while now. She'd be having a well-earned rest over winter, recharging her batteries until spring.

For the rest of the day, I dashed around cleaning and Gary went off on a final forage for chestnuts before his evening drive to Güimil. He wasn't in the least looking forward to it; against his better judgement he'd also agreed to take Paul's.

It was late afternoon when Paul turned up with his chestnuts. When I answered the door I was surprised to see that he'd brought them round in half a dozen mesh potato bags.

'Is Gary about?' he asked me.

'Yes,' I nodded. 'He's in the barn.'

I couldn't wait to hear how many he'd collected, so as he went into the barn I stood in the passage with the back door ajar and listened to the voices drifting through the slats and out into the lane.

'You're having a laugh,' I heard Gary say. 'They won't do like that. Haven't you got a sack?'

'They *are* sacks. They're just small.'

'You know what I mean,' said Gary. 'I mean a *proper* sack. I'm not taking them like that. I've got mine to carry as well remember. And it's not just me it's making it hard for, it's the chestnut bloke as well.'

'I don't see how.'

'It gets busy. The queue goes out of the door and down the street. If you've got six bags to weigh that's like having six turns – it's selfish. And then he's got to add them all up.'

'I thought I'd be doing you a favour. Easier for you to carry, you see.'

'Rubbish. Have you got a sack or haven't you?'

There was a pause. 'I *have*, but…'

'But *what*? Come on, spit it out!'

'I've got a sack, but I don't want to use it. It's a good sack.'

I waited for the explosion. I only counted to two.

'For fuck's sake man! You'll be losing a sack, not a member of the family! Now do you want me to take your chestnuts or not?'

Paul humphed. The barn door began to creak open, but Gary spoke again.

'Wait. Before you go let's weigh them. It'll be a lot easier while they're still in the bags.'

'I think there are roughly sixty kilos altogether. They're ten kilo bags.'

'They weigh ten kilos when they're full of potatoes. Yours are three quarters full of chestnuts. They'll weigh less.'

'Why will they? Ten kilos is ten kilos…'

'Paul. Believe me, I know what I'm talking about. Let's see, shall we? Pass me the biggest bag.' There was a shuffling and a clank. 'Nine kilos. See?'

Paul humphed again.

'So, if that's the biggest you're going to be looking at between fifty and fifty-five quid.'

'I still think you're wrong. I was banking on sixty. We'll have to see how you get on.'

When Paul's footsteps had disappeared out of earshot, the barn door creaked open. Within seconds Gary came through the door.

'You'll never believe what he…'

'I do. I had the door open. I heard every word.'

'You heard about his sack then? It's a sack, for God's sake! Why does he want to hang on to a fucking sack?'

I giggled. 'He told you why. He doesn't want to use it – it's a good sack.'

'Stick the kettle on, will you? If I hadn't got to drive over to Güimil I'd be having a beer.'

I was pouring water into the mugs when I heard footsteps. Paul was on his way back down the lane. I peered through the frosted panes at the bottom of the window. Sure enough, I could make out the blur of a large brown shape. I turned to Gary with a grin.

'He's back, he's back,

With a very important sack,

No time to say a last goodbye,

He's back, he's back, he's back.'

Gary chuckled in spite of himself. 'Very funny. I'd better go and get them in the van before he changes his mind.'

This time I followed him out through the door. Paul was standing outside the barn with a hessian potato sack which was less than half full. He didn't look pleased.

'Much better,' grinned Gary. 'That'll do nicely.'

'It's too big for the chestnuts,' groaned Paul. 'It's such a waste of a sack.'

'You'll be able to get another in May,' I said brightly. 'There'll be loads knocking about when the neighbours have planted their spuds.'

It was past six o'clock when Gary arrived home.

As I waited for him to put the van away I was brimming with excitement. I couldn't wait to hear how he'd got on.

'Well?' I asked, when he came into the kitchen. 'How did you do?'

'Not bad. Not quite as many as last year. Eighty three quid.'

'Crikey, Gary, that's brilliant.'

'It's not to be sniffed at. I thought we could p'raps spend some of it on a small electric radiator. They've got them for about thirty quid in the *ferretería*. It'd take the chill off the bedroom for Miranda and Ron.'

'That's considerate. Good thinking. And what about Paul?'

'Ten euros.'

'You're joking.'

'He's lucky to get that. Sit down and I'll tell you about it, let me get myself a beer.'

He opened the fridge and took out a can of lager. I fidgeted impatiently while he flicked it open and took a long swill.

'There were only about a dozen folks in front of me when I got there. I thought, "brilliant, I'll be back in the van in half an hour." So, I waited for, oh, twenty minutes or so – it seemed longer though, *I* can tell you. I was bloody freezing waiting out in the cold.'

'Go on.'

'It was the same man as last year, but after the first three or four people he went off somewhere and a woman took over. She was still serving when it was my turn.' He paused for another swallow of beer. 'Anyway, I gave her mine first and she rummaged about and pulled a few out from the middle and nodded, then she hoisted the sack onto the scales – I was surprised she could manage, she was only four-foot-nothing and...'

'*Gary.*'

'Then she pointed to the next sack and I told her "*separado*".'

'*Aparte.*'

'Eh?'

'That's what I'd have said.'

'Well it wasn't you – it was me, and she understood me perfectly. She counted out my money and then I passed her Paul's. She stuck her hand in and rummaged about and... well, I've never felt such a fool. She pulled a fistful out and I'm not kidding – some were that small we wouldn't have bothered with them for the freezer. I wanted to drop through the floor.'

I thought of last year's social pariah. She probably hadn't dared show her face in public once half of rural Galicia had got wind of her tiddlers. I couldn't bear the thought of Gary going through the same ordeal. 'What happened next?'

'I explained that they weren't mine, they were my neighbour's and I was ever so sorry and I would never have brought them if I'd known.'

'Poor you.'

'I'll say. So, I picked up the wretched sack and was about to walk away when she waved her hand at me and pulled out a mobile phone.'

'Oh dear.'

'Exactly. I didn't know if she was calling the *Guardia* or the local heavies or what. Anyway she tapped in a number and when they answered she spoke really quickly in *galego* and all I could make out was "small chestnuts", then she smiled at me and nodded and rang off.'

'Then what?'

'She gave me a ten euro note.'

'Thank goodness. Everybody will have seen you coming away empty handed except for some money. At least you've saved face.'

'That's what I thought. I tell you what though, I felt like keeping the ten quid myself.'

'I'm not surprised. I wonder what Paul will say when you tell him.'

'I already have. He was up at the church on his phone when I drove back into the village. His face dropped a mile when I gave him the tenner. I told him it was poor form and he was lucky to get anything after the way he'd cheated. Was he grateful? Was he buggery. He said, "I knew I shouldn't have parted with that sack."'

On Sunday morning the sun was doing its level best to make an appearance in a sky peppered with pale grey cloud. I only hoped that if it was going to rain it would have the decency to hold off until Tuesday; Lenda had been promised a walk through the woodlands and games in the garden with her yet-to-meet *invitados*, Miranda and Ron. Scholes, on the other hand, couldn't have cared less about who was visiting; he'd already laid claim to the heated bedroom and the fluffed-up duvet, draped with a fleecy throw.

Anxo had been an outgoing dog with a friendly nature, whereas Lenda, though sociable, was really quite shy in comparison and I wondered how she and our friends would get on. I needn't have worried. Lenda took to Ron and Miranda at once and she was an instant hit with them.

'Oh wow,' said Miranda. 'Isn't she pretty? I wasn't expecting her to be long-haired.'

'Neither was I,' I laughed. 'It's not what I'd have chosen, what with the landscape and the climate, but we'd driven for miles and waited hours in the perishing cold before we met her. Even if she'd had two heads I think we'd have made do.'

We spent what remained of the afternoon wandering round the village and the garden. When we stopped by the chooks' pen our guests had quite a surprise.

'Oh,' said Ron. 'Where are all your big orange hens?'

'Gone off to colder climes,' laughed Gary.

Ron and Miranda looked puzzled.

'Ignore him,' I said. 'They went in the freezer because they'd stopped laying. We're having one tonight in a curry. They're very tasty – we've already eaten two.'

'I like the little cockerel,' smiled Miranda. 'What's his name?'

'Wayne,' I sniggered, 'but that wasn't our choice. The little one with the Elvis hairdo is his sister, Waynetta. And the stripy one's Humbug, she's the first hen we've bred ourselves and she's laying every day.'

'Oh, look,' said Miranda, pointing over to the chestnut tree. 'Two little ones! And that's Mrs Brown, isn't it? Are the young ones her chicks?'

'Yes,' I nodded. 'I've called them Nutmeg and Juanita. Nutmeg's the orangey-brown one and Juanita's the one with the quiff.'

'Do you ever choose the names, Gary?' asked Miranda.

'Yes,' he nodded proudly. 'I named Mrs Brown.'

After a brief visit to Warren Place and Death Row to see the rabbits, we came back downstairs onto the ground floor of the barn.

'Look – kittens!' whispered Ron, nodding towards the woodpile where Hairy Fred and Splodgy, who I'd started to call Princess, lay dozing. Miranda managed a fleeting glimpse before they shot off to the upper level and out through the slats onto the lawn.

'They're lovely,' smiled Miranda. 'Aren't you tempted to adopt one?'

'We wanted to take them both,' said Gary, 'but you've seen how easily spooked they are. Hairy Fred's out of the question, but Liza says there's still hope for Splodgy…'

'Princess,' I corrected him.

'Princess, then. To be honest, I think the pair of them are a lost cause.'

After a welcome feast of chicken jalfrezi with pilau rice and naan breads we retired to the living room. Too stuffed to manage kulfi we voted to have it the next evening, dolloped on pumpkin pie.

'So what time's Gary's appointment tomorrow?' asked Miranda.

'Ten thirty,' said Gary. 'I'll have to be off just before nine.'

'It's a pity we can't have a proper day out,' I added. 'I thought the three of us could go for a stroll with Lenda in the morning. Gary should be back around one, so we'll still be able to have a drive out in the afternoon.'

'That'll be lovely,' smiled Miranda. 'It's just nice to see you both and we love being here in the village. I thought you were going to cancel when I got your text and saw the word "hospital". It was a relief when I read it properly and realised it was only routine.'

Gary looked at me accusingly. 'Only routine?'

'Calm down,' I said. 'It was too complicated to explain in a text and Miranda would've been worried if I'd said you were having a scan.'

'A scan?' chorused Ron and Miranda.

I nodded. 'It's a long story. Gary can tell you all about it while I go down and make us a brew.'

When I came back up with the teas and coffees, Ron and Miranda were listening wide-eyed as Gary gave them a blow by blow account of his ongoing saga of woe. His weird and wonderful symptoms caught their imaginations and for the next half hour we all chucked in our two penn'orth as to what might have been the cause.

Gary told them about Paul's pétanque court, his End of the World party and his chestnuts. I told them about the percussion, the chamber music and the *fiesta*. It would have been easy to go on talking for hours but, mindful of Gary's appointment, we agreed on an early night.

Next morning the rain was torrential. As soon as I walked through to the bathroom I knew that all hope of a walk through the woodlands was gone. The pitter-patter on the tiles above the terrace and the syncopated pinging on the metal chimney were a sure sign that the Galician weather was hell-bent on doing its worst. When I came out of the bathroom, Miranda was coming out of the bedroom clutching a towel.

'Morning,' she whispered. 'Is it okay to use the shower? We thought we'd get up early so we could wish Gary luck before he goes.'

'That's kind of you,' I smiled. 'I'll go and get us a brew on. Feel free to use the shower, Gary won't be up for ages yet.'

Down in the kitchen I stuck the kettle on the hob and yawned as I rolled myself a cigarette. Despite having an early night, I felt like a wrung out dish cloth. I'd tossed and turned for hours, worrying about Gary's scan.

Ten minutes later, Miranda came down from the shower. Unlike me, she looked as fresh as a daisy, her cheeks flushed and her hair still damp.

'Are you sure you don't want to go with Gary?' she asked. 'Ron and I would be happy to hold the fort while you're gone.'

I shook my head. 'If I went I'd only be in the way. I fuss too much and Gary gets snappy when he's nervous. I tell you what though, it's times like this I wish we both had a phone.'

'I can see that,' she nodded. 'I think it's a miracle how you manage with only one between you.'

'It's not really a problem under normal circumstances. It's times like today that it's a pain.'

'Well, it's easily resolved. Gary can always send a message to my phone today.'

'Thanks,' I smiled. 'I'm sure he won't need to, but it's good to know.'

By the time Gary came into the kitchen, Ron had joined us and the three of us were already on our second brew. It was a pity that Gary would have to sit and watch while the rest of us were eating breakfast, but at least, unlike last time, he'd be able to have a mug of black coffee or tea.

'What have you got on your feet?' I asked him.

He looked down at his shoes. 'Desert boots. Why?'

'I'll give you a clue, shall I? Desert boots. Traditional footwear of the Canary Islands. Gary, it's pissing it down out there.'

'I've only got to walk from here to the barn. Once I get to the hospital I'll park in the basement and go straight through the doors.'

'But if you stopped off in Lugo for a coffee, or… Oh, I don't know, Gary, I worry about you, that's all.'

'Liza. I won't be stopping anywhere. I'll drive straight to the hospital, have the scan and come home.'

While Ron and Miranda tucked into date and walnut bread with honey, Gary sipped miserably on his milkless, sugarless tea. The rain pounded against the window and dark clouds seem to engulf the entire village. It reminded me of a Baudelaire poem I liked, but I didn't bother to say so. I felt as though we were waiting for Doomsday all over again.

'Right,' I announced. 'I'm going to see to the chooks and the rabbits.' I pulled out my wellies from under the bench.

'I think I'll get off,' said Gary. 'If it stays like this the traffic'll be crawling on the N-540, you won't be able to see your hand in front of your face.'

As I untied my boots I watched him take down his wallet and phone from the telly shelf.

'Have you got the letter and your medical card?' I asked.

He frowned at me and I shuffled over to give him a peck on the cheek. 'Good luck then,' I told him. 'Mind how you go.'

He stuffed his wallet into the back pocket of his jeans and I went back to taking my boots off.

'I'll see you later then,' he said to Miranda and Ron.

I couldn't help wondering what they must think of me. I showed more affection to Scholes and Lenda than I did to Gary. Worse still, I was letting him drive all the way to Lugo on his own for a scan.

By the time I'd seen to the livestock, Gary had left for his appointment. Our guests gamely suggested they wash the pots and tend the fire while Lenda and I squelched over the fields. With our plans for a woodland walk well and truly scuppered, we spent the morning sitting in the kitchen catching up with more news.

By half past one we were ready for lunch, but there was still no sign of Gary. At a quarter to two we decided to start without him and I put his share of the sandwiches in the fridge. Once we'd eaten and the plates were stacked in the drainer I suggested we retire upstairs.

'There's only so long you can sit on these benches,' I said. 'After a while my bum goes numb.'

'I know what you mean,' said Miranda, 'and I've got more padding than you. Is it warm up there?'

'It will be once the heater's on,' I nodded, 'and it'll be so much comfier on the sofa. I thought you might want to nod off.'

'I'm fine,' she smiled. 'We were early to bed so I don't really need a *siesta*. I wouldn't mind reading for a while though, while my lunch goes down.'

'That's a good idea,' said Ron. 'I fancy reading too.' He looked at me. 'Do you mind?'

'Not at all,' I smiled. 'As long as you can put up with me clicking. I can sit and knit.'

'Ooh,' said Miranda. 'I had no idea you could knit.'

'I couldn't,' I laughed. 'I only started this summer. Come on, let's go up and get the heater on and I'll tell you about my plans for a stall.'

Miranda and Ron were thrilled with my prototype hedgehog.

'It's lovely,' smiled Miranda. 'It looks almost real.'

'It does,' agreed Ron. 'It's because of the spiky wool.'

'I'm pleased with it,' I said. 'I've got enough yarn to make six. But I'm going to need more than that to sell at the market. I wondered about doing some in psychedelic colours. I'll need to send a shopping list and a cheque to my Mum.'

'So when did you decide to do a stall?' asked Ron. 'I can just imagine Gary shouting, "Roll up, roll up! Come and get your hedgehogs!" I think it's his sort of thing.'

'Tell me,' I frowned. 'But I can assure you he won't be joining me. Don't say anything to him, will you? I haven't told him about it yet.'

'Really?' said Miranda. 'Whyever not?'

'Because he'll say it's stupid. He'll say, "you'll never knit enough to get a stall together. I know what you're like – you'll get bored."'

Miranda looked at me. 'And will you?'

'I s'pose I will, eventually, but I'll plod on regardless. I have to make a contribution, however tiny. It really galls me to be a dependent little wife.'

'But you're not,' said Ron. 'You work just as hard as Gary, if not harder. You're up at the crack of dawn doing your rabbits and your chickens. You see to the house and the laundry and the cooking and...'

'I know,' I nodded. 'But I feel guilty. We struggle for money and Gary's the one that brings in the cash.'

'You mustn't,' said Miranda. 'You worked above and beyond in Las Palmas. You did Saturday School and after-school classes. It's not as if you're lazy, it's down to opportunities. Eventually something will turn up.'

'I hope so,' I nodded. 'But in the meantime I can at least be making an effort. I've always been independent. I suppose it's a matter of pride.'

By half past two I was starting to worry; it seemed strange that Gary still wasn't home.

'I think I'll go up to the church to check the phone,' I said. 'I'd hate to think that he'd sent a message telling me to call and I'd missed it. It won't take me long.'

'Are you sure?' said Miranda. 'It's pouring down out there. Perhaps you should wait a while.'

I stood up and peered out of the window. Gunmetal clouds hung over the valley; the rain wasn't going to ease up any time soon.

'Why not give it another half an hour?' suggested Ron. 'The appointment might have been late, or perhaps he felt hungry. He might have stopped off for some lunch.'

The idea was preposterous and I knew it. Gary would drive from A to B and back again. Something was wrong, I could feel it. Had they found something and admitted him straight away? My stomach was churning and my mouth felt dry. I regretted now that I hadn't gone with him; how could I be such a terrible wife? In spite of his miserly ways, his IDS and his childish sense of humour, he was a good husband. I didn't always show it, but I loved him and couldn't bear the thought of him being ill. Whatever the outcome of the scan, I was determined I'd try harder to be patient from now on. I looked at Miranda. 'Can I have your phone? I won't settle 'til I know what's happening. It'll put my mind at rest if I go now.'

I sighed as I thought of the rigmarole ahead of me. An umbrella was no good when the rain blew in from the south across the valley; I'd need to don the full waterproof ensemble all for a two-minute trek up to the church. As I leaned over to the coffee table to stub out my cigarette I froze suddenly. I'd never been so happy to hear that oh-so-familiar screeching of brakes.

'Whatever's that noise?' frowned Miranda.

'It's Gary,' I grinned. 'He's home.'

'You see,' smiled Ron. 'There was nothing to worry about after all. And you didn't even have to get wet.'

'Shall I go down and put the kettle on for him?' asked Miranda.

I shook my head. 'I wouldn't bother. I've a sneaking suspicion he'll want a beer.'

I listened as the van reversed into the barn. I heard the engine die, the door slam closed, then the groaning of the barn doors as Gary swung them to.

Three minutes later he appeared at the top of the stairs. For a split second I didn't know whether to laugh or cry. His so-called rain mac was plastered to his body, his jeans and desert boots were drenched and his nose was tinged blue with the cold.

'My God!' I exclaimed. 'What's happened? Don't just stand there, Gary! You're dripping all over the floor.'

He said nothing, and only then did I realise he was shivering too violently to speak.

'Take your coat off, Gary,' said Miranda kindly, 'then come and stand by the fire.'

'You look perished,' added Ron. 'Let me go and fetch you a towel. We don't want you catching a chill.'

'So what happened?' I asked again.

He looked at me helplessly and shook his head.

'Go and get in the shower,' said Miranda. 'The hot water will warm you through.'

Fifteen minutes later, Gary was back in the living room looking decidedly warmer in a chunky jumper, sweatpants and his comfy battered mules. Ron turned up the butane heater and pulled it over to the armchair. I passed him a can of lager and a cigarette and we all waited patiently until he was ready to speak. Eventually he stubbed out his ciggie and cleared his throat.

'When I got to the hospital it wasn't quite ten, so I went for a coffee. At about quarter past I went and put my card in the machine but it popped straight out again without giving me a ticket. I must have tried it half a dozen times, turning it round, turning it over...'

I sighed impatiently and he gave me a hard stare.

'Sorry,' I muttered. 'Carry on.'

'Somebody else came up and shoved theirs in and it worked fine, so I tried again. *Nada*. In the end I stopped a woman in a white coat and said, "I don't think my card's working." She took it off me, pushed it into the slot and out it popped again. She asked where I needed to be, so I showed her the letter. "Here, look," I said, "the Centro de Especialidades – that's where I need to be." She took the letter off me, peered at it and shook her head. "You're in the wrong place," she said. "It's the specialist clinic in Praza do Ferrol. It's inside the city walls."'

We all gasped.

'Oh dear,' I frowned. 'So what did you do?'

Gary scowled. 'If you'll let me finish...'

'Sorry,' I said for the second time. 'Go on.'

'Well, by now it was gone half past ten so I was already late for the appointment, but I thought as long as I didn't get stuck in traffic I could still get there for eleven and everything'd work out okay.'

Miranda and Ron nodded. I rolled my eyes.

'I thanked her and legged it through the corridors, down the escalator and back to the basement. I only realised I'd left her holding the paper as I was starting the van.'

We all groaned.

'It didn't matter. I knew I wanted the Centro de Especialidades in Praza do Ferrol. Anyway, the drive back into the centre wasn't as bad as it could have been. The lights were all in my favour but the traffic was moving slowly because of the rain.'

'Still torrential?' I asked, without thinking.

This time he nodded. 'You know what those tiled pavements are like, the water looked like it was sliding down the streets.' He paused for a swig of lager. 'I hadn't a clue where Praza do Ferrol was, so I parked in that place where there's a man to give you a ticket instead of a machine. I thought he'd be bound to know.'

'Good thinking,' said Ron. 'And did he?'

'Yes. He said, "Ah, the clinic!" He told me his sister had been there. Or was it his wife? Anyway, it was only about five minutes away, but the rain was coming down in stair rods. I was like a drowned rat by the time I got there, but I thought that'd work in my favour. I hoped they'd take pity on me if I laid it on thick about the traffic and the rain.'

'Crafty,' laughed Miranda. 'Did it work?'

'Sort of. The woman on reception was ever so sympathetic, but she couldn't find me in the computer. She asked me for my paperwork, but of course I'd left it in the hospital, so I gave her my card. She took one look, shook her head, and said I was in the wrong place.'

'No!' we chorused.

'Oh, yes. So I said, "isn't this the Centro de Especialidades?" "Yes," she said, "but this is a *private* clinic. You want the health service clinic in Praza do Ferrol."'

'But didn't you look at the street sign?' I asked, incredulous.

'No. Why would I? The bloke had told me to go down the main street, left here, right there and I'd see the clinic on my right.'

'Ah,' I nodded. 'I see.'

'So she gave me directions and off I went again. It was still chucking it down and by now it was getting on for mid-day.'

'I'm surprised you didn't give up,' said Ron.

'Believe me, I was tempted, but I'd got that far so it made sense to see it through to the end.'

The story had been intriguing so far but I was growing impatient. Gary had been home almost an hour and we still didn't know whether or not he'd had the scan. Eventually my frustration got the better of me.

'So have you had the scan?'

'No.'

My heart sank.

'Anyway, I found the health centre and you'll never guess? It was the place where we went for your mammogram.'

'Never. Well fancy that.'

'I explained what had happened and they said I'd need another appointment. They gave me a letter to take back to the hospital and told me to hand it in at the main desk.'

'Wow,' said Miranda. 'So you drove all the way back again?'

Gary nodded. 'I've got an appointment though. I go back on December the tenth.'

I sighed. Poor Gary. My heart went out to him. He'd be lucky to have the results this side of Christmas. I was beginning to wonder if the saga would ever end.

Whilst summer had reluctantly relinquished its reign to the season of mists and golden harvests, autumn allowed its crown to be usurped suddenly and cruelly by winter's grasping claws. As November drew to a close, the first frosts descended. The rimy air hung like a starched sheet

315

over the village and the wind blew across the valley in icy shards.

In spite of the freezing temperatures, Hairy Fred and Princess still slept in the woodpile. They were almost six months old and, unlike Sophie, were as good as feral. I was growing resigned to the fact that I was never going to tempt them indoors.

The Book of Life

The Book of Life, from age to age
Is penned by Fate, at every stage,
Such myst'ries found on each new page;
Its dénouement we cannot gauge.

Let not your heart be filled with dread
For chapters that might lie ahead,
Dwell not on what's been done or said;
Those pages need no more be read.

The past can never be reversed,
The future cannot be rehearsed,
Move on, for better or for worse,
Through each new page of prose and verse.

The story, be it good or ill,
Moves on apace, will not stand still;
Each perfect joy, each bitter pill,
Is inked by Fate's enchanted quill.

So let the Book of Life be penned
Through every changing course we wend;
Long may we travel on, my friend,
Until the final chapter's end.

Chapter 18

Home Territory

On the first of December we were off to the market *and* the ex-pats' get-together. Buying a couple of hens had been the only purpose of the outing until Gary, quite out of character, had suggested stopping by the hotel. At first I'd wondered if the previous month's jaunt had rid him of his parking-in-Monterroso phobia, but I should have known better. He'd had a text message from a Dutchman about a lads' night out.

'White rabbits,' I smiled, when he came into the kitchen.

'It's not fair,' he yawned. 'You always say it first because I'm only half awake.'

'Rubbish,' I laughed. 'It's because *you* always forget.'

'Not *always*. I remembered as soon as I opened my eyes this morning. I'm looking forward to seeing Marcus and making plans for the match.'

'I'm sure you are – *after* we've been to the market. Our first priority is to buy my hens.'

'I've been thinking about that.'

'Oh yes?'

'Yes. Wouldn't we be better buying them from the *agro* shop? That's what we did last time. They were ten euros apiece on the market and in the shop they were only seven. I don't know why we don't just do the same again.'

'Because we're not buying *raza galegas,* Gary. It's false economy. I don't want to shell out fourteen euros for hens that have got to be killed in two years. We'll go down to the livestock section and we'll look for something that lays for longer. A few extra euros will be money well spent.'

The approach into Monterroso seemed less busy than was usual for a market day and I wondered if all but the most seasoned of the locals had stayed huddled around their fires. As we neared the first set of traffic lights I was surprised when Gary indicated right.

'What are you doing?' I asked him.

'I'm going to park in front of the medical centre. It's Saturday, they'll only be open for emergencies. We'd have to be bloody unlucky to get a ticket today.'

It was a stroke of genius. By weaving through the back streets we were able to skirt the hub of the market. All around us the sweet scent of woodsmoke did little to lessen the icy chill. Down on the tiny green, the stallholders were out in force, defying the wintery weather. The morning thaw had left the grass wet and springy, but the ground was still patched with frost beneath the latticed shade of the trees.

Ignoring the usual cages of fat orange hens and brown rabbits, I hovered around the more intriguing specimens. Gary pulled me away from the quails and red-legged partridges and I carried on walking until my eyes came to rest on a litter of guineapigs in a cardboard box.

'Guineapigs,' said Gary, stating the obvious. He frowned and stared at them. 'It seems strange that rural Galicians would be bothered with pets.'

'True,' I nodded. 'Perhaps they rear them to eat?'

'Don't be silly. Nobody eats guineapigs.'

'Of course they do. In Peru, it's a staple *and* in other South American countries, I'd imagine. I'm sure I read somewhere it was catching on in posh restaurants too.'

Gary frowned. 'That's madness. *And* it's cruel.'

'Of course it isn't. It's only the same as us breeding rabbits. It's not as cruel as locking them up for a lifetime in a tiny cage.'

'I still don't think they're for eating. I'm sure you're wrong.'

'Let's find out then, shall we? If I'm right, you can put the chooks and rabbits to bed for a week.'

'What if *I'm* right?'

'I'll sit in the barn and read *Marca* for two hours a day.'

'Very funny. Go on then, ask the nice lady. She's not serving anyone now.'

I strolled over and gave the woman my brightest smile. '*Crías los cobayos para comer*?'

She didn't even have to answer my question; the look on her face said it all. I mumbled a white lie about seeing it on the telly and sloped off with my tail between my legs. Gary made no effort to disguise his delight. Ignoring his smug expression I made a beeline for a crate of handsome white hens.

'Look,' I said. 'White leghorns. I had a couple of black ones in England. They were ever so tame.'

'Were they good layers?'

'Excellent. Never missed a day. They didn't go broody either. What do you think?'

'I think it's up to you. You're animals, I'm veg.'

'You said it. Come on then, let's see how much they are.'

'*Cuánto cuestan las gallinas blancas*?' I asked the woman.

'*Las livornesas*? Ten euros each.'

The price was over the odds and I knew it, but the hens were exactly what I wanted and I didn't care.

'Okay,' I smiled. 'I'll take two please.'

Gary raised his eyebrows. 'Only two?'

I nodded. 'A couple will be plenty. We've already got Mrs Brown, Waynetta and Humbug. Come March, Juanita and Nutmeg will be laying too. Seven hens'll be enough for Wayne to cope with. He's only small.'

I carried my cardboard box proudly the short distance back to the van.

'What are you doing?' asked Gary, as I yanked the passenger door open and placed the box on the seat.

'I'm not putting them in the back. The poor things will be sliding all over the place. Apart from that, we might be an hour at the ex-pats' thingy. Gladys and Mabel will be warmer in here.'

'Gladys and Mabel?'

'Yes. That's what I'm calling them. '

'Gladys and Mabel aren't hens' names. They sound like two old dears.'

'Let's hope they will be one day, shall we? I'm expecting them to keep on laying for a damn sight longer than two years.'

When we pulled up outside the Hotel Río Ulla, Nina and Marcus were out on the terrace with Lulu. Once again I couldn't believe how much she'd grown.

'Lulu's getting fat,' I told Marcus.

'She is not fat,' he laughed. 'She is well grown.'

'Hmm,' I frowned. 'If you say so. I hope she doesn't grow anymore.'

By the time we left the hotel, the arrangements were in place. The match was in the evening on the thirteenth of December, and Lugo would be playing Real Betis at home. At around four o'clock, Marcus would drop off Nina and Lulu, and collect Gary. They'd arrive at the ground in plenty of time for the kick-off at a quarter past six. While they were out, Nina and I would be busy. We'd take the dogs over the fields to run off their excitement then return to the warmth of the kitchen to cook a scrumptious Greek meal.

While Gary was out shopping on Monday morning I fetched my Greek cookbook from the pantry; the task of choosing the matchday menu had fallen to me. On Nina's insistence, I'd send her a message and she'd buy the meat from her local butcher; the produce was locally reared and slaughtered and very reasonably priced. I'd shop for the other ingredients and prepare the entrées and desserts in the morning. We'd only have the main course to prepare for the evening, leaving more time to gossip and have fun.

I thumbed through the recipes, surprised by the number of choices. The ingredients, though simple, were laced through with herbs and rich spices. As the fire crackled I began to feel festive, yearning for the fragrance of cinnamon and cloves. Last Christmas had arrived so soon after losing Anxo and I couldn't have felt less like celebrating. Gary had missed out on the usual festivities while I'd struggled to cope with my grief. I resolved that this year we'd have a proper Christmas. I'd put up the decorations and the tree, we'd have turkey dinner and treats and nibbles. We'd play board games, watch movies and I'd be happy-go-lucky, festive and fun.

When Gary came back with the shopping I announced my plan.

'I'm going to put the Christmas decorations up at the weekend.'

'Really? I'm pleased to hear that. It seemed weird not celebrating last year.'

'I know. It wouldn't have seemed right though, because of Anxo, but this year I'll make it up to you. I want to go into Antas on Thursday morning to get some stuff.'

'Thursday? That's no good – it's a bank holiday.'

'I know that. And Saturday's a bank holiday as well.'

'Is it? Oh, yes. Why they can't have two days together is beyond me.'

I giggled. 'You say that every year.'

'I ask you this every year as well, but bear with me – one's religious and one's political, is that right?'

I nodded.

'Go on then, which one's which?'

'The sixth is the political one – that's Constitution Day. It's a massive thing for the Spanish 'cos it celebrates democracy after years under Franco's rule.'

'Right. I remember some of the older ex-pats in Las Palmas telling us about how they used to break the curfew and sneak down to the beach. I can see why folks that were around then would want to celebrate. I can't imagine living like that now.'

'I know. And more so the Galicians. It's hard to believe it was forbidden to speak *galego*. I reckon he came down on his own people really hard.'

'I s'pose that's why they have so many fiestas and party their way through to next morning. They must be making up for lost time. What's the religious one?'

'That's to do with the Virgin Mary. It's the *Día de la Inmaculada Concepción*.'

'That doesn't make sense.'

'What doesn't?'

'The Immaculate Conception. Jesus was supposed to have been born at Christmas. That means he arrived less than three weeks after he was conceived.'

'It's doesn't mean when *Jesus* was conceived. It's talking about Mary. Catholics believe she was born completely pure and free from sin.'

'Hmm. You know *my* thoughts on religion. I wish I hadn't asked. Anyway you still haven't told me why you need to go into Antas when there aren't any shops open. Are you going to fill me in?'

'I want to go scrumping.'

'Scrumping? For apples? We've still got a boxful in the barn.'

'Not apples, holly. I want to pinch some for the Christmas decorations. You know the big bush by the pharmacy where we fetched it before?'

'Ah, right. I remember we'd been here two years and you'd never noticed it. You must walk round with your eyes shut. If I hadn't told you it was there you'd never have known.'

I giggled. 'Your memory isn't as bad as I thought it was. I'm impressed. Didn't the balustrade look lovely when I'd finished, with the holly and ivy and pine?'

'It did. Very tasteful. I must admit though, I used to like the Christmas tree as well.'

'Then you won't be disappointed. This year I'm going for the rustic look *and* the Christmas tree with all the trimmings. I know it wasn't much of a festive season for you last year, so I'm going to make up for it. I'm going to give us a Christmas to remember. Trust me, it's going to be great.'

I spent the whole of Friday and the best part of Saturday making our home look festive. Up in the living room I stood the Christmas tree between the two windows and draped it with lights and baubles exactly as I'd done the year we'd moved in. Along the balustrade I fastened sprays of holly and pine with red ribbon, and in the dining room I wove ivy and strings of gold beads around the wrought iron chandelier. On the back door, I hung a wreath of holly, ivy and pinecones and, in the passage and kitchen, I hung garlands of foliage studded with baubles and ribbons along the beam.

As I stood back to admire the effect I thought of Paul in his dark, dreary kitchen. We hadn't seen much of him since the chestnut debacle and I wondered if he was feeling embarrassed or even put out.

'I've been thinking,' I said, when we settled down with our beers that evening. 'Why don't we ask Paul if he'd like to join us for Christmas? It'll draw a line under the chestnut business and show him there's no offence.'

'But there is,' frowned Gary. 'It made me look a prize pillock. Apart from that, for two years running I've only taken the best chestnuts. I don't want a reputation for being a cheat.'

'You won't have. Like you say, your chestnuts were good ones and you explained that the others were someone else's. If you'd really meant to cheat you'd have hidden them at the bottom of your sack.'

I reached for my tobacco and waited. Eventually he spoke.

'I s'pose you're right. I wouldn't want to be sat in that miserable kitchen eating my Christmas dinner. I'll ask him tomorrow, do my bit for good will.'

At breaktime on Tuesday, Gary brought news.

'Paul said thanks, but he won't be able to make it on Christmas Day.'

'Oh dear. He's not still miffed about the sack, is he?'

'No. It's nothing like that. He won't be here.'

'Won't be here? Has he already been invited somewhere else?'

'No, I meant he won't be *here* – in Galicia. He's going back.'

'Back to England? You do surprise me. I thought he was here for good.'

'It's only a visit. He'll be back on the twenty-fourth of January. He's visiting family and friends.'

'Bless him. I'm glad he'll be with his nearest and dearest for Christmas. The twenty-fourth you say? That's the day before Burns Night. I could do us a supper when he gets back.'

'If you want to. As long as you don't push the boat out. Come the new year we need to be stricter with the budget. I know I've been earning us some money but…'

There it was again. I was beginning to feel inadequate. I was the wife who stayed at home and wore a pinny. My market stall really couldn't come soon enough.

After lunch, I nipped up the lane to see Paul. My invitation was well received.

'A Burns Night supper? With haggis? It sounds lovely. The thing is, I'm bringing a friend back with me so there'd be two of us, would you mind?'

''Course not,' I laughed. 'The more the merrier. I'll pull all the stops out and we'll have a proper Scottish bash.'

Instead of returning straight home, I strolled up to the church to make a phone call. I'd need suet if I was going to make haggis. I'd also need more tinsel yarn if I was going to knit enough toys for a stall.

The phone only rang twice before someone answered. 'Hello?'

I took a deep breath and crossed my fingers. 'Hello, Mum.'

On the tenth of December Gary was off to the hospital. Again. This time I made sure I checked and double-checked the letter. The appointment was at ten-forty, in room B404 of the *Gastroenterología* department. It was the same room as the consultation back in September. Gary knew exactly where he was going and *nothing* could possibly go wrong.

I spent the morning making *glyko portakali* for our Greek night; the boiled strips of orange peel in spiced syrup would make a moreish festive treat. I was beginning to look forward to match day almost as much as Gary and with the temperatures moving ever closer to zero I was more than happy to be staying at home.

It was almost twelve-thirty when the van screeched into the lane. I knew that all was well when Gary came in smiling. He didn't go straight to the fridge for a lager; instead he said, 'Are you making a brew?'

'So when will you know?' I asked, as I passed him his coffee.

'It's usually about a fortnight, but there's Christmas and *Reyes* so I've got to go back on the twenty-first of January. And I'll get the results of the endoscopy as well.'

'Crikey,' I said. 'I'd forgotten all about that. Hopefully it'll be good news and we'll be able to relax and enjoy next year without it hanging over our heads.'

'Let's hope you're right. It's been a weird few months and there were times I really felt in limbo. I'm already looking forward to a fresh start in the new year.'

On the thirteenth of December I was up before daybreak. I'd spent the evening baking baklava, honey cookies and pitta breads, and this morning I was making hummus. When Gary appeared in the kitchen the sun was only just rising. I wondered whether it was excitement or the blender on full throttle that had stirred him from sleep.

Throughout the morning, Gary went on and on and *on* about the evening's fixture; by the time Nina and

Marcus arrived, it felt as if every fact and figure was imprinted on my brain. At the end of the previous season Real Betis, who were from Andalucía, had been relegated from the first division to the second. They had won their last two matches against Llagostera and Mallorca and were currently fifth in the table. This would be their seventeenth match of the season and they would move up to fourth place if they beat Lugo today. Lugo were tipped as the underdog, despite being on home territory. They were halfway down the table and had lost the previous week's match, playing away to Sporting Gijon. They needed a win and were sure to be playing their hearts out. According to Gary (and I almost believed him) it was going to be a very exciting match today.

As soon as the men left for Lugo, Nina and I donned our hats and fleeces. There were still two hours until sunset but the air was already bitingly cold. It made sense to cut our losses before the temperature dropped even more.

We were nearing Másimo's *hórreo* when Lulu lunged forward, tugging Nina with her. Instead of releasing her grip on the lead in order to keep her balance she slid a short distance until her feet went from under her. She was still holding the end of the lead when she landed on her bum. When Nina stood up she was laughing. 'So much for our fun afternoon.'

'Come on,' I laughed. 'Let Lulu off the lead and we'll cut through Dry-Your-Laundry Field. If you slip over again you'll have a softer landing on the grass.'

'Dry-Your-Laundry Field? Why do you call it that?'

'See the big trough coming up on the left?' I said, pointing to the *río*. 'That's where our neighbour Carmen does her laundry. A couple of years ago we thought we'd got campers when Carmen hung her clothes out along the stone wall to dry.'

To say that the grass would be soft had been an error of judgement; the field was sheeted in ice where the *río* had burst its banks. While Nina and I tottered over the glassy surface, Lenda and Lulu were in their element, charging off into the distance then hurtling back towards us, oblivious to our nerves. The experience was a nightmare and when we reached the eucalyptus wood we agreed, for the sake of safety *and* sanity, to head home. In twenty minutes, frustrated and frozen, we were back in the warm.

'So what are your plans for the summer?' I asked as I made us a coffee. 'Will you be spending it here?'

She nodded. 'Marcus wanted to make a vegetable garden – you know, on the overgrown strip below the orchard? I told him I didn't think it was a good idea.'

'Why not? Were you thinking of using it for something else?'

'No, it's not that. I don't fancy digging and weeding and... well, it's not really my thing.'

I nodded. 'I can understand that, but if Marcus is happy to take it on himself, then surely it wouldn't be a problem?'

'Oh, but it would. I'd have to use what he'd grown. It would limit my choices and, to be honest, I like to shop.'

I giggled. 'I don't. I always send Gary. Have you thought about fencing it off and keeping hens?'

'That's another thing Marcus suggested. I told him it wouldn't be practical. Who would look after them when we go back to the Netherlands? And so he came up with another suggestion...' She paused and grimaced. 'Bees.'

'Bees!' I enthused. 'That's wonderful! Oh you *are* lucky. I've wanted bees since we came here, but as far as Gary's concerned it's a "no". I've told him he needn't be involved, but he's adamant. Between you and me, I think he's scared.'

'Scared?' echoed Nina. 'What makes you think that?'

'He doesn't like insects. He flaps at wasps, and you should see him around mosquitoes… Oh, and there was the dragonfly incident in England.'

'Go on.'

'My house backed onto a river, so I tended to get gnats and things in the summer. One evening we were sitting in the kitchen and Gary said, "What's that in the window?" There was something buzzing behind the curtain and I went over to have a look. I pushed back the fabric and out shot a massive blue dragonfly. Gary screamed at the top of his voice and ran out onto the patio. Now he tells everyone it divebombed him on purpose and aimed for his head.'

It was almost nine thirty when the men arrived home from the football. Neither Marcus nor Gary asked how our evening had been. As they tucked into pitta bread, hummus and olives, each was determined to regale us with the details of the game.

'The first half was boring,' said Marcus. 'There were no goals.'

'Lugo played well though,' added Gary. 'They gave Real Betis a run for their money. Both teams seemed evenly matched, that's why the score was nil-nil.'

'The second half was better,' said Marcus. 'After fifteen minutes, Betis scored.'

'It was a pity,' said Gary. 'Lugo didn't get back into their stride after that, so Betis won one-nil.'

'Not an exciting match then?' I ventured.

'Not really,' said Gary. 'I've seen better games.'

'And,' added Marcus, 'there was no atmosphere in the stadium.'

'You're right,' agreed Gary. 'Only a third of the seats were full.'

'And it was freezing,' said Marcus.

'You're not kidding,' nodded Gary. 'That's the trouble with seated stadiums – you can't move about and stamp your feet.'

'It sounds awful,' I said.

They both nodded.

'I bet you're sorry you went now.'

They both shook their heads.

'Not at all,' said Gary. 'It was well worth twenty euros.'

'Definitely,' nodded Marcus. 'We will go again.'

The next morning Gary slept later than normal. With a dog, a cat, rabbits, chooks *and* kittens to see to I had no such choice. It was past ten o'clock when I came back from the fields with Lenda. Gary was in the kitchen drinking his cuppa. His ashtray, devoid of cigarette ends, told me he hadn't been up very long.

'Morning,' I smiled.

'Morning,' he yawned. 'Wasn't it a good night?'

'It was,' I grinned. 'And I'm glad you enjoyed the football. Mind you, I think we'd have been spectators at a very different kind of match if Nina and Marcus hadn't left when they did.'

He chuckled. 'I know what you mean. The away side nearly kicked off. He doesn't half knock the wine back, doesn't he, old Marcus? It's a good job Nina only had a couple of glasses. If she hadn't stepped in he'd have still been quite happy to drive.'

'Madness. And the legal limit's lower here than in England – he'd have been way over. He might have escaped the local police between here and Monterroso, but the Guardia are crawling all over the main roads at this time of year.'

'He's lucky to have Nina. She's very patient with him. Nice girl.'

'She is. It was lovely to spend time with her. She's good fun. I asked her if they'd like to come over and join us for Christmas dinner but they're going back to Holland to be with her mum.'

'Oh well. It looks like it'll only be us then. Never mind.'

'It'll still be fun. We can play Scrabble and crib…'

'And we can watch *Withnail and I*.'

I giggled. It would be the tenth, eleventh, or perhaps even the twelfth time we'd watched Gary's best-loved movie. It was only fair that I chose a favourite too. 'We can play Buckaroo.'

He waved his arms in the air. 'Ooh! Ooh!'

'What are you doing?'

'That's you. Every time the donkey bucks and the stuff flies off, that's what you do.' He waved his arms again. 'Ooh! Ooh!'

I picked up the tea towel and stepped towards him, poised to strike. 'How does it go again?'

As Gary 'ooh-ed' and flailed, I thwacked him repeatedly until tears of laughter ran down my face. All of a sudden I was pleased we'd be on our own for Christmas. I loved our crazy life.

When Gary came in at breaktime he seemed pensive. I wondered if he was disappointed about our quiet Christmas after all.

'Penny for 'em?' I asked him.

He paused for a moment.

I smiled my encouragement. 'Go on.'

'I've been thinking… No, you'll say it's daft.'

''Course I won't. Or maybe I will, but you won't know unless you tell me. Come on.'

'It was yesterday, on the drive to Lugo. Marcus was talking about keeping bees.'

I stubbed out my cigarette. This sounded promising. Suddenly I was all ears.

'He sounded so excited, passionate even. And I was thinking, I haven't really got any hobbies, have I? I think it'd do me good to have one too.'

It was getting better by the minute. I smiled again.

He looked at me oddly, sensing my anticipation. 'Oh no,' he frowned. 'If that's what you're thinking you've got the wrong end of the stick completely. I wasn't about to suggest I keep bees.'

'No?' I said, disappointed.

'No. I was thinking of something crafty – you know, like you with your knitting. I'd like to have a go at carving – there's no shortage of wood.'

'That's a good idea. Won't you need special chisels?'

'Not necessarily. I thought I'd try something different. I'm going to use the angle grinder instead.'

On Christmas morning, I banged and clattered and generally made as much noise as possible down in the kitchen. I wanted Gary to get up early, so we could open our presents. I was filled with childlike excitement at the thought of the enormous parcel from my Mum.

Along with the suet, there were yarns in abundance: pink and silver, turquoise and purple, emerald and scarlet... the tinsel selection was too good to be true. If that wasn't enough, there was plain wool, an owl pattern, more stuffing and some cute wobbly eyes.

Later that morning the turkey sizzled and I clicked away with my needles, to a background of carols and the sound of the angle grinder out in the barn.

On the 31st of December I was singing 'Auld Lang Syne' when Gary came into the kitchen.

'Morning,' he yawned as I passed him his cuppa. 'What's got into you?'

'It's New Year's Eve,' I grinned. 'I'm getting into the spirit – out with the old and in with the new.'

'Right. I'm with you. It's a bit early for singing though – save it for midnight. What's it mean, anyway, "Auld Lang Syne"?'

'Old times past, apparently. Up until a couple of years ago I thought Auld Lang Syne was a bloke.'

'So did I. I think a lot of folks do, to be honest. Didn't Robbie Burns write it?'

'He did. He wrote the 'Address to a Haggis' too.'

'Ah, the haggis – now you're talking. I was thinking about that. How will you make it? Don't you need a pig's bladder or something to cook it in?'

'You're thinking of *sobrasada*. Think Scottish, not Spanish. It's a sheep's stomach. I don't fancy my chances of finding one locally. I thought I might cheat and steam it in muslin like a Christmas pud.'

'Yes, please. Sounds far preferable. There're some things we're just not meant to eat.'

'Trust you. I might do it this weekend. You can drive in on Friday and get me some mince.'

When he came in at breaktime, Gary was wearing a manic grin.

'Och aye the noo!' he proclaimed as I passed him his coffee.

This was clearly to do with my morning crooning. I had only myself to blame.

'I take it there's something you want to tell me?'

'Och aye! If ye dinnae mind.'

I sighed impatiently. 'Well, go on.'

'I've found us a caber for Burns Night.'

'You what?'

'A caber. Come on, I'll show you. It's in the barn.'

It was warm by the fire and I was about to protest, but something about his enthusiasm was contagious. 'Go on then, MacDuff. Lead on.'

Upstairs in the barn he pointed to a tree trunk leaning against the wall.

I stared at it. '*That*?'

He nodded.

'You're having a laugh.'

'Why?'

'It's about six foot long and a foot wide. You'd struggle to pick it up let alone toss it. It's an accident waiting to happen if you ask me.'

'Rubbish. Look, I'll show you...'

'No, it's alright. Let's leave it 'til Burns Night, shall we? God forbid that we spoil the surprise.'

On the sixth of January I wasn't expecting any presents from *los Reyes Magos*. We'd had a wonderful Christmas; so much so that I knew it couldn't be paralleled, so this year we wouldn't be doing anything special to celebrate the feast of the Three Kings. Apart from that, I had a market stall to prepare for; I had four spangly hedgehogs already and by the end of the week I was aiming to have finished number five.

After coffee break, I went upstairs to take down the decorations. I sighed as I looked at the over-decked tree and the profusion of foliage above the stairs. It was going to take me the best part of the day to dismantle my festive festoonery and I wasn't relishing such an arduous start to the year. I bundled the sprays of holly and conifer into a binbag, then lifted the tree, complete with its trimmings into the middle of the room. Once the lights were packed safely away I started to pull off the baubles. Realising I'd forgotten to bring a box to put them in, I continued regardless; sliding them from the ends of the branches and dumping them in a diffuse mass on the floor. When the branches were bare I eased myself up off my knees, ruing the sins of indulgence which pinched at the waist of my jeans. I stood up, stretched, and groaned when I heard the padding of paws on the staircase. Scholes would have a field day when he spotted the glittery baubles strewn all over the floor. I couldn't believe my eyes when I looked behind me. Princess was standing watching from the top of the stairs. Rather than panic and dash back through the cat-hole, she sloped slowly and deliberately behind the chair.

Pretending to ignore her completely, I picked up the binbag and crept back downstairs to the kitchen. I hoped against hope that if I left her for an hour while I saw to the dinner she might jump onto the sofa and decide that she liked it inside in the warmth.

Once the spuds were simmering away, I took the binbag out to the barn and brought in a small cardboard box from the recycling. Back in the passage, I paused and listened, puzzled by the terrible clattering that seemed to be coming from upstairs. It didn't take me long to work out the cause of the commotion; someone was playing with the baubles I'd left on the floor. I didn't think for a moment that Princess could be the culprit; Scholes must have come in through the cat-hole while I'd been out in the barn. Suddenly I heard a hiss-splash-hiss from the kitchen. I recognised at once the sound of the spuds boiling over and rushed through the door. I shifted the pan from the ring and took a plate of cold cuts out of the fridge.

When Gary came in for his lunch, I didn't say a word about Princess. I didn't want to raise his hopes until I was certain she was still upstairs.

'Aren't you having any lunch?' he called as I went back through to the passage.

'I'm alright for a bit,' I shrugged. 'I'll have my meat in a butty when I've finished clearing the decorations. I've still got the baubles to pack and the tree to fold up. I shan't go so over the top next Christmas. It might look nice but taking it all down's a pain in the bum.'

I grabbed the box and opened the stairs door, wishing it didn't creak quite so loudly. The hinges had needed oiling since way back in summer. It was one of those jobs that just didn't get done. When I reached the third stair I peered through the balustrade. There were baubles everywhere but no sign of Scholes *or* Princess. I tried not to feel too disheartened; I hadn't really expected her to stay for long. When I reached the top stair I sighed at the chaos before me. The tree was on its side and the branches looked squashed and misshapen. Only then did I spot Princess, lying curled up on the chair.

When I came out of the bedroom next morning, Princess was asleep on the sofa. Scholes seemed indifferent to her presence and had maintained his position on the bed.

'Morning Princess,' I said softly, in an effort not to spook her. To my amazement, Princess began to purr.

For the rest of the week, Princess was there on the sofa when I rose every morning, and by breaktime, even from the kitchen, I'd hear thumping and clattering as she batted her single red bauble around the floor. By late afternoon she'd be gone through the cat-hole and there would be no sign of her for the rest of the evening. I had no idea whether she returned late at night or in the early morning, but she was always in her place on the sofa when I opened the bedroom door.

On Saturday morning, I mixed mincemeat, offal, suet, oats and spices, then squoze them into the shape of a short, fat sausage and tied it firmly inside its muslin craw. When Gary came in for coffee it was bubbling away on a trivet inside my biggest saucepan, while I tried to turn a blind eye to the streaks of sooty condensation running down the tiles.

'Is that the haggis?' he frowned, as I passed him his coffee.

'It is. What's up? You're frowning. I thought you'd be excited. Don't worry about the muck on the tiles – I'll give them a wipe down when it's done.'

'It's not that. I'm frowning because of the timing. We've had a message from Paul.'

'Oh shit. You're going to tell me he's not coming back for Burns Night, aren't you?'

'Correct. His Mum's been off colour so he's staying with her 'til she gets better. He's hoping to be back before the end of February. And he wished us a belated Happy New Year.'

Since Princess had ventured in through the cat-hole, she'd quickly become a fixture. I was growing increasingly fond of her and after a fortnight I realised that she'd made an impression on Gary too.

'I think I'll get Princess a dropper,' he announced when I passed him the shopping list on Monday morning. 'It's two weeks today she moved in with us. I think we can safely say she's ours.'

'Whoa,' I frowned. 'Don't go getting your hopes up. It's the middle of winter and the living room's cosy. If she's still here in springtime *then* it'll be safe to say she's ours.'

'She can have a dropper though, can't she? Whether she stays or not, she'll still need to be treated for fleas and ticks and worms.'

I could have hugged him. Only a year ago he'd protested when I'd said I wanted to give Fred his treatments. Since then he'd come to accept that the animals needed protecting. Our Galician journey had been about so much more than house renovations and self-sufficiency; it was about understanding the countryside and developing empathy for the natural world.

'It's a good idea,' I nodded. 'The thing is, Gary, I'm frightened of getting attached to her. I'm fond of her already, and if she stays we'll have to spay her. She won't be a kitten for much longer but after what happened with Fred... well, I'm wary, you know.'

'I can understand that. Look, why don't we set a deadline? She moved in at *Reyes*, so let's say the sixth of February. If she's still here then, we'll book her in at the vets and we'll have her done.'

On the twenty-first of January, Gary came home from the hospital with the best news ever. He'd been signed off by the specialist, who had found no problems with the endoscopy or the scan.

Liza Grantham

Welcome, Haggis!

Hello there, Haggis! In you come,
So fine upon your platter!
A shame we couldn't pipe you in,
But hey, what does it matter?

To see your ample, meaty form,
And unctuous juices seeping
Turns all our mouths to gleeful smiles,
And sets our hearts a-leaping!

Since auld lang syne your likes were carved
By muscled arms of workers,
For haggis feeds the men of toil,
And not the scrawny shirkers.

And so shall we our spoons dig in,
No time to say our graces,
Then we'll sit back, our bellies full,
With smiles upon our faces.

The vegans turn away in scorn,
Their indignation simmers,
And see the looks of yearning on
The faces of the slimmers.

The vegetarians all sneer
At us, as though we're sinners,
Meanwhile the health freaks eat their leaves
And tasteless fat-free dinners.

The fine Scots folks who haggis eat
Are strong and mean and mighty:
'Tis nowt to toss a caber from
The Highlands down to Blighty.

So, Haggis, feed those gathered here,
And make us hale and hearty,
And warm the cockles of our hearts,
And brighten up our party.

Then afterwards we'll all break wind
And fill the room with laughter,
For no-one here wants flimsy food;
It's haggis that we're after!

Chapter 19

No Mean Feat

The arrival of February brought signs of rebirth in the garden. Daffodils were pushing up through the soil in the tubs and borders, and the tips of crocus leaves were sprouting between the rocks that covered Anxo's grave. Over the five fields, the gorse was already in bud and down by the steppingstones, clusters of frogspawn floated blancmange-like beneath the surface of the stream.

Down in the chicken run, all seven of the hens were laying and over in Warren Place, Doe rabbit had been mated again.

Though the outside world was abundant with signs of new life, I was determined that the same would not be the case for Princess. She'd been living with us for almost a month and it was safe to assume she'd be staying. Spring was in the air and at nine months old her first oestrus was imminent. I rang the vets to make the appointment; on the eleventh of February Princess would be spayed.

Over the last four weeks, Princess's movements had continued to follow the same pattern. We had no idea where she spent her time during the afternoons and evenings, and still didn't know whether she resumed her place on the sofa in the early hours of the morning or as soon as we'd retired for the night. Once, when the sun had been unusually warm for February, I was sure I'd spotted her in the bracken on Field One during Lenda's evening walk. Gary had said it was my imagination; he didn't believe for a moment that Princess would wander so far.

Princess loved to be petted and always purred loudly when we fussed her. She'd gladly roll over for a belly rub, sticking her 'arms' up as if to say, 'scratch under here'. Although she was comfortable in our presence, we still hadn't managed to hold her; the minute I put my hands around her ribcage, she'd wriggle violently, in a good-natured but most emphatic refusal to be picked up. Every day I'd make time to sit by her on the sofa, but try as I might, I hadn't yet succeeded in coaxing her onto my lap. I was confident that eventually she'd trust me enough to be handled, but it wasn't going to be any time soon. I had to accept that whilst she looked every bit the chocolate box cutie, Princess was essentially feral and if we were going to get her into the cat carrier we'd need a fool proof plan.

We wracked our brains and came up with all kinds of solutions. As far as I was concerned, my mouse-in-a-sock ploy was favourite, but Gary dismissed it instantly, convinced I was mad.

'So let me get this right,' he frowned when I told him. 'You'll release the mouse from the trap into a sock.'

I nodded.

'But it'll be dead.'

'No it won't. Those plastic traps don't kill them instantly. Sometimes they clatter about for hours before they die.'

'That's cruel.'

'No it isn't. It's no different to your mole trap principle. I run outside and let them go at the entrance to Corner Field. It's kinder actually, it gives them a chance.'

'*If* you're there when it happens.'

'Yes, well…' I took a deep breath. '*Any*way, once the mouse is wriggling inside the sock, which is now inside the carrier…'

In the end we'd decided we'd tempt her inside with some ham.

As every ailurophile knows, cats have an innate psychic ability and are adept at reading human minds. The cat-hole would therefore need to be blocked on the morning before the appointment; if Princess sensed something was afoot she might not come home in the night. Unlike Fred, she wouldn't be shut in the bedroom. A wet duvet had been a pain back in May but how much worse would it be in February? I wouldn't stand the remotest chance of getting it dry.

At daybreak on Tuesday morning, Princess was asleep on the sofa. It was clear that she'd used the litter tray and the towel blocking the cat-hole remained undisturbed. She'd been confined for twenty-four hours and had made no attempt to skedaddle. We were over the first hurdle and everything was going to plan. Scholes followed me down the stairs and into the passage, weaving and wailing persistently until I let him out through the door.

Shortly before eight-thirty, I went to the fridge and took out the ham.

'What are you doing? asked Gary. 'She's not due at the vet's 'til ten.'

'I know that, Gary. I'm being prudent. She's still half feral and it might not be easy to catch her. Apart from that, we still don't know whether your ham strategy is actually going to work.'

'You mean you didn't test it beforehand?'

I stared at him in disbelief. 'So that she's already wise to it you mean? Honestly Gary, sometimes you... look, it doesn't matter. The bottom line is we don't know if it'll work so we need to allow ourselves a margin of error. Trust me, it makes sense.'

Clutching the ham, I went up to the living room, where the cat carrier had been left open all night in the middle of the floor. I went over to Princess who was still curled up on the sofa. Her eyes soon opened when she picked up the scent of the ham. I gave her a morsel and she wolfed it down eagerly, then started to nudge at my hand with her head. Calling her gently, I backed over to the carrier and knelt on the floor. She was beside me in seconds, rubbing her cheek against the packet. This time I took out a full slice and dangled it at the door of the carrier before tossing it in. Princess didn't follow; she simply lay down on the floor. With only inches between her and the carrier I was sure it was going to be a doddle. I couldn't have been more wrong. A terrified cat develops joints in places it didn't previously have them. It snakes, twists and doubles back on itself like a master of contortion and, if all else fails, it uses its claws.

Fifteen minutes later I was back in the kitchen.

'It's impossible,' I sighed. 'Look at the state of my hands – she's like a wild cat. I'm going to have to put gloves on and try again.'

'Can't you chuck a towel over her?'

'Gary. I'm not *chucking* anything over her. She's scared enough as it is. I'll try again in a minute. I'm going to fetch the gardening gloves from the barn.'

When I returned to the living room there was no sign of Princess. Cursing myself for leaving the door open I went into the bedroom. Sure enough, Princess was hiding under the bed. I turned when I heard footsteps behind me. Gary was standing at the door.

'Have you got her?'

'What does it look like?' I frowned, walking past him back into the living room. 'I'm going to let her calm down for a minute. She's stressed.'

'You're making it too complicated. You're clumsy at the best of times. My reactions are quicker – let *me* have a go.'

'I really think…'

Whatever I thought was of no consequence to Gary. He ignored me completely and walked in. As the door closed behind him I took off the gloves, sat down on the arm of the sofa and stared at the door. I heard the bed being dragged across the floorboards and Gary's best effort to adopt a dulcet tone.

'Prinny. Come on, Prinny-Princess. That's it, come on…'

There was a creak of bedsprings.

'*That's* it, Princess. Now, if I can just reach…'

There was a thud.

'Shit! *Prin*cess! What did you move for? No-one's going to hurt you, for God's sake.'

The bedsprings creaked again and Gary's footsteps thudded across the floor.

As he came through the door, I smiled at him sweetly. 'Any luck?'

'Nearly. I got on the bed and reached right under. I'd have had her if your bloody Doc Martens hadn't been in the way.'

I pouted. 'I don't suppose any of *your* shoes are under the bed?'

'That's not the point. The fact is…'

'We're going to have to do it together. I'll bring the carrier. Come on.'

Once we were both in the bedroom I adopted a no-nonsense approach. 'Right,' I said firmly. 'You'll need to be right under the bed, so you'll have to get down on your belly. Your body will be blocking *that* end so you'll be able to shoo her in *this* direction. Does that make sense?'

He nodded.

'Good. Hopefully she'll shoot out towards the carrier and I'll be able to shunt her in. Just make sure you're in the right position before you shoo her. If you're really slow and careful she might even dive in by herself.'

As Gary lowered himself onto his knees, I could see that he'd misunderstood me. He was positioned at the wrong end of the bed. If he edged his way under from there, Princess would leap out at the headboard end and I was on the opposite side of the room. I was about to say so, but before I had chance to speak, Princess made her move. She leapt up onto the bedside table then lunged in panic onto the duvet. As Gary slid out, Princess dived under the bed again.

'Now what?' scowled Gary.

I scowled back. 'The same again, but this time *I'll* get under the bed.'

'Please yourself.'

By the time I'd squeezed myself under the bed, Princess had darted under the bedside table.

'Right, the carrier,' said Gary.

'No,' I whispered. 'Don't you bloody dare. You can pass me a pillow and I'll press it against the legs and *then* you can bring the basket. Well come on, what are you waiting for? Slide me a pillow under the bed.'

Two minutes later I was lying prostrate against the floorboards, pushing the pillow for all I was worth against the legs of the bedside table. It felt like my arms were coming out of their sockets as I reached forward and pressed.

It seemed an eternity before Gary finally brought the carrier over to the table.

'Right,' I said breathlessly. 'The second I move the pillow, shove the carrier in its place.'

For once, Gary didn't dawdle. Within seconds, Princess was caught.

Over the next fortnight I kept Princess indoors while her wound began to heal. For the first week it was red and slightly inflamed but I wasn't too worried. I trusted that the antibiotic I was mixing into sardines would do its job. In the second week the wound lay flat and the scab had darkened. In only a couple more days she'd be safe to go out. As the day of release loomed closer I was becoming increasingly nervous. Princess was back to her purry old self and was desperate now for her freedom, but I couldn't help wondering if the nightmare still preyed on her mind. We'd stalked her for almost an hour, then bundled her into the carrier. Had she really forgiven us for subjecting her to her ordeal?

Before she'd come in through the cat-hole, Princess had been feral. All she'd known were hedgerows, outbuildings, forests and fields. She could catch mice and birds, climb trees and play with her mum and her brother. When she returned to her familiar environment, would she be reluctant to come home for fear of being imprisoned again?

In the last week of February, Gary made me see sense.

'You can't keep her in forever, Liza. She's spending all day on the windowsill, staring outside. This is her home and I'm sure she won't leave us, but if she does that's her choice – you've got to let go.'

When I called Gary in at breaktime, Princess was out in the garden. I could see her from the back doorstep, sprawled out on the threshing floor enjoying the sun.

'I'm glad she's outside,' I smiled, as I passed him his coffee.

'So am I,' he nodded. 'But if you ask me, she's not the only one that needs releasing. I think it's about time you let something else out too.'

For a moment I thought he was talking about Waynetta. For the last two days she'd been flitting up into the trees in the daytime. I was sure that when the weather grew warmer she'd go back to roosting there for the night.

'Oh no,' I frowned. 'Not Waynetta? I'm sure it's only a matter of time before she tries absconding again.'

'I wasn't thinking of Waynetta. I'm talking about something you've had locked up since the beginning of the year.'

I looked at him puzzled. 'I don't understand.'

'I'm talking about the haggis, Liza. It's been shut in the freezer for weeks now. I can't help thinking it's time it came out.'

I giggled. 'Trust you. I thought you were being serious. I started to feel guilty without knowing what I'd done. I hadn't forgotten about it. I was waiting 'til Paul came back. I was expecting him to be here by now.'

'So was I. I was looking forward to tossing the caber, but we can't wait forever. It's March next week and haggis is supposed to be a winter warmer. If it was left to me I'd be defrosting it this weekend.'

I thought for a minute. I'd told Paul I'd do us a haggis and I knew he'd been looking forward to it, but Gary was right, we couldn't wait forever and we didn't know how long he'd be caring for his mum. All of a sudden I had a brainwave. I knew just what to do.

'I've got it,' I said. 'See what you think. It's three years since we had a St. Patrick's bash. Now we know a few people we could have one this year.'

He nodded slowly. 'Ri-ight. But I don't see what that's got to do with the haggis.'

'We'll have a meal and music, but instead of Irish, we'll do Celtic. It'd be very Galician. We could invite people with instruments and still sing Irish songs.'

'I've got you. It sounds good in theory, but we don't know any musicians, only Paul.'

'There's Rudi.'

'Rudi? From Quercus Sonora? *He* wouldn't be interested, he's a classical violinist. It wouldn't be *his* sort of thing.'

'Rubbish. It'd make a nice change for him. He and Sandra are down to earth sort of people – they'd think it was fun.'

'If you say so. There's no harm in asking, I s'pose.'

'Brilliant. I'll send them a message and I'll ring Helen and…'

'Hold on a minute. There's Adey as well.'

'Adey?'

'Yes. Adey from the Ghost House. He plays the guitar.'

'Really? You never said.'

'Didn't I? Well I have now. And he doesn't *just* play the guitar, he sings as well. He used to busk apparently, so he must be okay.'

'Splendid. That's settled then. You can ring Adey and I'll contact Helen and Sandra. It looks like you might get to toss your caber after all.'

On the first of March I brought my box of stuffed toys into the dining room. I'd been knitting like fury since

October and my family of hedgehogs and owls had really grown. I decided to spread them all out on the table and see how I might best display them. If they looked sufficiently impressive, I'd be off into Antas on the tenth to do my first stall.

For the best part of an hour I played with arrays and clusters, grouping them by size and colour and mixing and matching to achieve the most eye-catching effect. However I arranged them, the toys looked great but I couldn't help thinking I needed more of them. Of course, I'd seen folks selling as little as a few eggs or cheeses, but that didn't matter. They were old, they were local and they spoke *galego*. I was a different animal entirely. I was younger, pink-haired and English, and I stood out like a sore thumb. If I was going to hold my head up at Antas market I was going to have to go the extra mile to impress. Another half a dozen would make all the difference, and it was worth being patient. I could knit my heart out for a few weeks longer and be ready for the market next month.

Satisfied with my plan, my thoughts turned to the final hurdle. Gary was still clueless about my intentions. I couldn't keep my secret for much longer; it was time I told him my plan.

When we settled down with our beers that evening I was ready to take the bull by the horns.

'There's something I've been meaning to tell you,' I ventured.

He looked at me suspiciously. 'Oh yes?'

'Yes. And before I go ahead and share it with you…'

'*Share* it with me? What kind of pretentious rubbish is that?'

I tutted. 'Before I *tell* you, I want you to know that I've already decided and it's no good trying to get me to change my mind.'

His expression changed. If I wasn't mistaken he looked concerned. 'Go on.'

I swallowed. 'You know the toys I've been knitting?'

'Ye-es.'

'I'm going to have a stall and sell them on Antas market. There, I've said it. What d'you think?'

A look of relief came over his face. 'I think it's a great idea. They're good, especially the hedgehogs. I wasn't sure when you said you were going to do them in different colours, but they've turned out really well.'

I smiled gratefully. 'Thank you. I thought you'd say it's a daft idea. Do you think it costs much to have a stall?'

'I doubt it. I think you'll find it doesn't cost anything at all.'

'What makes you say that?'

'Well, we've seen folks with only a few bulbs of garlic or a dozen eggs to sell, haven't we? It wouldn't be worth their while if they had to pay for a plot.'

'You're right. I hadn't thought of that. We'll have to check though. I was thinking of starting in April, so perhaps you could ask at the *concello* next time you go into town.'

On Monday morning, Gary had a surprise for me when he came home with the shopping.

'I called in at the *concello* and you don't need a permit. You can set up anywhere you like, but you have to be mindful of the regular stallholders because they have priority. That means you'll be stuck on the very end, all the way past A Banca, if you go on the main street. The side street by the butchers has spaces and there's loads of room in the *auditorio* as well.'

'The *auditorio*?'

'That's what the woman called it. She means the covered space near the pharmacy that we've always called the bandstand. I reckon you'll be better off setting your stall up in there.'

'Did she happen to mention whether the trestles are provided? I forgot to mention it earlier – I don't suppose you thought to ask?'

'I did actually, and no they aren't. You don't need to worry though – I've bought you a present. You can call it your early Easter egg. Come on, it's in the barn.'

My surprise was just inside the doorway, leaning against the wall. It was a grey square wrapped in polythene. For a split second I thought it was a giant paving slab. I stared at it for a moment until the penny finally dropped.

'It's a table!'

He gave an exaggerated roll of his eyes. 'You don't say.'

I didn't want to seem ungrateful but it was really too small for my purposes. Present or no, there was no point in beating about the bush. I turned to him. 'It doesn't look very big.'

'What are you like? That's only half of it. It's folded up, silly. It was only forty-five euros from Ferretería Patao. I've got you a thermos flask too.'

I beamed at him. 'Thank you. It's so thoughtful of you. I honestly wasn't expecting it. I don't know what to say.'

'Don't say anything. It's only to stop you bottling out at the last minute – I know what you're like for changing your mind.'

As we were coming out of the barn a voice called, 'Elisa!' Maruja and Flea-pelt were making their way down the lane. As they drew closer, I saw that Maruja looked tearful. She wasn't usually given to displays of emotion and I wondered what the matter was.

'*Hola*, Maruja,' I said. 'You look worried. Is something wrong?'

Liza Grantham

'Pastor's gone missing. He isn't in the cowshed or the farmyard. He's been gone since yesterday evening and I'm beginning to think we won't find him alive.'

Since Pastor had taken ill in September he'd never completely recovered. He'd stopped making his daily rounds with Luna and hadn't regained his full weight. He was old now, and his days were numbered, but when the time came it would still be upsetting. He was part of the fabric of the village and, more than that, he was a friend.

I shook my head sadly. 'I haven't seen him. We walked all the way round the five fields this morning. If he'd been out there, Lenda would have been sure to raise the alarm. Maruja, I'm so sorry. I do hope he comes home.'

As dusk descended, I mustered up courage to make the final trek out to the garden. March was the month that served up the full gamut of weathers: biting cold dawns that gave way to glorious sunshine or days upon days of the trademark Galician rain. I zipped up my coat and dug my hands deep into my pockets; tonight was the former and I wondered when the frosts would finally end. Out in the lane I heard a gate clang and felt sorry for Maruja. She had a herd to tend to and chickens and rabbits, yet five days a week, morning and evening, she traipsed through the village to see to Solina's hens. As I opened the gate, I heard footsteps approaching. I turned round and saw Maruja on the corner by the annexe. As she came towards me I guessed she had news.

'Javier's found Pastor,' she told me. 'He was lying in the field near the bus stop. He was cold and wet, but he was still breathing. We've put him in the straw in the cowshed. He's eaten some stew, and he looks a bit brighter. Elisa, I think he'll make it. I don't think he's going to die.'

354

On St Patrick's Day morning I was filled with excitement. At the eleventh hour, Rudi and Sandra had replied to my text. They'd been in Madrid since the new year, but now they were back in Galicia and would love to come to our do. Adey, Paul and Helen had accepted our invitations as soon as we'd asked them. We'd have a haggis, a Bailey's cheesecake and a grand assortment of instruments. With all the ingredients for a great party I couldn't wait for our Celtic fusion bash.

At six o'clock I flitted nervously between the living room, the kitchen and the doorstep. A little before half past, all three of our ex-pat guests turned up.

Adey was just as much fun as Gary had promised. He had wicked blue eyes and an irreverent sense of humour. He regaled us with tale after tale of the ex-pats he'd worked for. He had nicknames for all of them and I found myself wondering what names he'd come up with for us.

By half past seven there was still no sign of Rudi and Sandra and I was beginning to think they'd changed their minds about coming. Feeling slightly deflated I went downstairs to check on the food. Satisfied that everything was cooked to perfection, I called up the stairs for everyone to move through to the dining room. I was piling vegetables into serving dishes when there was a knock at the door. Sure enough it was Rudi and Sandra and they were *both* carrying violin cases. I was quick to forgive their lack of punctuality; we were going to be blessed with some proper Irish fiddling after all.

'Perfect timing,' I lied, as I ushered them up the staircase. 'We're just sitting down to eat.'

'Already?' said Sandra. 'I'm sorry. When you said six o'clock I thought you meant any time after that. In Spain it's different you see – people don't usually eat until after ten o'clock.'

As it turned out their Spanish body clocks were as flexible as their time-keeping; neither Rudi nor Sandra had any trouble in polishing off their grub. The haggis was delicious, even without its traditional casing; it wasn't long before only its juices remained on the plate.

Back in the living room we chatted for a while until Paul, Adey and Gary took up their instruments. I sang with gusto, as they belted out all my traditional favourites, but I couldn't help feeling puzzled when Rudi and Sandra made no attempt to take out their violins.

As time ticked on, our merrymaking became more raucous and I wondered if Gary had been right after all. Rudi was a professional musician who now found himself surrounded by a bunch of inept and rowdy amateurs. I hadn't taken him for a prig, but perhaps I'd been mistaken. I knew how disappointed our other guests would feel if he'd changed his mind.

It was Adey who finally plucked up the courage to ask. 'Are you getting your violin out then, Rudi? It's not the same without a fiddler – are you going to join in?'

Rudi smiled. 'I'd like to,' he said, 'but it's impossible. I don't know how to play these tunes.'

'You don't have to play them by ear,' explained Paul. 'I play them that way because I know them, but I've brought the music with me. The folder's in my bag.'

'It's not that,' said Rudi. 'I can't do it, even with the music. I *will* play something Irish for you, but I can't join in with those songs.'

I looked at Gary and he shrugged his shoulders. I noticed that Adey, Paul and Helen were looking bewildered too.

Sandra had picked up on our confusion. She looked at Rudi fondly. 'Perhaps you should try to explain?'

Rudi smiled his agreement and we waited, intrigued.

'Okay,' he began. 'You know that I play in an orchestra?'

We all nodded.

'Well that's my problem. I'm over-trained. A classical violinist has many years of instruction. Every day of their lives is practice, practice, practice. Over time it is as if I've become… well, brainwashed. When it comes to being a fiddler I don't know where to start.'

'Wow,' said Adey. 'That's amazing.'

'It is,' agreed Paul. 'What is it exactly that you can't do?'

'Well,' began Rudi. 'The hardest part is the vibration of the strings. In classical music the notes are played with vibrato, unless the dynamics say otherwise. I do this without thinking, and I move from the elbow to make long strokes of the bow. With the fiddle, the notes are quicker and compared to the violin they hardly vibrate. The strokes are shorter and the fiddler moves more from the wrist than the elbow. It's exactly the same instrument, but a completely different technique.'

For a moment we all fell silent, trying to take it all in. Eventually we all began to speak at once.

'Unreal,' said Adey. 'Who'd have thought it?'

'I'd no idea,' said Paul. 'I just thought, well – a violin, a fiddle – it was all down to the name.'

'I knew it would be different,' I said, 'insofar as a fiddle player might struggle to play classical music, but I hadn't thought for a moment it could happen the other way round.'

'I know what you mean,' agreed Gary. 'You tend to think of a fiddler as a second rate violinist. It hadn't occurred to me that it's a completely different art.'

'So what would it sound like?' asked Adey. 'You know, if you played the Irish stuff as if you were playing classical violin?'

'I'll show you, shall I?' grinned Rudi. He looked at Sandra. 'Shall we do it now?'

She nodded shyly. 'I'm not very good,' she told us. 'Rudi only started to teach me two years ago. I still have a lot to learn.'

'You're doing really well,' Rudi assured her. 'Tonight will be a good experience for you. When you play in front of an audience your confidence improves.'

'What are you going to play?' asked Adey.

'We've learned an air,' said Rudi. 'I found one that was popular, but easy to learn for Sandra. You might know it. It's called 'Sheebeg and Sheemore'.[4]

It was after two in the morning when we finally waved goodbye to our visitors. Scholes had come home long before the party had finished. He'd glared at us all disapprovingly before walking as bold as brass across the living room and putting himself to bed. Throughout the evening there had been no sign of Princess, but I wasn't expecting to see her until morning. Since we'd unblocked the cat-hole she'd immediately returned to her normal routine.

I was feeling the worse for wear when I walked into the living room next morning. I groaned at the sight of the cans and bottles and overflowing ashtrays; there was always a downside to hosting a do. As I crossed the room, my heart skipped a beat when I looked at the sofa. It was nothing to do with the crumbs or cigarette ash; Princess hadn't come home.

For the rest of the day, I traced a circuit along the lane, around the garden, up to the living room and back again. How could I have been so thoughtless? It had taken months for Princess to trust me and I'd betrayed

---

[4] Also known as *Sí Bheag, Sí Mhór*, composed by Turlough O'Carolan and inspired by the legendary Fairy Hills in Co. Leitrim, Ireland.

her for the sake of a party; when would I ever learn? That night I wept silently into my pillow; I'd lost Princess in the very same way I'd lost Fred.

The next morning you could have knocked me down with a feather when I came out of the bedroom. Princess was out for the count on the sofa. This time I wept with joy.

Liza Grantham

Hey Diddle Diddle

Hey diddle diddle,
The maestro will fiddle,
Mad Cow will be over the moon!
We'll clap and we'll stamp
And we'll beat on the drum
When the maestro is playing the tune!

Hey diddle diddle,
Oh my, what a riddle!
The maestro felt such a buffoon!
We clapped and we stamped
And we beat on the drum,
But he just couldn't pick up the tune!

Hey diddle diddle,
You'll laugh 'til you tiddle;
Mad Cow tried her hardest to croon!
'Twas nowhere as good
As a fiddle, of course,
But the maestro could not play the tune!

Hey diddle diddle,
Oh, please say you'll fiddle,
And don't burst the party balloon!
So he played with true flair
Such a sweet Irish air,
And Mad Cow was over the moon!

Chapter 20

No Smoking

On the first of April, I went out to the bench as the sun rose. Lulled by the cockerels and the cuckoo, I sipped on my coffee and smoked my first cigarette of the morning. Spring had truly arrived and around me the world was awakening. The frosts were gone now, and signs of new life were abundant. The *aldea* in springtime was enchanting, and dawn was my favourite time of the day.

Inside the barn, a thud and a snuffle roused me from my reverie. The countryside was stirring to life, and so was Hairy Fred. Since Princess had moved in, I hadn't stopped feeding him, despite being resigned to the fact that he would probably never be tamed. Over the last couple of weeks he'd become noticeably fatter. At nine months old he was a young adult. His growth rate was slowing down and his optimum calorie intake was less than it had been as a kitten. It was about time I started cutting his rations down.

Unlike Hairy Fred, Doe's babies were still in the rapid growth stage of infancy. At four weeks old they were eating like gannets and pooing accordingly. Doe, who had never been blessed with the greatest of maternal instincts, had already relinquished all responsibility; there were no top-ups from the milk bar and the cost of feeding them – economic or otherwise – fell to me.

Down in the chooks' pen I waited for Waynetta to flap her way down from her damson tree. Just as I'd predicted, she'd returned to her favourite roost once the temperatures had risen. I'd been expecting her to be pecking about on the ground already; she was usually up with the lark. I cast my eyes around the enclosure, thinking she must be grubbing for an early breakfast. There was no sign of her, so after letting the rest of the birds out I squeezed myself behind the henhouse and peered at the foot of Paul's tree. To my surprise and disappointment, Waynetta wasn't there.

'White rabbits,' said Gary, when I came back into the kitchen. 'I win.'

'What? Oh yes, white rabbits. Good for you.'

'What's the matter? You seem distracted. You're usually on the ball.'

'I *am* distracted. It's Waynetta. She's missing again.'

'Well, at least we know where to find her this time. She'll be back under the apple tree round Paul's.'

'She isn't. I've already looked.'

'And she's not up the damson tree?'

I shook my head.

'She won't have gone far. I bet she's sitting on a load of eggs like last time. I'll have a look while you're out with Lenda if you like.'

'Thanks. I won't hold my breath though. It wouldn't surprise me if the fox has had her. It's that time of year.'

When I came back from the fields with Lenda, Gary was waiting outside the barn.

'Any joy?' I asked him.

He shook his head. 'Nothing. I've looked round Paul's and along the track and all over the garden. If she's sitting on eggs she's bloody well hidden. All we can do now is wait.'

On the last afternoon before the market in Antas, I made preparations in earnest. I ironed my jeans and laid out a big chunky jumper. I polished my Doc Martens and applied apple green colouring to my freshly bleached hair. I set up my table in the living room and covered it with a white cotton cloth. It was five weeks since I'd spread out my toys on the dining table, and I was pleased with how well my collection had grown. As well as the owls and hedgehogs, there were now eight little felt ponies, thanks to another crafty parcel from my Mum. Edged round in contrasting blanket stitch with matching tails and manes, they were going to make a bright and colourful addition to my stall.

For the next two hours, my creative muse ran riot. I rummaged about in the chests and cupboards, then tacked and trimmed and tweaked until my fingers were sore. The ponies stood in a fruit-box paddock, on shredded green tissue while the hedgehogs nestled on scrunched up sacking dotted with appliqué leaves. The owls made the perfect centrepiece, perched in the bottom half of the Christmas tree, peering out with their beady eyes.

I'd been knitting for only eight months, yet my work looked far from amateur. I'd come on in leaps and bounds since my scarf-cum-britches back in August and was sure that my first foray into entrepreneurship would be a roaring success.

Happy with the results, I dismantled it all and stuffed everything into binbags. After three trips downstairs and out to the barn, the bags, the table and a folding chair were piled up in the back of the van.

'I still think I should join you,' said Gary, when we settled down with our beers that evening. 'You're too serious for a market stall – you haven't got the gift of the gab.'

'Rubbish. I just don't play the fool like you do. I'll manage perfectly well without you, thank you. The last thing folks want is some nutter acting the goat.'

'That's the idea, silly. You've got to grab people's attention, look…' He stood up, put one hand on his chest and moved the other in sweeping waves. 'Roll up, roll up! *Come* and get your 'edge'ogs! *Beau*tiful 'edge'ogs!'

'Haven't you forgotten something?'

'What?'

'The punters are Spanish.'

'Alright then.' He took up his demented Thespian stance again. '*Venga*! *Venga*! What's hedgehog?'

'*Erizo*, but please don't bother. I've got the idea.'

'I was trying to be helpful. You're a fine one to talk anyway. You've changed your hair colour so you'll stand out.'

'That's different. I want to make a visual impact not cause a breach of the peace.'

When morning came round I hadn't expected to feel nervous, but Gary stepped in to walk Lenda while I shuttled up and downstairs to the loo. On the drive into Antas, for once I sat quietly. I was having a crisis of confidence about my knitting; were my toys really good enough to sell? I considered voicing my doubts but thought better of it. A repeat of the previous night's performance was more than I could bear.

As we carried our load from the van, the drizzle fell and the breeze was icy. I was having misgivings even before I'd begun to set up my stall. The *auditorio* was a spacious rectangular area with a paving slab floor. It was walled on two sides, but the front and back were completely open. The wind blew through as if it were gusting through a tunnel. Had it not been for the showers, the main street might have been a better location after all.

'Where do you want to be?' asked Gary as we hovered uncertainly at the back.

I cast my eyes over the space before us. 'There,' I said. 'By the wall.'

'Are you sure?' he frowned. 'Wouldn't you be better further forward? There, look – next to the fruit stall? Folks might not see you if you're tucked away at the side.'

If I was honest, that was exactly what I wanted, but I was here for a purpose and common sense prevailed.

'Okay then,' I nodded. 'I'll go over there.'

While Gary set up the table, I opened the bin bags. As he locked the legs into position I pulled out the tablecloth and the tree.

'Do you really need the cloth?' he asked me. 'It's going to flap about when the wind blows. You could end up losing all your stuff off the stall.'

'It'll be fine,' I said tersely. 'Right, I've got everything. You can go now, thank you. I'll see you at two.'

For a moment he hovered and I wondered if he was going to be awkward. Instead, he patted my shoulder and said, 'Okay then. Good luck.'

Once the cloth and the tree were in place, I began to set out the toys. I stood the hedgehogs on one side on their sacking and arranged the ponies on the other in their tray of straw. As I turned to pick up the owls, the wind gusted through from the back entrance, lifting the tablecloth and sending a flurry of hedgehogs and ponies tumbling down onto the slabs. I dashed forward, scooping them up where they'd landed before they were blown further across the floor. The wind was going to be a problem; I didn't want to spend the next four hours trying to catch my stuff as it took off from the stall. I was wondering what to do when the man from the fruit and veg stall came over.

'You're in the wrong place there,' he said cheerily. 'Come on, I'll give you a hand to move.' He glanced around him, then pointed. 'Over there might be better, between me and the *charcutería*. We'll act as a windbreak for your stall.'

As we began to gather up my things, Fruit Man asked me how long I'd lived in Galicia and if I was born in London. By the time I'd been relocated my nerves had subsided. Fruit Man had been kind and helpful and there was really nothing to worry about after all. I sat down on my folding chair and took out the flask and tobacco from my rucksack. With the hairy start behind me I was beginning to look forward to the morning. I might even feel like chatting and smiling once I was plied with a fag and a brew. I rolled a cigarette and held it to my lips between my cold, trembling fingers. Inhaling deeply I flicked open the lighter, but Fruit Man dashed over before the flame had even touched my fag.

'Stop!' he said gravely. 'You can't smoke in here.' He pointed behind us. 'Look, there's a sign on the wall.'

I glanced over to wear he was pointing. Sure enough, a big white sign said, '*Prohibido Fumar*.'

I gaped in horror. Four long hours without nicotine lay ahead of me. It felt as if the bottom had dropped out of my world.

'Sorry,' I mumbled, as Fruit Man walked back to his stall.

Five minutes later, he returned with a small bag of cherries. 'Here,' he smiled kindly. 'These are for you.'

For the next half hour, I munched on the cherries and waited patiently for my customers. People wandered in dribs and drabs through the *auditorio* but, be it due to the weather or the no-nonsense Galician mindset, none of them seemed willing to browse. People paused to admire my toys en route to the food stalls on either side of me. Some of them even paid compliments but no-one wanted to buy.

With little else to do I poured a coffee and resigned myself to a morning of peoplewatching. If nothing else I'd be able to study the experts and see what clever ruses they used to tempt people over to their stalls.

Fruit Man did a steady trade from the outset. His customers all walked away with bulging carrier bags and it was only minutes later before others came smiling up to the stall. The way he laughed and joked gave me the impression that everyone knew him, but perhaps he simply had a talent for making them feel like his lifelong friends.

Throughout the morning, Cold Meat Man chain-smoked and chatted jovially as he served his customers. I wondered whether he'd earned special privileges or merely had a blatant disregard for the law. I watched longingly as the cigarette dangled from his bottom lip and wiled away the time imagining every possible outcome in the event that the ash might drop onto the food. Would he make a big show of discarding the meat quickly, then surreptitiously return it later to the stall? Would he brush it aside with his hand and proclaim blithely that it was of no consequence? Was I suffering so acutely from withdrawal symptoms that I'd lapsed into a trance-state and he wasn't really smoking at all?

Although he hadn't once smiled at me or bid me good morning, at mid-day he came over with some *jamon ibérico* on a hunk of fresh bread. He must have noticed me staring and assumed I was coveting his cold cuts. I thanked him politely, fighting the temptation to ask for a drag on his ciggie instead.

Over by the entrance, facing out onto the pavement, a young woman with a toddler in a pushchair was selling adults' and children's underwear. Her stall was sheltered by a canvas awning, adorned with enormous flesh-coloured knickers and support bras, all flapping about in the wind. The child had grizzled for most of the morning and was growing increasingly restless. I would have loved to abandon my stall and take the pushchair for a lap round the block, if only to stretch my legs and get some blood back into my feet which were numb with the cold. When the child began to scream hysterically, the mother was torn by her loyalties. I pitied and admired her in equal measure; it was no mean feat to cope with the weather, a toddler *and* a stall. I picked up the prettiest of the ponies and took it over to the little girl. She stopped sobbing and grasped it in her tiny chubby fingers. She giggled sweetly, and her mum smiled and beckoned me to her as I turned to go back to my stall.

'Wait,' she called. 'Come and choose a *regalito*. The least I can do is give you a gift.'

I thanked her, surprised by her kindness and, not wishing to take advantage, looked for the cheapest items on sale. I spotted a tray at the front marked '2 EUROS' and began to sift through an assortment of pretty cotton briefs in pastel shades edged with lace. What should have been a simple exercise left me totally flummoxed; the sizes ranged from medium to extra-large. I chose a pink and grey pair three sizes too big and was pleased with them regardless. They'd be tantamount to bloomers and perfect for dog walks in winter. I was sure they'd stay up if I wore them under joggers or jeans.

Shortly after, Cold Meat Man came over with another piece of bread, this time topped with chorizo. Since his last visit I hadn't been staring and I wondered if he was on a mission to help me fit into my drawers.

On the opposite side of the road, the not-so-cheap shoe stall stood deserted apart from its owner. The poor young woman, barely visible beneath layer upon layer of clothing, looked frozen to the marrow. My heart went out to her as she nodded at people who ambled along the pavement. In a way, we were kindred spirits; I was certain she hadn't sold a single pair of shoes all day.

At a quarter past one I could bear it no longer. My feet felt as if they were detached from my body and, having drained every drop of my coffee, there was nowhere left to warm my hands. If I cleared away now I wouldn't be able to escape from the bandstand, but at least I'd be able to wait for Gary in the corner, out of the wind. As I began to take the owls out of the tree, Fruit Man came over. 'I like the hedgehogs,' he smiled. 'How much are they?'

The hedgehogs were seven euros, but I thought of his earlier kindness. 'Five euros,' I said, feeling ashamed.

He passed me ten euros. 'I'll take two for my little girls.'

Dear old Fruit Man. He was my knight in shining armour and he'd saved the day.

I was folding my plastic table when I spotted Gary coming through the back entrance. Whether it was due to telepathy or morbid curiosity, I couldn't believe my luck.

'Alright?' he asked brightly. 'I thought I'd come half an hour early – help you out with the last minute rush.'

'Not funny,' I gruffed. 'I'm bloody frozen and I'm dying for a fag.'

'I bet you're starving as well, aren't you? It's a long time to go without grub.'

'I'm alright. I've had some fruit and a couple of butties. Look, grab some stuff will you? The sooner we get home the better – I need to warm up.'

As we carried the bags back to the van it was clear that my load hadn't lessened since earlier that morning. I had to get it over with; it was only a matter of time before Gary noticed as well.

'I didn't sell much,' I ventured.

'No?'

'No.'

'Well, never mind. You'll do better next time. I s'pose the bad weather will have kept folks at home.'

I took a deep breath. 'I sold a couple of hedgehogs to Fruit Man. I only charged him ten euros. They were for his two little girls.'

'That's nice. You've made a friend as well then. What else did you sell?'

'Nothing. That was it.'

'That was it?'

'Yes. But like you say…'

'You've stood in the freezing cold for four hours and only made ten euros? Oh well, at least it's paid for your flask.'

Back in the *aldea* I was surprised to see smoke coming out of our chimney. Gary had a habit of coming up trumps when I least expected it. We were almost halfway through April, but a roaring fire couldn't have been more welcome today. A proper mug of coffee and a warm by the range soon had me feeling chipper. I'd stepped bravely out of my comfort zone and I'd sold a couple of hedgehogs. On top of that, I'd had a free lunch and won a pair of oversized britches. On reflection it hadn't been such a bad day.

Next morning I awoke with a pounding in my temples and a burning sensation at the back of my throat. My pyjama top clung to my back as I shivered beneath the duvet. Four hours in the biting wind and damp had done even less for my health than it had done for my bank balance. One thing was certain; I wouldn't half be glad of my big knickers today.

A week later, I was still getting over the lurgy. The market had left me under the weather but not despondent, and despite my affliction, I was willing to give it another try. In the meantime I'd been wracking my brains for other ways to bring in some money. We were coming up to the fourth anniversary of buying the house and it was about time I earned a crust. If the market stall took off, it would only ever give us pin money; I wanted to pay for essentials and to do so I'd need a proper job. Up until now I'd avoided returning to teaching, but if I was serious about making a financial contribution I could no longer rule it out. I didn't drive, so finding work at one of the academies in Lugo was out of the question. I could, of course, offer private lessons, but local parents had *huertas* to plant and livestock to tend to; they wanted tutors who were prepared to drive out to them. I was wondering about asking for work at the poultry farm on the way into Antas. The eggs were dispatched all over the region and the free-range hens could be seen from the roadside, pecking contentedly in acres of grass. Thoughts of them roused me back to my duties. The sun had risen and it was time to go and feed hungry mouths and beaks.

It was almost three weeks since Waynetta had gone missing and I was under no illusions; she wouldn't be coming back. Hairy Fred, however, had continued to visit us morning and evening. He had also continued to grow.

When I opened the door of the barn, I was expecting to find him waiting, but when he jumped down from the log pile, he gave me the shock of my life. Yesterday he'd been enormous. This morning he was horrifically thin.

'Oh my life!' I exclaimed. 'Whatever's happened, Hairy Fred?'

As the poor chap hovered by the food bowl, the realisation hit me. It wasn't the best news ever, yet I chuckled regardless; I couldn't believe what a nitwit I'd been.

When I came back into the kitchen, Gary was making his cuppa. I was still wearing a grin.

'Morning,' he yawned. 'What's tickled you?'

'Hairy Fred,' I giggled. 'You know how I've been telling him to diet? It looks like he's taken me at my word.'

'Eh?'

'He's lost weight overnight. Wait 'til you see him, he's as thin as a lath.'

'That's impossible. Yesterday he was gigantic. You thought he might have perry-something-itis and I said he looked like he was going to pop.'

'He has – sort of. I can't believe I could be so stupid. If he'd had short hair I'd never have missed it. I didn't think…'

'For God's sake, Liza, *what*?'

'Hairy Fred's a girl.'

His mouth fell open and for a moment I wondered if it was ever going to shut. Eventually he spoke. 'I can't be*lieve* it. He never stood still long enough to see… and even if he had, he's so hairy and… shit.'

'What?'

'He's got kittens. And Sophie'll have kittens. Thank God we managed to have Princess done.'

'Crikey. I'd forgotten about Princess. She's an aunty. However am I going to tell her? Her brother's become a mum.'

The next morning, Gary was smiling when he came in for his coffee at breaktime. I thought for a moment he was going to tell me he'd seen the new-born kittens, but when he pulled the phone from his pocket I knew it was nothing to do with Hairy Fred.

'I've had a message from Matt,' he announced. 'Do we know of any cleaners? That's all it says.'

'For the Ghost House?'

Gary sighed. 'Well I don't suppose he's expecting someone to drive all the way to Málaga, do you?'

'There's no need to be sarky. Do you think it's a one-off or will he want someone on a regular basis?'

'How would I know? I'm not psychic. All I know is what it said in the text.'

'Sorry. Look, never mind that, what did you tell him?'

'I didn't tell him anything. I don't know any cleaners, do I?'

'But Gary! How can you not have...' I stopped in mid-sentence as I noticed the grin playing around his lips.

'How could I not have thought of you? Honestly Liza, after the market fiasco I know you're prepared to do anything to earn a crust.'

'So did you tell him I'd do it?'

'No, I didn't. You're very wayward and I know how fiercely you cling to your independence. Don't get me wrong, I respect you for it, but I thought you'd want to ring him yourself.'

I stubbed out my cigarette and studied his expression. There was no mistaking the sincerity in his eyes.

'So you don't think I've turned in to a submissive little housewife?'

He raised his eyebrows. 'You're joking aren't you? Life would be a lot easier if you had. Now, are you interested in the job or aren't you? 'Cos if you are I suggest you get your arse up to the church.'

When we sat out on the bench with our beers that evening, I was still on cloud nine about my good luck. I could hardly believe that I'd finally found myself a job. Eighty euros a month wasn't a lot, but it was better than nothing. Perhaps I could make it up to a hundred or even two, once my market stall took off.

I looked at Gary. 'This cleaning job, will it help?'

'What d'you mean, "help"?'

'You know, the money – eighty euros a month. Will it make a difference?'

'What sort of a daft question's that? Of course it'll make a difference – it'll pay for your bacca and beer.'

I gave him a smile as warm as the evening sunshine. My earnings would be more than pin money; I'd be buying essentials after all.

It's April, and the call of the cuckoo from the oakwood reminds me how much I love Galicia in the spring. The sun is low in the sky now, yet its radiance still casts a welcome warmth across the threshing floor where Scholes is stalking the lizards that dart in and out of the wall. Princess, though mesmerised, watches from the safety of the stone table, unsure of Lenda who is sprawled out on the grass by my feet. Down in the chooks' pen, Wayne adds his lusty crow to the final village chorus, and over in Warren Place, Bravo Buck thumps on the roof of his hutch, eager to be reunited with Doe.

I sigh in contentment as I gaze out across the valley, where the far-off mountains are crowned with pine. There are times when life seems as mysterious as whatever lies beyond those mountains, but Fate continues to lead us, hoping, trusting, believing, in Galicia, our home.

At Market In Antas

At market in Antas it's drizzling again,
I'm under the bandstand, avoiding the rain.
I've just set my stall out in spite of the weather,
Already I'm reaching the end of my tether.

The wind's blowing fiercely, my stuff's on the floor;
As fast as I catch it, it's flying once more.
Thank goodness for Fruit Man who runs to my aid,
I'm soon relocated with nerves somewhat frayed.

I light up a ciggie, I'm instantly calmed,
But Fruit Man runs over, he looks most alarmed.
In here it's No Smoking, the sign's on the wall.
I stub it out quickly and tend to my stall.

I look at Cold Meat Man who chain smokes all morning
And doles out chorizo from under his awning.
I wonder what makes him exempt from the rule,
I want to protest but it's best to keep cool.

I notice Big Pants Girl has come with her child
Who's bored in the pushchair and growing quite riled.
I take her a pony, she looks up and beams.
Mum gives me some knickers with lace down the seams.

I see that Cheap Shoe Girl's been shiv'ring for hours;
There aren't many people out due to the showers.
I'm sure that like me she's sold nothing all day,
At quarter past one she starts clearing away.

I give up at half past, my takings are zero,
But Fruit Man comes over, oh my, what a hero!
He looks at the hedgehogs and tells me they're pretty,
Buys two for his daughters; I'm sure it's just pity.

Liza Grantham

At market in Antas I've stood here for hours,
I've suffered the wind and the cold and the showers,
I've not had a ciggie all morning since ten
But I'm pleased with my knickers so I will come again.

Liza Grantham was born in 1965 in the East Midlands brewery town of Burton-on-Trent. She worked for over twenty years as a primary teacher in England and Gran Canaria before moving to rural Galicia where she continues to live, love, and learn.

All titles in the **Mad Cow in Galicia** memoir series are available in paperback and e-book from Amazon stores, or as a free download on Kindle Unlimited.

Follow Liza Grantham on:
https://www.facebook.com/thepinkissimopoet/
https://allauthor.com/lizagrantham/
https://www.goodreads.com
https://www.amazon.com

And, if you love reading or writing memoirs, join the friendliest and most generous group on Facebook:
http://www.facebook.com/groups/welovememoirs

PRAISE FOR *MAD COWS AND ENGLISHMEN*

'Outstanding writing that conjures your imagination and passion.'

'Definitely a very unique book. It paints a wonderful picture of life in Galicia. The icing on the cake was the wonderful poetry that interspersed the chapters.'

'Humorous, educational and true!'

'A beautifully written book, and a light-hearted romp through the Galician countryside, with a lot of laughs and some wonderful poetry along the way.'

'This book is written from the heart!'

PRAISE FOR *HOW NOW, MAD COW?*

'Peppered with funny stories, local characters, intrigue, and exploits, this is an amusing and captivating book.'

'Liza is an absolute gem at telling about everyday life in Galicia! It makes you want to go and see for yourself. Top 10 Writer of the 21st century! A definite must read.'

'The fabulous cast of characters, both animal and human, are brought to life in Liza's masterful hands. Her descriptions take you to rural Spain, her characters are so perfect you can hear them speak.'

'Told with warmth and humour and kindness, their stories are enchanting and the characters of the village, animal and human endlessly amusing.'

PRAISE FOR *'TIL MAD COW COMES HOME*

'Liza has a wonderfully engaging style of writing; her anecdotes often had me in fits of giggles.'

'I expected this to be nothing more than 'brits buy a ruin in the Sun' escape-lit but it was so much more.'

'Written with humor, this is so easy to read.'

'A great story and very well written.'

'The book is wonderfully calm and enjoyable.'

Printed in Great Britain
by Amazon

23841583R00223